# The Restoration of Human Affairs

# The Restoration of Human Affairs

*Utopianism or Realism?*

EDITED BY JAN HÁBL

SCIENCE CONSULTANTS:
Mária Potočárová, PhD (Science)
Peter Cimala, ThD
Pavel Černý, ThD

PICKWICK *Publications* · Eugene, Oregon

THE RESTORATION OF HUMAN AFFAIRS
Utopianism or Realism?



Pickwick Publications
An Imprint of Wipf and Stock Publishers
199 W. 8th Ave., Suite 3
Eugene, OR 97401

www.wipfandstock.com

PAPERBACK ISBN: 978-1-6667-1414-2
HARDCOVER ISBN: 978-1-6667-1415-9
EBOOK ISBN: 978-1-6667-1416-6

*Cataloguing-in-Publication data:*

Names: Hábl, Jan, editor.

Title: The restoration of human affairs : utopianism or realism? / edited by Jan Hábl.

Description: Eugene, OR : Pickwick Publications, 2022 | Includes bibliographical references and index(es).

Identifiers: ISBN 978-1-6667-1414-2 (paperback) | ISBN 978-1-6667-1415-9 (hardcover) | ISBN 978-1-6667-1416-6 (ebook)

Subjects: LCSH: Comenius, Johann Amos, 1592–1670. | Education—Philosophy—History—17th century.

Classification LB475.C62 R46 2022 (print) | LB475.C62 R46 (ebook)

Publishing supported by the University of Hradec Králové, Czech Republic, and Calvin University, MI

# Contents

Contents

# List of Contributors

**Radim Červenka** completed his PhD at Palacky University in Olomouc. He worked as a researcher at the National Pedagogical Museum and Library of J. A. Komenský, where he participated in the preparation of the Encyclopedia Comeniana project. He currently works at the Institute of Ethnology, Czech Academy of Science. He has published a number of works on sin and Utraquism in the sixteenth century, as well as on Comenius, including: "Duchovní město a Labyrint světa – text, kontext a obraz lidové kultury." [The Spiritual City and the Labyrinth of the World—Text, Context, and the Image of Folk Culture.] *Komparativní studie a edice* 2017, "Hříšný člověk v dílech utrakvistických autorů a Labyrintu Jana Amose Komenského" [Sinful Man in the Works of the Utraquist Authors and the *Labyrinth* of Jan Amos Komenský] (*Studia Comeniana et Historica,* 2016). He currently works at Institute of Ethnology, Czech Academy of Science.

**Pavel Floss** studied history and Czech at the Faculty of Philosophy and History, Charles University, Prague, 1957–1962, then worked as a Comeniologist at the Comenius Museums in Přerov and Uherský Brod from 1962–80. There he founded and edited the journal *Studia Comeniana et historica*, and organized international Comeniological colloquia in Přerov and Uherský Brod. In 1990 he started working in the Department of Philosophy, Faculty of Arts, Palacky University in Olomouc, and became a professor of philosophy in 1994. Together with a group of former graduates of the Department of Philosophy in Olomouc, he annually organizes the Summer School of Philosophy, founded by his brother, Karel, in Sázava in 1991. He is the author of several dozen professional studies in Comeniology and philosophy (which, in addition to Czech, have also been published in Slovak, Polish, German, French, Italian, Spanish, and English), and almost two dozen separate publications. From recent years these include: *Mikuláš Kusánský: Život a dílo renesančního filosofa, matematika a politika* [Nicholas of Cusa: The Life and Work of a Renaissance Philosopher, Mathematician and Politician], 2001, co-authored by Patočka; *Cesty evropského myšlení I, Architekti křesťanského středověkého vědění* [Paths of European Thought I, Architects of Christian Medieval Knowledge] (2004); *Poselství J. A. Komenského současné Evropě* [Message from J. A. Comenius to Contemporary Europe], (2005); *Meditace na rozhraní epoch [Meditation at the Intersection of Epochs]*, (Brno, 2012).

**Jan Hábl** is a pedagogue, and Comeniologue. After studying philosophy of education at the University of Wales, he worked as an English teacher, researcher at the Comenius Institute in Prague, and lecturer at the universities in Hradec Králové and Ústí nad Labem in the areas of pedagogy, anthropology, ethics, and educational history. He received his PhD in 2009. He is the author of several books, for example, *Labyrint upgrade: Jinotajný román (nejen) pro děti* [Labyrinth Upgrade: A Mysterious Novel (not only) For Children] (2015), *Even When No One is Looking: Fundamental Questions of Ethical Education* (2018), *Učit (se) příběhem* [Teaching and Learning Through Story] ( 2013), *On Being Human(e)* (2017), *Lessons in Humanity from the Life and Works of Jan Amos Komenský* (2011).

**Dana Hanesová** is Professor of Pedagogy at Matej Bel University in Banská Bystrica, Slovakia. Since 1993 she has lectured on several pedagogically-oriented disciplines, especially the didactics of religious education, as well as teaching English as a professional language, or as a foreign language to young school-age children, in the Department of Theology and Catechetics, Department of Elementary and Preschool Pedagogy, Department of Ethical Education, Department of Andragogy, and since 2018, primarily in the Department of Pedagogy. She is the author of several books and studies in the fields of pedeutology, subject didactics, religious pedagogy; for example, *Náboženská výchova v školách* [Religious Education in Schools] (2005); *Náboženská výchova v Európskej únii* [Religious Education in the European Union] (2006); *Sociálna a misijná práca s rómskou komunitou* [Social and Missionary Work with the Roma Community] (2006); *Pre-primary and primary teachers in theory and job-analysis* (2011); *Teachers under the Microscope* (2016); and *Children at the Threshold of Education* (2017).

**Pavel Hošek** works at the Faculty of Evangelical Theology at Charles University. His research focuses on the relationship between theology and culture, religion, and interfaith dialogue. He is the author of several publications, including: *Židovská teologie křesťanství* [The Jewish Theology of Christianity] (2011), *A bohové se vracejí. Proměny náboženství* v *postmoderní době* [And the Gods Return: Transformations of Religion in the Postmodern Era] (2012), *Kouzlo vyprávění. Proměňující moc příběhu a „křest fantazie" v pojetí C. S. Lewise* [The Magic of Storytelling: The Transforming Power of Story and the "Baptism of Fantasy" in the Conceptions of C. S. Lewis] (2013), *Cesta do Středu skutečnosti. Směřování* k *nebeskému cíli duchovní pouti* v *myšlení a díle C. S. Lewise* [The Way to the Center of Reality: Towards the Heavenly Goal of the Spiritual Pilgrimage in the Thoughts and Work of C. S. Lewis] (2014), *Islám jako výzva pro křesťany* [Islam as a Challenge for Christians] (2016) *Je to náš příběh* [It Is Our Story] (2018).

**David Krámský** is a researcher and pedagogue in the field of Philosophy, Ethics, and Methodology. He works at the Police Academy of the Czech Republic and the Charles University in Prague, where he primarily teaches courses in philosophy and ethics. He graduated from Charles University, where he obtained a PhD (2000) and docent (2018). His current focus includes two lines of research—applied ethics and moral psychology. He is the author of several monographs and many scientific articles.

**Jan Kumpera** graduated from the Faculty of Arts at Charles University in 1970 (history-English), and he worked at the Historical Institute of the Czechoslovak Academy of Sciences from 1970 to 1976. In 1971 he received the title of PhD from Charles University. He has been lecturing at the Department of History of the Faculty of Education in Pilsen since 1976. Since the 1980s, he has lectured (in English, German, and Russian) and worked at many foreign universities in Europe (Leipzig, Berlin, Bayreuth, Poznan, Pécs, Vienna, Linz, Amsterdam, London, Sheffield, Aberdeen, Rome, Moscow, St. Petersburg, and Kiev), in the USA (Boston), and Canada (Montreal and Calgary). He lectures on comparative European history, religious and cultural-historical issues of the early modern period, historiography, and didactic application of history. However, the focus of his work for the past almost forty years has been research in the field of Comeniology, and in education of history teachers.

**Miroslav Procházka** is an assistant professor and head of the Department of Pedagogy, part of the Department of Pedagogy and Psychology at the University of South Bohemia in České Budějovice. He publishes in the field of history of pedagogy, theory of education and pedeutology. He is the author of the professional monograph *Social Pedagogy* (Prague, 2012), co-author of the monograph *Hodnotenie kompetencií učiteľov v európskom a slovenskom kontexte* [Evaluation of Teacher Competences in the European and Slovak Context] (Prague 2016), and author of a number of chapters in professional monographs (e.g., "Komenský jako inspirace pro rozvoj myšlenek sociální pedagogiky"[Comenius as Inspiration for the Development of Ideas in Social Pedagogy] in *Pedagogika pedagogů* (2012), articles in professional journals and papers in the proceedings of domestic and foreign conferences.

**Karel Rýdl** studied German and historiography at Charles University in Prague (1972–79), then he worked at the university from 1981 to 2001 as a specialist in the history of education, training, and educational systems. Since 1986 he has devoted himself intensively to non-Marxist pedagogical concepts and, in particular, to alternative schools. From 2006 to 2010, he worked as a requested advisor to the Ministers of Education. Since 2003 he has been working as a professor of the history of pedagogy at the University of Pardubice. Professional specializations: Comeniology, Czech and world history of education in the modern age, alternative education and pedagogy, Montessori pedagogy, development of administration and management of school systems. To date he has published fifteen monographs (in Czech, German, English, and Italian), 130 scientific studies, and over fivee hundred professional articles.

**Radka Skorunková** works at the Department of Pedagogy and Psychology at the Faculty of Education, University of Hradec Králové. She teaches the psychological disciplines: general psychology, developmental psychology, social psychology, and psychopathology. She is the author of monographs, study texts, and professional studies in the field of psychology; for example, *The Relation among IQ, Study Achievements and Motivation to Study Teaching Programmes in the Educational Fields of Study* (E-pedagogium, 2018), *Sociální psychologie v pregraduální přípravě učitelů* [Social Psychology in Undergraduate Teacher Training] (Media4u magazine, 2018), *Inteligence a studijní* úspěšnost *ve vzdělávání* [Intelligence and Academic Success in

Education] (2016), *Základy vývojové psychologie* [Fundamentals of Developmental Psychology] (2013).

**David I. Smith** is professor of education and director of the Kuyers Institute for Christian Teaching and Learning at Calvin University in Grand Rapids, Michigan. He serves as senior editor of the *International Journal of Christianity and Education.* He has authored a number of books, book chapters, and articles in the areas of second language education and Christianity and education, including most recently *Teaching and Christian Practices: Reshaping Faith and Learning* (2011, with James K. A. Smith), *Teaching and Christian imagination* (2016, with Susan Felch), *John Amos Comenius: A Visionary Reformer of Schools* (2017), and *On Christian Teaching: Practicing Faith in the Classroom* (2018).

**Zuzana Svobodová** is an assistant professor at the Department of Medical Ethics and Humanities at Charles University, in the Department of Education at the University of South Bohemia, in the Department of Teaching of the Hussite Faculty of Theology, and in the Department of Theology and Philosophy Jabok—College of Social Pedagogy and Theology. She publishes in the field of philosophy of education, ethics and theology, for example: Nelhostejnost: Črty k (ne)náboženské výchově [Non-indifference: Essays on (non)Religious Education], Homo educandus [Homo Educandus] (together with Radim Palouš), *Vývoj a stav etického vzdělávání a teologickoetická reiterace lidských práv* [Development and Condition of Ethical Education and the Theological Reiteration of Human Rights] (together with René Milfait), *Paideia as Care of the Soul—The Potentials of Contemporary School* (2014).

**Jan Valeš** is a preacher and theologian of the Church of the Brethren (Církev bratrská). He teaches theology at the Evangelical Theological Seminary in Prague, where he heads the Department of Practical Theology. From 2007 to 2017 he was the director of this seminary. He received his doctorate in systematic and practical theology from Charles University in 2014. His sermons can be found on the website of his church (Sboru Církve bratrské v Praze 5). He publishes professional and popular articles such as: "*Jak první reformace nakládala s Augustinem a jeho spisy? U Husa, Mikuláše Biskupce a Rokycany*" [How Did the First Reformation Handle Augustine and His Writings?] (2009). "Wolfhart Pannenberg's imago Dei doctrine as interpreted by F. LeRon Shults and Kam Ming Wong" (2014). "*Křestní přípravy* *v evangelikálních církvích v ČR*" [Preparations for Baptism in Evangelical Churches in the Czech Republic] (2015).

**Miluše Vítečková** is an assistant professor and head of the Department of Primary and Pre-primary Pedagogy, part of the Department of Pedagogy and Psychology at the University of South Bohemia in České Budějovice. She publishes in the field of pedeutology and preschool education. She is the author of the professional monograph *Začínající učitel: jeho potřeby a uvádění do praxe* [Novice Teacher: Needs and Introduction to Practice] (2018), co-author of the monograph *Hodnotenie kompetencií učiteľov v európskom a slovenskom kontexte* [Evaluation of Teachers' Competencies in the European and Slovak Context] (2016), co-author and editor of the monograph *Osobnost předškolního pedagoga: Sebereflexe, sociální kompetence a jejich rozvíjení* [Personality of the Preschool Teacher: Self-Reflection, Social Competences, and Their Development] (2017), and author of a number of papers in proceedings of domestic and foreign conferences and articles in professional journals.

# Preface

"WHAT ARE WE GOING to do—watch! To consult on the reparation of human affairs in general: that is, with a greater degree of generality and availability to the public than has ever been used since the inception of the world. So, nothing new in terms of things, something completely new in terms of how things are done. For since the fall of the world people's minds have never been able to grasp such horror as the realization of their own evil, and to grieve over it and desire to somehow make a turn for the better, even the more capable ones from any age, country or condition who struggled to do so" (51).[1]

"So whoever belongs to the human race (whether placed in the highest class or lowest class, learned or unlearned, refined or simple, king or beggar, from whichever country, religion, situation, just if you have a part of human nature), know that this book was written for your benefit, dedicated to your profit, and sent directly to you. It is therefore not to underhandedly hide anything from you, nor flatter in anything, nor hatefully reproach for anything, but to present freely, honestly and openly everything that contributes to the common good. Receive it with grateful hands, eyes, and minds you Christians, Jews, Mohammedans or whoever you are, as a gift from heaven (as indeed it is) to you! In it you will find more wealth than the treasures of Croesus, or a thousand times a thousand royal treasuries. For she will show

1.. All quotations in the Preface are from Komenský, *Obecná porada o nápravě věcí lidských* [General Consultation Concerning the Restoration of Human Affairs], vol. I (Praha: Nakladatelství Svoboda, 1992). Therefore, only page numbers will be given in the text. Please note that Comenius is the Latin version of Komenský. Although English readers tend to know him only as Comenius, the Czech authors in this book are quoting from Czech versions of his writings and thus they are published (and listed here) under the name Komenský. The works Comenius wrote in Latin, as well as English translations of his works, are published and listed under the name Comenius.

to all the blind, light, to the lost, the way, to the sick, medicine, to the dead, life, to the despondent, strength to stand again, to the defeated, new victory, to the imprisoned, unlocked dungeons, to the shipwrecked, harbors, to the dying, salvation, to all the world she shows the way out of every labyrinth, relief from every Sisyphean boulder, the transforming of every tantalizing, fleeting pleasure into a truly eternal delicacy" (234).

"Only what is broken is fixed. Thus, when we propose a consultation on the repair of human affairs, we assume that they are broken, or out of order. Perhaps this does not require laborious proof, because laments that nothing is in its place and that everything deviates from the correct path (to the right or to the left), are universal. For people who see at least something, see that instead of wisdom there is ignorance or sophistry, instead of devoutness there is unbelief or superstition, instead of management of society there is anarchy or confusion, or tyranny and oppression. However, since we have decided to trace back everything from its very roots, we will first look at what it means, or what is said to be broken. Brokenness is said to be that which is, in and of itself, so changed that it no longer conforms to its own idea and cannot fulfil its function. But what is the purpose of our things? According to God's design this world, to which we were sent at birth, should be God's school, full of light, God's temple, full of piety, God's kingdom, full of order and justice." (84)

"On the whole, no matter what kind of iniquity appeared in the human race, or who started it, it immediately threw out roots like a malignant weed, immediately pushing up stalks and it could not be eradicated by any means whether simple or complex. . . . Not only do we constantly plot against God and ourselves (we have established many communities since then, and all together we are a great Babylon which must be scattered forever if we do not repent), but each of us also builds our own little tower of Babel. The whole world is indisputably full of confusion. Nimrod began to organize a hunt for people and established dominion over the nations God had uprooted, as others who followed after him did too; and we have never stopped promoting one over another so we can oppress whoever we are able to." (95)

"Although human affairs are corrupt, they have not fallen into complete depravity because, behind the yeast of errors, defects and confusion stands the dough of God's work." (102)

"A large part (if not the basis) of human corruption is that, while people quite diligently care for their external possessions and in practice assiduously apply the tenet: *I am a neighbor to myself*, they mostly neglect their internal assets. Hence Seneca's statement: One cares for one, the other for another, but nobody cares for themself! He is quite right—at least, that is still the case in the human multitude. Many pay attention to others, nobody to themselves; many teach others, no one themselves; many manage and improve others, no one themselves; many give alms to others, no one to themselves, etc. So, in order to stop the laments, everyone must begin with their own selves in everything that leads to reform. This only means to begin the work where it has to start, and select a firm center for completing the circle. For the universal reform cannot move forward unless each individual reforms themselves; after all, the whole is the sum of its parts. Public reform, that is, transformation, cannot be done as a business by a private business owner, but privately, yes! No one can be prevented from setting up a paradise in and around themselves, or establishing a kingdom within themselves or erecting an altar to God, acting in an entirely reasonable and devoted manner with things, with themselves and with God, [and] in that lies joy." (369)

"Outside of this path of returning to oneself and in oneself, to God and in God, there is no hope of any salvation, peace or happiness. Wherever one seeks for it unprepared within oneself, it won't be found, but in seeking that one will become tired, the tired one will regret, then cry, then despair, and in despair will die. Light is nowhere other than in the light, peace than in peace, and everything than in one." (373)

"It is desirable that the state of the world become as close as possible to a clock made precisely by the artist's hand and assembled everywhere such that everything is mutually connected in perfect harmony. This is the right place to repeat the wish. For what is a clock, if not a machine to measure time? And the flow of time does not come from the movement of the heavens, the measurement of time is by this device, the clock, which ingeniously, even to the imitation of the heavens, adds movement to parts that don't move by themselves (or which, in and of themselves would move without order and quickly break). And so too, universal reform seeks nothing other than that the will of God be done on earth as it is in heaven. As one who watches the clock moving precisely sees at the same time the movement of the heavens, even if they can't look at it, maybe at night, so also the one who sees Christ's kingdom established on earth sees in it, at the same time, the true and living picture of the heavenly kingdom." (262)

Jan Amos Komenský,
*General Consultation Concerning the Restoration of Human Affairs*

# Introduction

## *The Problem of "Human Affairs"*

BY JAN HÁBL

HUMANITY IS CHARACTERISTICALLY FULL of contradictions, among other things. On the one hand, as people we know a lot, we know how to do a lot, and we are able to do a lot, but precisely this capability is our greatest threat. Everything we have at our disposal, we can manage to misuse. We are the only beings who have the potential to both develop and destroy ourselves. It is therefore imperative that we look for a way to realize our potential humanely.

Almost four hundred years ago, John Amos Comenius named the problem of "human affairs" with extraordinary foresight. When he died in 1670, he left behind his magnum opus, unfinished, called *General Consultation Concerning the Restoration of Human Affairs*. In it he thoroughly reflects on the causes of all human depravity and calls humanity to a discussion on the remedy. His remedial efforts are based, among other things, on an assumption which may at first glance seem trivial, but in fact is profound and important: Humanity is not quite all right, yet isn't completely lost.[1] There is a way out, there is hope. There are two alternative counterparts to this formulated anthropology—on the one hand the pessimistic view, that human affairs are totally corrupt, lost, and without hope for improvement,

1. It is a paraphrase of this statement: "Though human affairs are corrupt, they have not fallen into complete depravity because, behind the yeast of errors, defects and confusion remains the dough of God's work." (Komenský, *Obecná porada o nápravě věcí lidských* [General Consultation Concerning the Restoration of Human Affairs], vol. I. (Praha: Nakladatelství Svoboda, 1992), 102.

and on the other hand, the optimistic view which sees human affairs as completely beyond reproach, and thus without need of any remedy, reform or improvement. Neither of these views seems realistic, down to earth, recognizing the contradictory reality of the human world. Nor does either of them have the motivational potential for any kind of repair—if a person is perfectly wrong, no remedy will help, and conversely, if a person is perfectly good, no remedy is necessary. Obviously, Comenius is neither an anthropological pessimist nor optimist.

The goal of this project is, with hermeneutical humility, to examine Comenius's notion of "human affairs" in an emendatory context. We want to look at the possibilities and limits of Comenius's restoration project. The research questions we ask in this book are the following: How relevant is Comenius's vision for the restoration of human affairs in the twenty-first century? Are the concepts of the *Consultation* realistic, or, more precisely, to what extent are they realistic in the sense of being universally valid and applicable to humanity? Or was Comenius's project sheer utopia? Is it possible for there to be any kind of repair of human problems at all? Or at least to move forward? Improve them?

We want to avoid simplistic interpretations and misinterpretations, as well as uninformed applications to the present. We in the Czech Republic witnessed this in the interpretations of the Modernist or Communist period. Many years ago, Jan Patočka drew attention to the violent hermeneutics of the so-called "incorporation of our perspectives" into Comenius, which usually served as a cover for their own self-admiration. We want to avoid that. Methodologically speaking, the fundamental imperative of this project is to let Comenius speak in his contextual integrity.

## Structure of the Monograph

This book is divided into three parts that correspond to three interpretational perspectives:

(1) *The Historical Perspective*. The goal of this section is to examine and understand the historical context of the *Consultation*. What were the historical connections or relations out of which the *Consultation* was formed? The sources and influences? What shaped Comenius's concept of humanity and its remedy? Was his vision unique, or were similar projects characteristic of his time? What was the historical fate of the *Consultation*

after the death of Comenius? How has history evaluated Comenius's *Consultation* in the context of the debate between utopianism and realism?

Jan Kumpera opens the topic with a fundamental probe into the roots of Comenius's emendatory thought. In his chapter entitled "The Czech Comenius: A Utopian Visionary or Pioneer of European Integration?" he notes that Comenius's vision comes partly from the legacy of European humanism and at the same time follows the best of the traditions from the Czech Reformation, which in the mid-fifteenth century gave birth to the peace plan of the Hussite King George of Poděbrady. Comenius's spiritual architecture likewise reflects his heritage from the Unity of Brethren (church), which sought to restore the individual by means of education and Christian love. In summary, Jan Kumpera demonstrates that Comenius's project represents the most significant and original Czech contribution to the treasury of European political philosophy of the early modern period, which despite some utopian features does not lose its exigency even at the threshold of the third millennium.

In the second chapter, entitled "The Golden Dream of Humanity or the Picture of Reality in Comenius's Pansophy?" Radim Červenka puts together an anthropological analysis of the ambivalence of the realist and utopian aspects of emendatory efforts of the time and compares them with those of Comenius. The author explains here the tension between two anthropological poles typical in 17th century thought. On the one side is the "golden dream" of the ideal state of humanity, and on the other is the everyday reality that it is imperfect, distorted and corrupt. Červenka shows how Comenius, in his universal restoration project, takes into account the doctrines of the sinfulness of humankind and of salvation. Humanity is corrupt, but has soteriological potential. The corruption, depravity, is real, but at the same time each one has the possibility, or even the necessity, of actively overcoming it and thus participating in human salvation.

The third chapter, "'It Would Be Good to Have a Paradise': Comenius on Learners Past and Present," borders on both historical and pedagogical studies. In it, David I. Smith analyzes Comenius's notion of an educational "paradise" or "garden" which, in his universal restoration, was to link the physical, cognitive, relational, moral and spiritual dimensions of learning. In his reflection on the "paradise garden" (*hortum deliciarium*), Comenius explicitly refers to the story in Genesis about the garden of Eden (*paradiso voluptatis*), in which the first people were to find beauty, virtue, meaningful work and fellowship with God. The author wonders what can be taken from this reference into our present context, when the Christian narrative framework is no longer a given. Then Smith, on the basis of his current experience with student learning, demonstrates that Comenius's concept of learning which includes the triad of perception-understanding-belief in a moral-spiritual context, does remain valid today.

(2) *The Pedagogical-Psychological Perspective*. Karel Rýdl opens this section with his "Only an Educated Person Can Change the World in the Spirit of Humanization." This chapter focuses on the external events which influenced Comenius's life stories and his thinking about the meaning of human existence, and also reflects on pedagogical humanization in connection with Patočka's conception of "open" and "closed minds."

The chapter by Miroslav Procházka and Miluše Vítečková, "Comenius's Notion of the Educational Reform of Society in the Context of His Social and Pedagogical Thinking," is an analysis of selected connections in the fourth and fifth parts of the *Consultation*—Universal Education (Pampaedia) and Universal Restoration (Panorthosia). The authors follow the relationship of crisis-behaving society with the creation of a social, human communal environment in which education could be used to orient people towards tolerance, peace, and mutual communication. In light of the social significance and character of education, Comenius's *Consultation* is presented as a kind of primary and original appeal for socio-educational work. In the second part of this chapter the authors present the results of their research investigation, in which they observe how the message of Comenius's *Consultation* has been preserved and passed on in the opinions of contemporary students. The research was conducted among students of teacher education in the Faculty of Education at South Bohemia (Jihočeské) University in České Budějovice.

Dana Hanesová's chapter clearly states its content in the title, "'Preventing Humans from Becoming Unhuman': Comenius's Restoration from the Perspective of a Contemporary Educator." The author presents a brief overview of the period background and characteristics of the anthropological foundations of Comenius, as well as key points of the current humanistic orientation of pedagogy. She compares their mutual anthropological and ethical intersections by means of the Central Axiom Method. Subsequently, she points out possible overlaps in Comenius's pedagogy, based on the synthesis of educational reality with the transcendental anchor of humanity.

Radka Skorunková closes this section of the book with her chapter "Comenius's Educational Plans from the Perspective of Developmental and Social Psychology." The psychological perspective through which the author views Comenius's work brings a unique interpretation. The author deals mainly with the psychological aspects of human selfishness, which J. A. Comenius considered the source of all problems in human society. She comes to the conclusion that Comenius's educational plans, whose goal was the attainment of a "common good," are utopian in terms of psychological knowledge—given both the innate and the acquired psychological sources of human behavior. Nevertheless, the author sees Comenius's humanization efforts as meaningful in terms of motivation. Although the emendatory goal cannot be achieved, one's efforts to improve oneself have a humanizing effect.

(3) *The Philosophical-Theological Perspective.* In the opening chapter of this section, "On the Philosophical Foundations of Comenius's Emendatory Work," Pavel Floss examines the philosophical and specifically anthropological foundations of Comenius's project. He shows that the concept of a humanity whose supreme activity is the fundamental and universal reform of human affairs, was born in Comenius's contemplation on key themes of European thought from antiquity to its present day. Floss comes to the conclusion that, in our present day as civilization is in the midst of crisis (ecological, social, educational and moral), Comenius's indomitable reformatory program is an extremely timely and inspiring appeal.

"On Earth, as It Is in Heaven: The Theological Basis of Comenius's Universal Restoration" is the title of the second chapter in this section. Here Pavel Hošek presents the theological standpoints which led Comenius to the formulation of his plan for universal restoration. The main thesis of Hošek's essay is the assertion that Comenius's distinctive theological points of view are inseparable from his pedagogical and emendatory proposals, and that if we look at his pedagogical proposals apart from the wider theological framework in which they are anchored, we will inevitably arrive at a considerably distorted interpretation of his whole philosophy and the real motives of his emendatory efforts. Pavel Hošek thus successfully documents the theological sources of Comenius's optimism, irenicism, universalism, etc.

In his study of "Comenius's Notion of Happiness and Its Platonic-Aristotelian Connotations," David Krámský analyzes Comenius's distinctive linking of morality, education and the ethics of virtue. He points to Plato's inspired notion of virtue: moderation, bravery, wisdom and justice, but backs it up with Aristotle's emphasis on *praxis*. For virtues are cultivated only through actions, and as such they are to Comenius the sovereign subject of education, that is, the restoration of humanity. A partial plan for the essay is to also show—based on his interpretation of Comenius's ethics of virtues—the experience of shame as one of the ways of exercising *fronésis*, the practical reason leading a person to God and thus to a good life.

The fourth chapter is the text by Zuzana Svobodová, "The Concepts of God and Truth in Comenius's Metaphysical Writings." Here the author presents a unique summary of the structure and contents of Comenius's metaphysics. It is based primarily on a book of Comenius's *Writings on the First Philosophy* (*Spisů o první filosofii)*, published in 2017, with an emphasis on the analysis of Comenius's concepts of God and of truth. The author also analyzes the sources of Comenius's metaphysical thought and points out the differences between the sources and those who initiated them. She thus reveals what makes Comenius's concept of metaphysics unique. The aim of Zuzana Svobodová's text is to show the relevance of Comenius's concept and outline its possible use for today's education.

The final chapter in this philosophical-theological section is that of Jan Valeš, "Things Essential, Ministerial, and Incidental in the *General Consultation*." The text maps the influence of the ecclesiological teaching of the Unity of Brethren on questions about the so-called essential, ministerial and incidental things which are evident in the text of Comenius's *Consultation*. The author demonstrates that this influence does not only apply to Comenius's notion of the church and its renewal, but also to his anthropology and emendation.

# PART 1

## *Historical Perspective*

# Comenius, the Czech

## *Utopian Visionary or Pioneer of European Integration?*

Jan Kumpera

*"We Europeans are surely sailing as if on the same ship."*
—Jan Amos Comenius[1]

The title of the following study, or rather reflection, on the current legacy of Jan Amos Comenius is intentionally slightly provocative. As a visiting professor teaching historians abroad, I was pleased that sometimes the name Comenius (never the Czech Komenský) said something to future teachers of history, even though many of them regarded him as German, Polish, British, Dutch, or even Italian, and in Egypt—simply as a "Christian European reformer" without specific nationality (which is actually very flattering). If the young international students knew him at all (or if they were like Czechs, matter-of-fact about their luminaries), they put him in the category of "outstanding teachers." Certainly, Comenius is unquestionably the father (or, at least, one of the fathers) of modern pedagogy and didactics, but no less beneficial are his emendatory projects and vision. And so our compatriot stands, as a political thinker and reformer, undeservedly in the shadow of his own pedagogical legacy. We may also be convinced about this by taking a look at the heading "Comenius" in world encyclopedias. At the same time, Comenius himself always understood didactics and

1. Komensky, "Europae lumina."

pedagogy as part of the great reform that he thought about and added to throughout his long and complex life.[2]

The culmination of his efforts in this respect was the great architecture of thought, the *General Consultation on the Restoration of Human Affairs*, with its message—despite its Old Testament rhetoric and biblical pathos—for the future. This work, although unfinished, can be considered as a late flower of the Czech Reformation,[3] as well as the "most comprehensive and courageous synthesis the Czech thinker ever ventured."[4] It expresses the utter conviction of the need for a global reform of education and training, understood as the foundation of all further reformative steps towards the peaceful coexistence of humanity. I will try to illustrate this idea, imparted by my feeble self to our domestic and international students, in the following lines. Nevertheless, the answer to the question of Comenius's utopianism (which is, in any case, both noble and winsome) I leave to the kind readers themselves.

The problems of war and peace, in connection with the pursuit of dialogue between scholars and politicians, run through the life and creative labyrinth of Comenius himself, whose irenic thinking underwent remarkable development. The beginning of this winding journey in search of a just peace, was evangelical irenicism as presented to Comenius by his teacher at Heidelberg University, David Pareus.[5] And it was the Czech reformer who then, in exile, became a fervent apostle of the reconciliation of the divorced Protestant churches, especially of the Calvinists and Lutherans (but he reaped ungratefulness from fundamentalists on both sides). He was in this regard the most prominent spokesman of the Czech exile, who saw in the united front of the Protestant states (*corpus evangelicorum*) the prerequisite for victory over "Antichrist" and "Babylon" (Habsburgs and papal counter-reformers). From this point of view it is dubious to speak of Comenius's pacifism—his disappointment over the Westphalian peace is well enough known. For that matter, his position of authority also protected Comenius from the last desperate attempt of the Czech exiles to overthrow the Habsburg rule of Bohemia in 1654.[6]

2. Zemek and Kumpera, *Komenský známý neznámý*.
3. Zemek and Kumpera, *Jednota bratrská*.
4. Patočka, *Doslov*, 533.
5. Kumpera, *Jan Amos Komenský*, 25, 33, 186.
6. Kumpera, *Poslední pokus*.

Although Comenius never gave up his vision for a "just peace in freedom," and thus remained an opponent of "bad peace,"[7] he changed his ideas about war. As a theologian and bishop of the Unity of Brethren, he had always condemned war as a fundamental violation of "the peace of Christ," but as the political representative of the Czech exile he admitted the war solution as a necessary evil, essential for upholding a "just peace." Under the influence of his personal experiences and many disappointments, however, in the 1640s he began to be aware of the hopelessness and ruthless cruelty of all war—and, touched by the shattered English hope—also revolutionary violence.

Thus Comenius, as also a political philosopher, raised again the question of resolving contemporary power and religious disputes. At first, he saw war as the worst of possible solutions, but gradually dismissed it entirely as "bestial."[8] According to Comenius, therefore, it is necessary to resolve disputes through negotiation, and it is necessary to bring to the negotiation table every one of the politicians involved without regard to national or religious affiliation. That was expressed in practice, for example, in Comenius's active participation in the Torun Peace Colloquium in 1645, at which religious peace in Poland was to be agreed upon.[9]

It was no accident that Comenius's *General Consultation on the Restoration of Human Affairs* was born right in that period,[10] and from the 1640s its author also devoted a huge amount of energy to a most varied set of reconciliation appeals, addressing the representatives of European states and churches. Comenius tried to gain political support (more or less in vain), and therefore mainly addressed in his proclamations and various dedications the current prominent rulers—the Swedish Charles X Gustav, the English Charles II Stuart, the Transylvanian George II Rákóczi, and at the end of his life in particular, the French King Louis XIV.[11] At the same time—from that period until his death—the Czech reformer was thinking about an astonishing peace architecture, whose foundation was to be an international conference, and its supporting pillar a newly established institution, overseeing the preservation of a just peace and removal of possible new disputes. In *The Way of Light*, created and written in London in

7. Kumpera, "Tranquilla Libertas."

8. Kumpera, *Jan Amos Komenský*, 203.

9. Kumpera, *Jan Amos Komenský*, 98–99; Kumpera, *Komenského Vlastní životopis*, 64–67.

10. Kumpera, *Jan Amos Komenský*, 223–28.

11. Kumpera, *Jan Amos Komenský*; Polišenský, *Jan Amos Komenský*

1641–42, Comenius rightly regarded as a prerequisite for peace the "elimination of hatred and its causes, i.e., mutual hostilities"[12]

The peace project, however, only took its concrete form in the unfinished sixth part of the *Consultation—Panorthosia* (Universal Reform), which best outlines Comenius's vision of a comprehensive and lasting peace solution for all people—conditioned on the reforms of the mutually interdependent triad Education-Religion-Politics.

His proposal for the establishment of an international peace institute is revealed in its most complete form in chapter XVII, with the indicative title "On the Universal Bond between States, the Court of Peace" (*De Politiarum Vinculo Universali Dicasterio Pacis*).[13] As Comenius wrote, "this committee could also be called the Directorate of World Power, the World Senate, or the Areopagus of the World" (*Dicasterium pacis, Potestatum Orbis Directorium et Senatus orbis, vel Areopagus Orbis*). He also suggested the labels "Worldwide Advisory Council" (*Orbis Terrae Consilium*) or "World Court of Justice" (*Orbis Dicasterium*) and for its members he recommended the title "Peacekeepers" (*Regnorum Irenarchae*) or "Chief Arbitrators of Peace" (*Pacis Arbitri Summi*) Their work should be "right politics," ensuring "peace in every realm of the world." Comenius summarized their duties in a special ten commandments that he stated in the form of clear and practical requirements: "Their special duties will be to carefully pay attention to

I. themselves as the measure and example of justice,
II. then to justice itself, in every situation of human society,
III. but especially to the courts and town halls as the seat of justice,
IV. to the judge as the minister of justice,
V. to the implementation of the law itself, as used by one or another,
VI. to rights or books containing rights,
VII. to interpreters and commentators, notaries,
VIII. to measures, weights, coins, public roads, etc. as instruments of public justice and safety,
IX. to the other two councils as helpers in the guarding of order,
X. finally, to God Himself, eternal guardian of justice."[14]

12. Kumpera, *Jan Amos Komenský*, 309–10; Kumpera, *Cesta světla*; Kumpera, *Komenského Vlastní životopis*, 38.

13. Komenský, *Všenáprava*, 357–59.

14. Cf. Komenský, *Všenáprava*, 357.

In this declaration he emphasized the preservation of truth and justice and cooperation with the other two worldwide institutions—the "College of Light" and "the Consistory of Holiness," that is, with the representatives of the sciences and the church. The "peacekeepers" should then become "the leading guardians of the common good, to prevent the return of wars, storms, bloodshed, or the opportunity for them to return . . . and will build everywhere everlasting barriers against all wars," nevertheless, according to Comenius, it would be necessary to establish individual subordinate "peace tribunals" at an even lower level—in individual countries, nations, cities, "for administering justice and for preventing injustice, quarrels and disputes or for their quick resolution."[15] Only in this way could civil wars, which the Czech reformer considered an especially great curse, be prevented. For that matter, his personal experiences in the Czech Estates Uprising, the English Revolution and in Poland were very painful.[16]

Comenius also reacted very interestingly to the contemporary problems starting from the European expansion overseas: "If the native land is not enough to feed everyone, then it will be the responsibility of the peacemakers to take action . . . by establishing colonies abroad . . . not in a rough way, through robbery (as did the Spanish, Portuguese, French, English and Dutch, etc. not long ago), but according to the example of Abraham and Lot (Gen. 3:18) for mediation of a peaceful arbitration." Of course, Comenius was also aware of the need for sanctions against "violators of peace and rest," and for those to be "as far as possible without violent means," but unfortunately, he was not able to develop his project in this respect. What is interesting, however, is the explicit rejection of the death penalty: "this sacrosanct administration should not be tarnished by capital punishment."[17]

Comenius also realized the necessity in actuality of unifying international legal norms, "therefore a universal law must inevitably be established which will serve the whole human race in every case." The international law thus agreed upon would respect, in addition to natural law, the "law of God!" i.e., the highest morality in Comenius's view. While "the world's highest marshals of governance and peace" will have great jurisdiction to support the authority of the other two worldwide institutions, "the College of Light and the Consistory," nevertheless "universal government does not belong to anyone other than Christ and . . . if anyone else seeks universal

15. Komenský, *Všenáprava*, 358–59.

16. Kumpera, *Jan Amos Komenský*, 45–44; Kumpera, *Komenského Vlastní životopis*.

17. Komenský, *Všenáprava*, 358.

rule, that one seeks Babylon and re-establishes confusion." Thus power is always held in trust and must be subject to control and higher moral principles.[18]

Chapter XXIV, "Reform of World Management" *(Reformatio Politiarum)*, is also devoted to the Peace project, relatively well thought-through and formulated by Comenius.[19] Here in the introduction Comenius stated that "the aim of human society is general peace and safety, and the welfare of humanity should be the highest law of any republic and any kingdom." Therefore it is necessary to stop wars, "for war does not bring any good." The Czech reformer also recommends disarmament, because "the removal of weapons" reduces the "opportunity to return to hostility and war." Although this chapter is again unfortunately only an outline of thoughts, it also contains concrete reflections on the character of the selected "peacekeepers," at whatever level of peace tribunal they are operating. Comenius's requirements were really high. That is, they should be at the same time "preachers, legal experts, philosophers, doctors against tyranny—upright men, wise, pious, brave, and vigilant," enjoying the universal respect of kings as well as common people. It also addressed the issue of the placement of the peace tribunals—he considered the appropriate places to be locations which were easily accessible for communication, yet isolated from the daily hustle and bustle ("perhaps a monastery surrounded by fields and with income"). Comenius did not forget to communicate with the public, and therefore advised holding "an annual public balance party," in which the peace tribunal would present the results of their work.[20]

The decisive impulse for reversing the existing unfavorable development of humanity must, however, be brought about by the worldwide council of politicians, which Comenius called for in various appeals and to which he also wanted to present his *General Consultation*. This idea was most precisely developed in chapter XXV of "Universal Reform," bearing the name "World Diet or Ecumenical Council, Guarantee of Universal Reform" (*Comitia Orbis Seu Consilium Oecumenicum, Universalis Reformationis Auctoramentum*).[21] According to Comenius, there existed only one "universal medicine" against "universal confusion," and that was "the universal council (*Tali universali Concilio prorsus opus est, tanquam*

18. Komenský, *Všenáprava*, 359.

19. Komenský, *Všenáprava*, 406–18.

20. Komenský, *Všenáprava*, 406, 410, 413, and 417.

21. Komenský, *Všenáprava*, 418–30.

*universali adversus universales Confusiones remedio . . .).*" First of all, therefore, "men of enlightenment, superior to other mortals in wisdom, piety, and prudence, philosophers, theologians and politicians" must be convened from all over the world "to discuss how to finally fully provide, secure, and spread salvation to the whole human race." The ones to call together this meeting should be "kings and republics from the Christian world in unanimous agreement . . . after the defeat of tyranny", and furthermore "the whole world should be invited, that is, every tribe and nation . . . through the best people from their midst, who are learned, spiritual and political . . . representatives of universities, churches, kings and republics, that is, through philosophers, theologians, and politicians."[22]

Comenius also drew attention to the necessary linguistic competence of the delegates. He proposed Venice as the most suitable place to convene such a world peace conference, because of its availability and the tolerance and neutrality of the Venetian Republic. Comenius also recommended "a universal erasure of the past (*universalis amnestia et oblivio*)," a kind of thick line behind the past as a necessary prerequisite for overcoming mutual animosities. Negotiations must proceed without prejudice and in an atmosphere of freedom, and they should aim at "abolishing tyrannies in politics (*Abolenda in Politia Tyrannis*)" and "a new civil society (*Nova Politia*)." The Czech thinker also understood religious freedom and respect for the person as a free being created in the image of God, to be included in these terms. This chapter is actually just a kind of rough draft, but is nonetheless crammed full of ideas. The international negotiations should result in the establishment of three supreme bodies: "the College of Light, the Consistory of Holiness, and the World Court (*Collegium lucis, Consistorium Oecumenicum* a *Dicasterium Orbis*)." The latter institution should represent a kind of world government, capable of "restraining the power of external disruptors of peace (*externi turbatores pacis*)." Its world headquarters should be in London because of its convenient location, but other branches should exist in each of the four continents (Europe, Asia, Africa, America), and at a lower level in every country and larger city. Every peace court would have its president and three secretaries, at the world and continental courts each nation would be represented by one assistant judge (in the case of a large country, two). To avoid disagreements, the presidents of the world court would rotate regularly according to the major parts of the world. Once every ten years there should be another world peace

22. Komenský, *Všenáprava*, 418, 420.

conference, alternately taking place in Europe, America, Asia, or Africa. The rulers of the world should together take care of the enforcement of the project, never with violence, but by a persuasion campaign and the sending of special diplomatic missions to all nations of the world. In this context, Comenius recommended the introduction of a new international language, which would facilitate communication between the nations of the world. Comenius devoted the entire fifth part of the *General Consultation*—the *Panglottia* (*Universal Language*)—to this issue.[23] It is understandable that this idea of the international integration of humanity and the Christianizing of the world would flow out of Comenius, for—with all due respect for other religions, including Islam—the Bishop of the Unity of Brethren considered Christ's message of love and peace to be the foundation of his efforts. After all, according to Comenius, the establishment of world peace had to be part of the coming Kingdom of God, the millennium empire of Christ.[24]

The chiliastic ideas are even more intertwined with the political proposals and plans in the *Clamores Eliae* (*The Cries of Elijah*).[25] In this late work of Comenius, styled as a diary (written in both Latin and Czech), we also find many remarkable observations on the issues of war and peace, more interesting in their rawness and openness. "For the universal reconciliation of all" it will be necessary to overcome sectarianism, and do it "not by fire and sword, stormy wind or earthquake, but in the mild spirit of Christ" on the foundation of harmony and equality among people and nations.[26] Comenius was always a tough opponent of "crazy Machiavellians," and therefore did not recognize the justification of immoral means by a noble end; in an address to the rulers he called: "Let go of deceitful Machiavellian cunning, you politicians" for "the igniting of wars, hatred, differences, and fighting are works of the devil."[27] He was especially critical in his charges against tyrants, a group including "all who rage with physical violence (jailers, proscriptors, punishments) against those who differ from them (in faith or opinion)."[28] Politicians lack Comenius's humility, for "many want to rule and govern the world without God—with their

23. Kumpera, *Jan Amos Komenský*, 227.

24. Komenský, *Všenáprava*, 421–22; Válka, *Problém výkladu*.

25. Komenský, *Clamores Eliae*.

26. Komenský, *Clamores Eliae*, 14.

27. Komenský, *Všenáprava*; Komenský, *Clamores Eliae*, 48–49.

28. Komenský, *Clamores Eliae*, 19.

idol called the state's interest." A truly just peace cannot, therefore, occur "unless fraud and subterfuge are eliminated everywhere." In a private sigh Comenius here indicated his opposition to absolutism, which is called the "monopoly" of power and "beast-like rule." To fully reform the world, then, what is necessary is "that care is taken throughout the world for religion, justice, and education (guaranteeing freedom of religion, free access to justice, repudiation of weapons, tax relief, easier livelihoods, safe travel, preservation of marriage and an abundance of schools of every kind)."[29] He urged the rulers of the world to renounce war and atrocities, and as the Old Testament prophet Elijah cried: "Your kegs of gunpowder, bullets, cannons, swords, spears will never bring peace, instead they violate it—it has always been this way (*Vestra salopetra, tormenta, petardae, gladii, hastae nunquam res tranquillabunt, asperabunt magis, sicut tot seculis*)." And he added in his native Czech: "Make armories into libraries—the tolling of bells into music." Here too, he saw the only solution as the calling for a Council of the Whole World (*Concilium orbis totius*).[30] According to Comenius, "wars are a disgrace to kings and empires, especially Christian ones"; moreover, they are "not only futile, but cruel and destructive to mankind, the whole world is devastated by them." Paradoxically, in *Clamores Eliae,* Comenius revealed an ambivalent relationship to monarchs—he had no illusions about them, but he needed them to enforce his plans. And so, for example, both here and in several of his prefaces he turned directly to Louis XIV with an appeal for the convening of the World Peace Council.[31] It would be, for Comenius, as decisive as the second coming of Christ, which the new prophet Elijah should help with (there can be more than one Elijah—this role could be played by enlightened politicians or even reformers like Comenius himself). "Let Elijah invite all nations, languages, sects together so that, by this union, the distinction between Greek and Scythian, free and slave, European and American will disappear" urged Comenius, and like a biblical patriarch he cried: "Be reconciled everyone, all of you return from war to the gates (Isaiah 28:6), for wars are fought in the fields, they are discussed in the gates."[32]

The "reconciliation of the human race" thus became a focus of Comenius's attention, especially in the last period of his life, when he even offered

29. Komenský, *Clamores Eliae*, 20–21.

30. Komenský, *Clamores Eliae*, 20–23.

31. Komenský, *Clamores Eliae*, 25.

32. Komenský, *Clamores Eliae*, 31, 42–43.

to cooperate with all of his opponents (including the Jesuits and the pope) on the reformative work. His vision of peace was also intertwined with others of Comenius's late works—especially *Angel of Peace* (*Angelus Pacis*) and *The One Thing Necessary* (*Unum Necessarium*).[33]

Although Comenius never finished putting his peace project into its final form, his restorative ideas represent the most significant and original Czech contribution to the treasury of European political philosophy of the early modern period, and despite some utopian features, they do not lose their urgency even on the threshold of the third millennium. In addition, Comenius's visions excel in their kindness and Christian anthropocentrism, which distinguishes the Bishop of the Unity of Brethren from all the notorious theorists and practitioners of social engineering from the 19th and 20th centuries.

Comenius, however, only managed to start developing his peace project of European and world integration. Nevertheless the ideas and suggestions outlined witness to the great depth of Comenius's vision, which partly came out of the legacy of European humanism. At the same time, Comenius's efforts were tied to the best traditions from the Czech Reformation, which in the middle of the fifteenth century gave birth to the peace plan of the "Hussite" King George of Poděbrady. Comenius's spiritual architecture reflects the best of the legacy of the Unity of Brethren, seeking to rectify the individual by means of education and Christian love.[34] In the whole of Comenius's reformative work there is a clear three-fold identity that comes to the fore—Czech, European and Christian. Comenius's reform work is also intertwined with a requirement for religious freedom and tolerance for opinions.[35] Therefore it is possible to describe the Czech Comenius as a European whose intellectual legacy speaks even to today's contradictory situation with its integrational problems.

33. Cf. Kumpera, *Jan Amos Komenský*, 202–3, 306–7; Kumpera, *Cesta světla*, 173–206; Zemek and Kumpera, *Komenský známý neznámý*.

34. Zemek and Kumpera, *Jednota bratrská*; Zemek and Kumpera, *Komenský známý neznámý*

35. Kumpera, "Jaké dobro nám doporučuješ".

## Bibliography

*Europae lumina*. Preface to the work De rerum humanarum emendatione consultatio catholica, Academia: Praha, 1966.

Komenský, Jan Amos. *Clamores Eliae—Křiky Eliášovy* [The Lamentations of Elijah] (Selected edition of J. Beneš). Praha: Primus, 1992.

———. "Europae lumina." Preface to *De rerum humanarum emendatione consultatio catholica*. Academia: Praha, 1966.

———. *Via lucis* [The Way of Light]. Annotated ed. Brno: Miloš Palatka-Almi, 2009.

———. *Všenáprava (Panorthosia). VI. část Obecné porady o nápravě věcí lidských (De rerum humanarum emendatione consultatio catjholica)*[Universal Reform, part 6 of the *General Consultation Concerning the Restoration of Human Affairs*]. Vol. 3. Translated by J. Hendricha et al. Praha: Academia, 1992.

Kumpera, Jan. *Cesta světla* [The Way of Light]. Annotated selection from the works of Comenius. Brno: Almi, 2009.

———. *Poslední pokus českého exilu kolem Komenského o zvrat* v *zemích České koruny* [Last Attempt by the Czech Exiles around Comenius to Return to the Land of the Czech Crown]. Brno: Muzejní a vlastivědná společnost, 1988.

———. "'Jaké dobro nám doporučuješ?—Svobodu': Komenského politické ideály—utopie tehdy i nyní?" ["What Good Do you Suggest For Us?—Freedom": Comenius's Political Ideals—Utopia Then and Now?]. *Studia Comeniana et historica* 43.89–90 (2013) 4–19.

———. *Jan Amos Komenský: Poutník na rozhraní věků* [Jan Amos Comenius: Pilgrim at the Intersection of the Ages]. Praha: Amosius servis, 1992.

———. *Komenského Vlastní životopis: Autobiografie Komenského pro období 1628–1658* [Comenius's Own Biography: Autobiography of Comenius for the Period 1628–1658]. Praha: Odeon, 2017.

———. "Tranquilla Libertas: Frieden in Freiheit in Comenius's Vorstellungen" [Peace in Freedom in Comenius's Writings]. In *Comenius und Weltfrieden* [Comenius and World Peace], 445–56. Berlin: Werner Korthaase, 2005.

Patočka, Jan. *Doslov k Obecné poradě III* [Epilogue to Part III of the *General Consultation*], 533–62. Praha: Svoboda, 1992.

Polišenský, Josef. *Jan Amos Komenský*. 2nd ed. Praha: Statní pedagogické nakladatelství, 1972.

Válka, Josef. "Problém výkladu revelací v Komenského životě a díle" [The Problem of Interpreting the Revelations in Komenský's Life and Work]. *Studia Comeniana et historica* 7 (1977) 105–14.

Zemek, Petr, and Jan Kumpera. *Jednota bratrská: Zbožnost, mravnost, tolerance* [Unites Fratrum: Piety, Morality, Tolerance]. Uherský Brod: Muzeum Jana Amose Komenského, 2007.

———. *Komenský známý neznámý* [Comenius Known and Unknown]. Uherský Brod: Muzeum Jana Amose Komenského, 2018.

# A Golden Dream of Humanity or a Picture of Reality in Comenius's Pansophy?

Radim Červenka

## Introduction

The turn from the sixteenth to the seventeenth centuries, when Comenius lived, and which time his works necessarily reflected, was a period of considerable conflict related to the religious turbulence that triggered the European Reformation. Although John Amos Comenius was an author and thinker whose works surmounted his period in certain aspects, he was also fundamentally influenced by elements typical of many cultural expressions that today we usually label Renaissance, Humanism, Baroque, or Reformation. Despite their conflicting views, all of these cultural streams were linked to the roots of European culture laid in the Christian religion.

A typical element of the Christian religion is the interest in sin. It is not just a monopoly of the evangelicals, the attention given to the problem of sin distinguishes Christianity from other world religions.[1] The issue of sin also framed this chapter, since it does not apply only in the realm of theology, but is also a perspective through which can be seen the reality of human existence. The religious thinker John Amos Comenius saw it the same way.

His work is markedly distinguished by his period and ideological engagement, to which Comenius's universalist concept is largely due, and that

1. Blocher, "Sin," 129.

concept, in turn, is particularly characteristic of his *General Consultation*.[2] Thanks to this, it is possible to think of the legacy of the prominent Czech thinker not only as a unique cultural artifact, but also as a documentary of the time, enabling it to reflect an authentic view into historical thinking. The concepts formed by historical thinking are conditioned by the cultural context in which they are formed, both diachronically and synchronically. As a result, it means that each use of a concept anchored a certain tradition, is at the same time in some way modified or redefined by its current usage.[3]

The preceding interpretational framework is appropriate for our chapter, which will attempt to problematize Comenius's view of the "sinful reality" in several remarks. In the context of this theme, Comenius worked with traditional concepts (the seven sins, original sin), and in his own way transformed them into his thought system.

## Sin as a Picture of Reality

If we ask about the picture of reality in Comenius's consultative work, we seemingly paradoxically come across early modern concepts of utopias. Although the *General Consultation* cannot be declared a full-fledged utopia,[4] there are certain elements connected to utopian thinking in it. Comenius himself worked with utopian literature, so he was familiar with the genre and felt the need to comment on it. This is illustrated, for example, in his evaluation of Campanella's utopian visions in *The City of the Sun* .[5]

The utopian aspects of Comenius's works themselves are also an important starting point for us, as they are comparable to the ideal of the golden age of humanity, which has had a significant impact on the culture of the early modern period. Here we encounter the interpretation of Jean Delumeau, which was based on numerous reports seeking the idealized life in the most diverse forms of ideas about an earthly paradise. But such notions of the ideal are, according to the French historian, signs of grief over the loss of paradise.[6] This is related to the second fundamental interpretive concept of the dominance of pessimism in cultural expressions of the late

2. Čapková et al., "Philosophical Significance."

3. Newhauser, *In the Garden*, 2. Richard Newhauser bases his methodological anchoring of the interpretation of the concept of sin in history (Koselleck, "Begriffsgeschichte").

4. Čížek, *Conception of Man*, 135; Floss, "Jan Amos Comenius," 13.

5. See, for example, Komenský, *Obecná porada*, 2:240.

6. Delumeau, *Dějiny ráje*, 137.

Middle Ages and early modern period. In a wide range of analyzed works, Delumeau points to the pessimism of the authors regarding the nature of human existence. In other words, it is reasonable to assume that in these expressions are revealed a belief in the prevailing sinfulness of the real, contemporary authors.[7]

Both poles are anchored in their own religious backgrounds. The ideal refers to the loss of paradise caused by eating the forbidden fruit from the tree of knowledge, the original sin of the human grandparents. Although the event takes up only a few pages in the Bible, it was the basis of the perception of human nature and the relationship between God and humanity held at that time. Of course, the story itself was not reproduced only in the literal narrative of the Bible. Especially since the invention of the printing press, the whole message from Genesis has also been reproduced by authors other than learned theologians. This has led to a variety of reinterpretations, but they have remained a key to human notions about the world.[8] The sinfulness seen in reality is, then, the observable result of these events. On the one hand we see a theological concept, but it is used to explain existential questions. This leads to a mixture of social and purely religious issues captured in written culture.

John Amos Comenius also tied his work with emendatory ambitions placed on humanity to such a concept; in a specific way he established the problem of lost paradise and worked with it in his own way.[9] The resulting reform of human affairs was based on the theological background of Comenius's thought system. Similarly, Comenius's pedagogical concept was based on theology and it is precisely the power of hereditary sin that should be reduced by education. He emphasized the necessity of working with young people, since the reform of old people is already problematic.[10]

As was typical of him, Comenius also recognized the problematic nature of social reality. "Only what is broken is fixed. Thus, when we propose a consultation on the repair of human affairs, we assume that they are broken, or out of order. Perhaps this does not require laborious proof, because laments that nothing is in its place and that everything deviates from the correct path (to the right or to the left), are universal. For people who see at least something, see that instead of wisdom there is ignorance

7. Delumeau, *Hřích a strach*.

8. Crowther, *Adam and Eve*, 9–11.

9. Klosová, "Dva modely," 68.

10. Kišš, "Concept of Paradise," 108.

or sophistry, instead of devoutness there is unbelief or superstition, instead of management of society there is anarchy or confusion, or tyranny and oppression. However, since we have decided to trace back everything from its very roots, we will first look at what it means, or what is said to be broken. Brokenness is said to be that which is, in and of itself, so changed that it no longer conforms to its own idea and cannot fulfil its function. But what is the purpose of our things? According to God's design this world, to which we were sent at birth, should be God's school, full of light, God's temple, full of piety, God's kingdom, full of order and justice."[11] Especially illustrative is Comenius's belief about the universality of the problem of corruption. Comenius's conception of the starting condition began in the *Panegersia*, (one of the oldest parts of the *Consultation*), with the generally accepted view of reality, the corruption of the world, which does not need to be laboriously proven. With such a critical condemnation, Comenius approached that which motivated the writing of the contemporary utopias. The outline of the ideal society came out of the search for escape from the corrupt society, the typical means of expressing it was a path to another place where the ideal was realized.[12]

In explaining the problematic key categories of Comenius's so-called human affairs, he concluded that they had a historical dimension. He turned to the golden age of human paradise in the biblical past, where the whole problem began. He used the generally known story of the perpetration of the original sin by Adam and Eve to explain the historical background of his thought system. In the time of the Reformation, the reinterpretation of a notoriously well-known story was a frequently used method to explain theological ideas to a wider audience, and the story itself, for this purpose, could be put into a different form than that briefly presented in the Bible.[13] Comenius also did the same, combining a well-known biblical story with the intention of making its details accessible to the wider public, as was common among scholars of his time.[14]

11. Komenský, *Obecná porada*, 1:84.

12. Patočka, *Komeniologické studie*, 35; Klosová, "Dva modely," 65. Modern utopias were located in places detached from the surrounding world. Seafaring discoveries inspired the use of the island motif in, for example, Thomas More's *Utopia* and James Harrington's *Ocean Republic*. An early modern city enclosed in its walls could offer a similar function (Miller, "Snový svět idejí"). Comenius used the narrative possibilities of an enclosed city in his *Labyrinth of the World* (Červenka, "Hříšný člověk").

13. Crowther, *Adam and Eve*, 16.

14. Grafton, *Bring Out Your Dead*, 7.

In Comenius's interpretation, Adam was to observe, name, and manage the other creatures, which Comenius considered to be the beginning of philosophy. After the creation of Eve, human beings were charged with multiplying and filling the earth. This event stood at the beginning of the second of the human affairs—politics. The fundamental imperative for Adam was to keep away from that which was forbidden. It was the historic moment of the genesis of religion.[15] However, as is well known, Adam violated the religious command and here was the beginning of the corruption of humanity. Humanity itself, then, must try to restore the abovementioned three basic human affairs.

## Humanity in Conflict with the Seven Sins

Comenius's optimistic anthropology was thus complemented by the picture of problematic reality. One of the methods Comenius used to describe the situation was that of using the concept of the seven sins.

Historical research to date has considered the doctrine of the seven deadly sins to be a key moral code of Christianity, widespread and generally accepted in the Middle Ages. The meaning of the seven sins was closely linked with the medieval process of repentance, where sins served to formulate transgressions against social and religious order, followed by satisfaction and absolution.[16] But with the advent of the Reformation, the concept of the seven sins became increasingly marginalized as it was forced out by the more prominent Christian code, the Ten Commandments. Some researchers have interpreted the retreat of the seven sins in the early modern period as definitive, saying that rhetorical use in the sources of the time was only an echo of the original meaning of the whole concept.[17] But the entrenched concept found its place in many younger sources, thus it is possible to argue that its purpose changed in the thinking of the time. Although the seven sins were no longer a principal part of the process of repentance, their theological function was replaced primarily as a means of social criticism and political argumentation in the contemporary texts of the most diverse genres.[18]

15. Čížek, *Komenský a Bacon*, 65–70.

16. Koch, "Repentance," 258–59.

17. Bloomfield, *Seven Deadly Sins*, 200–201, 441; Bossy, "Moral Arithmetic," 220.

18. Newhauser, "Understanding Sin."

Not surprisingly, the traditional concept of the seven deadly sins was repeatedly also used by Comenius, as his extensive and universalist work is also a reflection of the typical elements of the thinking of the time.

In his pansophic "Spiritual World," Comenius spoke of the three basic religious combinations in which people occur.[19] After a combination, or a certain union, with God, a person must enter into a union with angels.[20] Only the combination with angels depends not only on the ability to deal with angels, but also with evil spirits such as the fallen angel—Satan. He traditionally threatens people by means of the specific sins which they embody. In other words, in Christian culture, Satan and the problem of sin are interconnected themes.[21]

The character of Satan, or the Devil, is a personalization of the temptation of sin in everyday reality. And this is also how Comenius described the seven deadly sins. In the framework of the suggested ability to deal with evil spirits (*daemonotechnia*) he described the method Satan uses to attack people and how people should defend themselves. Comenius used the number seven for the set of seven sins everyone should be on their guard against:

1. Guard against pride . . .
2. Guard against idleness . . .
3. Guard against inquisitiveness . . .
4. Guard against envy . . .
5. Guard against indulgence and worry about your stomach . . .
6. Guard against disobedience . . .
7. Guard against avarice . . .[22]

The specific sins contained in the doctrine of the seven sins enjoyed considerable variability. However, we can try to compare the specific sins Comenius used with the most widespread set of sins used in his time, which is the SALIGIA list. The name doesn't mean anything, it is an anagram of

19. "The Spiritual World" is a chapter in Comenius's *Pansophy*, a section in the *Obecná porada*.

20. Komenský, *Obecná porada*, 2:364.

21. Grollová and Rywiková, *Militia est*, 36.

22. Comenius used these Latin sins: "superbia, otia, curiositas, invidia, gula, inobedentia, avaritia" (Komenský, *Obecná porada*, 1:691, par. 1191.) See also Komenský, *Obecná porada*, 2:372.

the first letters of the Latin names of the sins included—*superbia, avaratia, luxuria, ira, gula, invidia, acedia.*[23] Four of the sins Comenius used are literally the same (*superbia*—pride, *avaritia*—avarice, *gula*—gluttony, *invidia*—envy), and one of them differs only in the choice of words. Comenius's *otia*—idleness fully corresponds to *acedia*—sloth. The sins of anger and fornication seem to be exchanged for inquisitiveness and disobedience. In the case of inquisitiveness, it is worth mentioning that it is one of the sins in Augustine's triad (*curiositas*), and this is surely where Comenius drew it from.[24] The use of extracts from Augustine's work is justified by both the fact that Augustine was for him a significant authority, and, above all else, the place in the *Pansofia* where Comenius uses the seven sins and reminds the readers of the sin of curiosity (inquisitiveness, *curiositas*).[25] Disobedience can then be included in the sin of pride, since it was precisely pride that led to disobedience in the biblical story of the commission of the original sin.

Satan tempting people through wrongdoing is, in Comenius's work, a realistic picture of the evil that threatens people and society. But even here we find Comenius's optimism in his emendatory effort. "People themselves make Satan into God by attributing to him power he does not have (for he can do nothing other than what he can use from nature, and even that is only with God's permission), they are overly afraid of him and don't stand up to him, but submit to him. Steer clear of him if you want to escape destruction."[26]

In accordance with his philosophy, in which he attaches great importance to the human will, Comenius presented the need for people to actively resist the temptation to sin.[27] He described in concrete terms how to defend oneself against attacks referred to as sins. A person can always face the temptations of evil spirits with the help of fasting and prayer. Theological coping with sin can be carried out with active or passive cleansing.[28] Comenius stressed the need for the active approach.

23. Grollová and Rywiková, *Militia est*, 51.
24. Newhauser, *In the Garden*, xi.
25. Komenský, *Obecná porada*, 2:206.
26. Komenský, *Obecná porada*, 2:372.
27. Čížek, *Filosoficko-teologická*, 72–74.
28. Marunová, "Tehdy celé stvoření," 12.

Comenius used sins in "The Moral World" too, where he presented his optimistic anthropology.[29] In Comenius's conception, humanity is blessed with free will, in contrast to every other creature (including angels) who have not been given such sovereign wills.[30] In spite of that, or rather, precisely because of that, he worked with the fixed categories of the Christian religion in this part of his consultative work. Sins have been an important category of Christian anthropology since the Middle Ages,[31] and, moreover, it is a widely understandable category that Comenius used repeatedly. A certain moral individualism based on the free will of human beings was significantly anchored in the evangelical morality of Comenius. The link between human morality and religious norms was one of the distinctive features of the reformational thinking,[32] in which Comenius was anchored, even though his optimism was very pronounced.

In "The Moral World," Comenius warned about the specific dangers that are directly contrary to morality, using the concept of the seven sins. Before getting into the list itself, he explained that our everyday reality is problematic: "We get involved in things that are not related to our true happiness, we let ourselves be fooled by a false good, and because we are primarily concerned with what we should not deal with until later, we don't live our lives, we only use them."[33]

Comenius further advised people to resist every vice, similarly to the place where he used the seven sins in "The Spiritual World," which is why the interconnectedness of the religiously and morally oriented parts of the *Pansophy* are evident here. However, in "The Moral World" he abandoned the number seven. The number of sins used could vary considerably, but of course the importance of the number seven was not insignificant. The number played an important role in communication between the clergy and the laity, especially in the context of pre-Reformation penitential practice, because it was anchored in folk culture.[34] According to Richard Newhauser, the transformation of science in the early modern era also revealed the abandonment of the number seven, since it was no longer used symbolically, nor had any practical importance. Seven became more of a

29. "The Moral World" is a chapter in Comenius's *Pansophy*.
30. Čížek, *Conception of Man*, 75–76.
31. Newhauser, "The Capital Vices."
32. Levi, *Renaissance*, 11.
33. Komenský, *Obecná porada*, 2:206.
34. Bossy, "Moral Arithmetic," 220.

tool of social criticism than of theology, and hand in hand with that ceased to mean specifically seven; the number could be reduced or increased.[35] It is thus possible to consider the hypothesis that in "The Moral World," where Comenius placed more emphasis on the social and anthropological aspects, the number did not carry so much weight. Comenius may have done it intentionally.

"What is sensual licentiousness? It is as harmful as the others, but more immoral. To be licentious is bestial."[36] When Comenius worked with the seven sins in "The Moral World," he also mentioned the sin of fornication, which was left out of the above-mentioned composition in "The Spiritual World." In the introductory passage, the part where the sin of fornication was analyzed, he emphasized that it is worse from a moral perspective than other sins. He paid special attention to fornication there, because he worked out that sin in two parts. In Comenius's original manuscript, one part was placed on its own page.[37]

Other sins Comenius dealt with in that same place in the *General Consultation* are drunkenness, avarice, and, lastly, pride. Besides the Augustinian curiosity (*curiositas*), which in the next part immediately followed the sections devoted to more traditional sins, there were the usual attributes of the seven sins. Just as there was no emphasis on the number seven in the original concept, we also find other deviations, for example, in the sin of gluttony. While in "The Spiritual World" Comenius used the traditional term of gluttony (*gulla*), in "The Moral World" he spoke of drunkenness in the paragraph "Against Drunkenness and Wastefulness" (*Adversus Ebrietatem et Helluationem*). The sin of gluttony involves excessive consumption of both food and drinks, especially alcoholic ones. "Drunkenness is nothing but merry madness. A drunkard is like a parched pumice stone, an eternally thirsty sponge. Drunkenness is a continuously smoking and reeking chimney that obscures the mind with a black cloud, exposes the body to harmful air, and afflicts the body in various ways until it finally brings it to the grave."[38] This allegory sums up the unfortunate way drunkenness

35. Newhauser, "These Seven Devils," 173–74.

36. Komenský, *Obecná porada*, 2:207.

37. This is from the section "Against Pleasure or Dissipation" (*Adversus Voluptates seu Luxuriam*). On its own page is another section, "Against Avarice" (*Adversus Avaritiam*) (Komenský, *Obecná porada*, 2:206–7, 254).

38. Komenský, *Obecná porada*, 2:207.

affects a person. Referring to Seneca, he warned that drunkenness opened the door to other vices, which was a typical *tópos* associated with this sin.[39]

In "The Moral World" Comenius, of course, also talked about the virtues that formed an important part of his emendatory system of thought.[40] It came out of the classical thinking about morality, as evidenced by the abundant quotations from classical authorities in connection with Christian thought, from which Comenius in no way deviated. His concept was, in that regard, based on traditional knowledge, which he redefined according to the needs of his text.

## Good Deeds, Repentance, and the Czech Reformation

The consultative character of the observed passages on sin once again adds to the important contextual dimension. Comenius's advice on what people should do with their problematic sinfulness was connected to the Unity of Brethren denomination. In the two-centuries-long historical development of the Czech Reformation, a distinctive approach to coping with sin was established. Its basic premise was an active approach to the problematic sinfulness of humanity. At first glance, the question could be raised whether the Czech Reformation, in this respect, denied a basic point of the European Reformation, namely, the doctrine of justification by faith alone, which was probably the most fundamental breaking point between the old Christianity and its new version proposed by Martin Luther.[41]

In the case of the notable John Amos Comenius, this typical motif of the Czech Reformation calls forth specific questions. Comenius spent the prime of his life in exile, having to rely on alliances with other evangelical streams. Although we might come to the conclusion that the Unity of Brethren subscribed to the evangelical conception of the doctrine of righteousness in the confession given by Comenius in Amsterdam in 1662,[42] in this regard he never fully abandoned the distinctive view of the Czech Reformation.[43] A comparison with other works from the period points out that is precisely Comenius's anchoring in the thinking of the Czech Reformation that in certain ways distinguished him from other similarly-oriented

39. Kümin, *Drinking Matters*, 9.

40. Hábl, "Even If," 54.

41. Hamm, "Was ist reformatorische?"

42. Beblavý and Říčan, *Čtyři vyznání*, 139.

43. Červenka, "Hřích jako hranice," 220–21.

thinkers of his time.[44] We also encounter this problem in his crowning work, the *General Consultation*.

In the *Panorthosia*, where he suggested how to stop all the great disputes, he also spoke about justification. Summing up a number of approaches by the most diverse of the reformers, he concluded that the whole dispute was nearly unnecessary. "So there is no need to argue whether we are justified by faith or by deeds. For the answer is: both. That is, the Scripture explicitly says both."[45] The environment of the Czech Reformation always emphasized the importance of faith leading to salvation, but did not neglect the need for a person's active participation through their deeds.

In connection with the active cleansing from sin, one must not neglect to repent. Comenius drew attention to the need for repentance, again in line with the teaching of other reformers, "Their teachings contradict the words of our God, who calls everyone and summons them to repentance. People under the influence of that teaching become idle, partly from fear, partly from despair."[46] Of course, he also refers to the Bible: "On the other hand, many of God's admonitions are delivered to men as if they depended purely on people's own will: 'Make yourselves a new heart and a new spirit' (Ezek 18:31; see also Deut 30:6 and 10:36). God thus commands repentance (Matt 3)."[47]

The traditional practice of repentance had three parts: (1) remorse, the so-called affliction of the soul, (2) confession of the sin, and (3) satisfaction, which is associated with the priest's absolution in the Catholic setting.[48] Of course, Comenius did not agree with this, and even explicitly criticized the act of confession to a priest, which he considered to be "Violence against truth and conscience."[49] Comenius thus clearly separated himself from the post-Tridentine Catholic concept of the practice of repentance, of which confession to a priest was an integral part. But we do find all parts of traditional repentance mentioned. In the above quotation he referred to the symbolism of the heart, which is very common in Comenius and it is reasonable to associate it with remorse for sin. Comenius emphasized the confession of sin, for example, in the pansophic dictionary under

44. Sousedík, "Comenius Prinzip"; Beneš, "Pojem harmonie."

45. Komenský, *Obecná porada*, 3:311.

46. Komenský, *Obecná porada*, 2:395.

47. Komenský, *Obecná porada*, 2:392.

48. Thayer, *Penitence*, 11.

49. Komenský, *Obecná porada*, 3:345.

the headword "confession." "Denial of sin is a doubling of sin." Nor did he neglect the satisfaction of sins. As we have already mentioned, when he spoke of the seven sins in "The Spiritual World," he recommended prayer and fasting, elements of the traditional satisfaction of sins, as a weapon against them.

## Conclusion

Eduard Petrů offered a hypothesis which stated that the ambition to realize the ideal in the everyday world was rooted in the traditions of the Czech Reformation. There was also an emphasis on the pursuit of active cleansing from sin. This approach, according to Eduard Petrů, prevented efforts to create utopian literature in the Czech environment.[50] Along these lines, we do not attempt to assess to what extent Comenius's work was or was not part of the efforts of the time in the genres of utopian literature. Nevertheless the ideal that Comenius aimed at also suggested a pessimistic view of everyday reality. Comenius perceived the sinfulness of humanity to be one of the important problems, but believed it must be dealt with actively. It was based on the established concepts of the Christian religion (the seven sins, original sin, the conflict with Satan), which, in the spirit of these traditional schemes, transformed into an appropriate form for the consultative character of his work. It was typical work for these concepts, as modern research on other sources has already noted (Crowther, Newhauser, Delumeau). Comenius's work in these component aspects falls into the views of the early modern European culture, as these researchers interpret it. Since these questions have their basis in religious thought, we come across Comenius's anchoring in the traditional Czech Reformation, whose last significant representative he was.

50. Petrů, "Komenský a absence," 68.

## Bibliography

Beblavý, Jan, and Rudolf Říčan, eds. *Čtyři vyznání: vyznání Augsburské, Bratrské, Helvetské a České* [Four Creeds: Augsburg, Brethren, Helvetic, and Czech]. Praha: Komenského Evangelická Fakulta Bohoslovecká, 1951.

Beneš, Josef. "Pojem harmonie u Wolfganga Ratkeho a u Jana Amose Komenského—blízké pojmy, vzdálená východiska" [The Notion of Harmony in Wolfgang Ratke and John Amos Comenius—Close Concepts, Distant Starting Points]. In *Idea harmonie v díle Jana Amose Komenského*, edited by Věra Schifferová, 89–94. Červený Kostelec: Mervart, 2014.

Blocher, Henri A. G. "Sin." In *The Oxford Handbook of Evangelical Theology*, edited by G. R. McDermott. Oxford: Oxford University Press, 2013.

Bloomfield, Morton W. *The Seven Deadly Sins: An Introduction to the History of a Religious Concept*. East Lansing, MI: Michigan State College Press, 1952.

Bossy, John. "Moral Arithmetic: Seven Sins into Ten Commandments." In *Conscience and Casuistry in Early Modern Europe*, edited by Edmund Leitees, 214–34. Cambridge: Cambridge University Press, 1988.

Čapková, Dagmar et al. "The Philosophical Significance of the Work of Comenius." *Acta Comeniana* 32.8 (1989) 5–16.

Červenka, Radim. "Hřích jako hranice mezi konfesemi a počátky reformace v předbělohorských Čechách" [Sin as the Border between Confessions and the Beginning of the Reformation in Pre-White-Mountain Bohemia]. *Studia Comeniana et Historica* 97–98 (2017) 211–23.

———. "Hříšný člověk v dílech utrakvistických autorů a Labyrintu Jana Amose Komenského" [Sinful Man in the Works of the Utraquist Authors and the *Labyrinth* of John Amos Comenius]. *Studia Comeniana et Historica*, 93–94 (2015) 46–64.

Čížek, Jan. *The Conception of Man in the Works of John Amos Comenius*. European Studies in Theology, Philosophy and History of Religions 15. New York: Peter Lang, 2016.

———. *Filosoficko-teologická koncepce člověka v emendačním díle Jana Amose Komenského* [Philosophical-Theological Conception of Man in the Emendational Work of Jan Amos Comenius]. PhD diss, Univerzita Palackého v Olomouci, 2014.

———. *Komenský a Bacon: Dvě raně novověké cesty k obnově vědění* [Comenius and Bacon: Two Early Modern Ways towards the Restoration of Knowledge]. Červený Kostelec: Pavel Mervart, 2017.

Crowther, Kathleen M. *Adam and Eve in the Protestant Reformation*. New York: Cambridge University Press, 2010.

Delumeau, Jean. *Dějiny ráje: Zahrada rozkoše* [The History of Paradise: The Garden of Delight]. Praha: Argo, 2003.

———. *Hřích a strach: pocit viny na evropském Západě ve 13. až 18. Století* [Sin and Fear: Guilt in the European West in the 13th to 18th Centuries]. Praha: Volvox Globator, 1998.

Floss, Pavel. "Jan Amos Komenský v duchovních zápasech našeho tisíciletí" [Jan Amos Comenius in the Spiritual Struggles of Our Millenium]. *Studia Comeniana et Historica* 61 (1999) 13–23.

Grafton, Anthony. *Bring Out Your Dead: The Past as Revelation*. Cambridge: Harvard University Press, 2004.

Grollová, Jana, and Daniela Rywiková. *Militia est vita hominis: sedm smrtelných hříchů a sedm skutků milosrdenství v literárních a vizuálních pramenech českého středověku*

[Seven Mortal Sins and Seven Acts of Mercy in the Literary and Visual Sources of the Czech Middle Ages]. České Budějovice: Veduta, 2013.

Hábl, Jan. "Even If No One Is Watching: Comenius's Anthropological Assumptions of Moral Political Practice." *Studia Comeniana et Historica* 89–90 (2013) 49–57.

Hamm, Berndt. "Was ist reformatorische Rechtefertigungslehre?" [What Is the Reformational Doctrine of Justification?]. *Zeitschrift für Theologie und Kirche* 83.1 (1986) 1–38.

Kišš, Igor. "The Concept of Paradise as the Theological Starting Point for Comenius' Pedagogy." In *Jan Amos Komenský—odkaz kultuře vzdělávání*, edited by Svatava Chocholová et al., 104–10. Praha: Academia, 2009.

Koch, G. "Repentance" [Pokání]. In *Slovník katolické dogmatiky*, edited by Wolfgang Beinert, 258–59. Olomouc: Matice cyrilometodějská, 1994.

Klosová, Markéta. "Dva modely dokonalé společnosti: Andrae a Komenský" [Two Models of the Perfect Society: Andrae and Comenius]. *Studia Comeniana et historica* 80 (2008) 63–73.

Komenský, Jan Amos. *Obecná porada o nápravě věcí lidských* [General Consultation on the Restoration of Human Affairs]. Vols. I–III. Praha: Nakladatelství Svoboda, 1992.

Kosselleck, Reinhart. "Begriffsgeschichte und Sozialgeschichte" [Conceptual and Social History]. In *Soziologie und Sozialgeschichte*, edited by Peter Christian Ludz, 116–31. Opladen: VS Verlag für Sozialwissenschaften, 1972.

Kümin, Beat. *Drinking Matters: Public Houses and Social Exchange in Early Modern Central Europe*. New York: Palgrave Macmillan, 2007.

Levi, Anthony. *Renaissance and Reformation: The Intellectual Genesis*. New Haven: Yale University Press, 2004.

Marunová, Magdalena. "Tehdy celé stvoření bude jedním tělem" [Then the Whole Creation Will Be One Body]. *Studia Thelogica* 18 (2016) 1–22.

Miller, Jaroslav. "Snový svět idejí a syrovost současnosti: městská historiografie raného novověku jako utopie?" [The Dream World of Ideas and the Rawness of the Present: Urban Historiography of the Early Modern Period as a Utopia]. *Český časopis historický* 106 (2008) 261–87.

Newhauser, Richard G., ed. "The Capital Vices as Medieval Anthropology." In *Laster im Mittelalter*, edited by Martin Rohde, 105–23. Berlin: de Gruyter, 2009.

———. *In the Garden of Evil: The Vices and Culture in the Middle Ages*. Turnhout: Brepols, 2005.

———. "These Seven Devils: The Capital Vices on the Way to Modernity." In *Sin in Medieval and Early Modern Culture*, edited by Richard Newhauser and Susan J. Ridyard, 157–88. Woodbridge: York Medieval Press, 2012.

———. "Understanding Sin: Recent Scholarship and the Capital Vices." In *Sin in Medieval and Early Modern Culture*, edited by Richard Newhauser and Susan J. Ridyard, 1–19. Woodbridge: York Medieval Press, 2012.

Patočka, Jan. *Komeniologické studie: soubor textů o J. A. Komenském. Díl 2. Texty publikované* v *letech 1959–1977* [Comeniological Studies: A Collection of Texts by J. A. Comenius. Vol 2, Texts Published in 1959–1977]. Praha: Oikoymenh, 1998.

Petrů, Eduard. "Komenský a absence české utopie" [Comenius and the Absence of Utopia]. In *Utopia* w *językach, literaturach i kulturách Słowian*, edited by Barbara Czapik-Lityńska, 67–73. Katowice: *Wydawnictwo* Uniwersytetu Śląskiego, 1997.

Sousedík, Stanislav. "Comenius Prinzip Natürlichkeit der Erziehung und sein Philosophischer Hintergrund" [Comenius's Principle of the Naturalness of Education and Its Philosophical Background]. *Theologie und Philosophie* 58 (1983) 34–47.

Thayer, Anne T. *Penitence, Preaching, and the Coming of the Reformation.* Aldershot: Ashgate, 2002.

# "It Would Be Good to Have a Paradise"

## *Comenius on Learners Past and Present*

David I. Smith

### Introduction

Some time ago, I visited a secondary school and observed a history class. Students sat in straight rows facing a screen where a long sequence of bulleted sentences offered factual information about a particular stretch of the American Revolutionary War. A dainty pink border around the slides offered some concession to aesthetics but felt jarringly at odds with the terse summaries of the suffering endured by combatants. There was potential here for a rich set of connections. Physical and ideological conflict, national identity, beliefs, religion, ideals of service and honor, violence, death, purpose—a host of potential links between the subject matter and life beyond the walls of the history classroom lurked amid the dry, descriptive sentences. Students no doubt carried with them their own convictions, resentments, and sufferings. Yet connections to contemporary social reality, to student's own faiths or fears, or to other dimensions of learning remained submerged. Students were asked to copy each sentence in silence, by hand, into their notebooks. They did so dutifully until they left the room to pay their dues to another branch of learning. I wondered what Comenius would have thought.

Comenius hoped to transform all schools in ways "useful for humankind," a universalizing impulse that for him was rooted in the particularity of Christian assumptions. The particularity of this root system may at first seem at odds with the vision that framed this volume, which was to address the question of whether Comenius had ideas that may still be taken as realistic (as opposed to utopian) and that are universally valid and useful for humankind. Grappling with the value of his pedagogical thinking for today requires engagement with the complicated relationships between belief and practice. I hope here to sketch a few of the problems and possibilities involved.

## Gardens

There is a little passage buried in a late chapter of Comenius's *Panorthosia* that hints at some of the promises and perils of drawing his pedagogical mind into dialogue with present-day education. The passage is not actually about schools, although it is about learning. In the midst of plans for the comprehensive reform of social institutions, Comenius offers a suggestion about gardens.[1] He thinks it would be helpful to have a kind of combined park/zoo/museum in each town. His reasoning is worth quoting in full:

> It would also be good to have a Paradise of delight [*Paradisum deliciarium*] in every kingdom, republic, and market town, that is: 1. All kinds of plant. 2. Minerals and materials dug from the ground. 3. Animals of the land, water, and air. 4. All kinds of artifacts. The rationale [*ratio*] is:
>
> 1. This would be one powerful restorative for cultivation [*culturae*] among all nations,
> 2. and also an outward symbol that the new Adam has opened up for us not only a heavenly paradise, but also an earthly one, Isaiah 11:6–9.
> 3. It would be a source of pleasure to the devout, as they rejoice in the reform of our affairs.
> 4. And it would be a beneficial medicine for the body, and for the human mind a noteworthy test of character [δοκιμασία], so as to be a spur to each person to plant such a garden of delight [*hortum deliciarium*] in themselves.[2]

1. Comenius, *Universal Reform*, 107.
2. Comenius, *Panorthosia*, 356. My translation.

Given his lifelong wrestling with pedagogical questions, it is no surprise to find that Comenius's purpose for bringing up this facet of town planning is pedagogical. The park/zoo/museum is to serve "cultivation," the fostering of community culture, a term with its roots firmly in the soil of agriculture.[3] As already implied by his choice of term for the growth process, it becomes clear as Comenius continues that the point of assembling representative samples of the vegetable, mineral, and animal kingdoms is not to amass information or to serve mere taxonomy. He hopes, rather, to prompt a more holistic formation of the self within its community. The goal is for the cultivation/culturing of the members of the community in a manner that draws together pleasure and delight, bodily health, spiritual discipline, virtuous character, social reform, harmony, and awareness of the larger story of redemption and reformation within which individual experience is to be embedded. The habitual holism of Comenius's thinking becomes visible as soon as we try to specify his suggestion in more recent, more analytic categories: roughly, he wants us to establish external/inward, literal/symbolic gardens/parks/zoos/museums so that we can grow in faith/joy/health/hope/virtue in our minds/spirits/bodies/cultures/societies through God's/our agency. The present-day reader must decide whether to read this as hopelessly fuzzy thinking or as an invitation to learn how to think things together that have been too sharply separated in our own habits of thought.

The choice of the term "paradise of delight" for the proposed institutions invokes a rich narrative palimpsest.[4] It has its roots in the Genesis narrative of the Garden of Eden (*paradiso voluptatis* [Gen 2:15 Vulg.]) in which the first humans were to find beauty, virtue, meaningful labor, and communion with God. It echoes the imagery of the Hebrew wisdom literature, in which evocations of growth in wisdom invite us to picture ourselves as flourishing trees (e.g., Job 15:32–4; Ps 1; Prov 13:12). The idea of planting a garden of delight *within* oneself appears in patristic passages, as when, for instance, the Epistle to Diognetus promises devout wisdom-seekers that they will "become a very paradise of delight" and will "make a grove to spring up and flourish within themselves, which yields all manner of nourishment and adorns them with fruits of every kind."[5] This patristic imagery of spiritual formation was linked to formal learning through medieval

3. Eagleton, *Idea of Culture*.

4. Smith, "Biblical Imagery."

5. Staniforth, *Early Christian Writings*, 150.

appropriations such as the *Hortus Deliciarum* of Herrad of Landsberg,[6] arriving eventually through further mediations at Comenius's talk of schools as gardens, gardens as schools, and the self as a place to plant gardens. The further backdrop of the Hebrew prophets, in which the garden of Eden is refigured as an image of societal shalom, of peaceful, just community flourishing, adds a social justice element to the image. The "garden of delight" invoked in Isaiah 5:1–8 is associated with justice in place of bloodshed and distress, a connection that recurs, for instance, in Isa 58. The Isaiah passage referenced here by Comenius, Isaiah 11, focuses even more cosmically on the removal of violence and destruction in a harmonious, renewed creation, the lion lying with the lamb and the earth filled with the kind of knowledge of God that yields peace. The traditioned image of the "paradise of delight" thus spans (with echoes in Comenius's present proposal) individual spiritual growth (the garden "in themselves") and ethical maturity ("test of character"), the just ordering of society ("the reform of our affairs"), and a horizon of ultimate renewal ("a heavenly paradise, but also an earthly one"). Comenius is recommending quite literal institutions, actual gardens and informative displays built with sweat and scholarly diligence, made up of material things. They equally exist as narratively embedded signifiers, invoking the underlying story arc of creation and its restoration from fallen fragmentation to wholeness.[7] They might be said to combine the realistic and the utopian; they do so because of the underlying conviction that the realistic is not synonymous with the empirical and that the restoration of all things is part of the trajectory of the real world.

The connections among the spiritual, the material, and the narrative horizon are carried not only by the choice of biblical nomenclature ("paradise of delight") and the explicit reference to biblical symbolism ("the new Adam," Isaiah 6), but by an implicit assumption of harmony between various facets of existence that structures the rationale for the proposed gardens. The redemptive symbolism is offered as part of the actual meaning of the garden—an outward symbol and a provocation to spiritual growth are what the garden would *be*, just as surely as it would be a source of knowledge and bodily exercise. This does not seem to require the inclusion of Bible story exhibits or brochures with accompanying homilies. The garden itself, with its array of the fruits of creation, is understood as pointing beyond itself, and those of serious mind are challenged to receive it as such. This will

6. Green et al., *Hortus Deliciarum*.

7. Smith and Felch, *Teaching*.

be a test of their character and discernment. Walking among the world of creatures and of human industry should prompt us to inner piety; if it does not, something in us has failed a crucial test. Inner piety should prompt us to rejoice in the reform of ourselves and our society, and so is in the end inseparable from outer service and bodily wellbeing. The animal, vegetable and mineral; the arts and crafts and the realm of nature; the bodily, the spiritual, and social; the earthly and the heavenly; the mundane, the civic, and the religious—these are narrated as facets of a complex simultaneity, a harmony in which each may readily invoke the others. The gardens, like the world that they figure, are not simply convenient visual aids to spice up the cold, hard facts of reality. They are to be taken as "self-transcending" and "inherently educational."[8] All of the above articulates why it would be "good" to locate such a microcosm of the harmoniously ordered cosmos at the heart of each local community, lest we forget that our common life should echo the divinely centered harmony of the whole and fall back into discord. Given the cosmic nature of the stakes, the proposal can only be offered with universal intent to "every kingdom, state, and market-town."

## Problems

We see here the strikingly organic character often noticed in Comenius's reflections on school and society. Yet the brief for the chapters in this volume asked not about coherence of thought, but for ideas that might be "realistic" and "universally valid" in the present-day context. Once we put the question this way, complications emerge.

To begin with, a present-day understanding of what it would mean for Comenius's suggestions to be "realistic" might be alien to his own. If, for instance, we are tempted to think of the rise of the natural sciences and the emancipation of philosophy from theology as the foundations of a rational, realistic outlook, then there are aspects of Comenius's thinking that must seem irrational and unreal. The medieval cosmos, with its vision of a narratively ordered reality anchored in divine providence and constantly gesturing beyond itself to its sacred horizon of meaning, and the Renaissance faith in the correspondences to be found between the world's disparate elements, have in modern societies given way to the modern idea of the universe, in which things are taken to be just things and their

8. Hábl, *Being Human(e)*, 81–82.

relationships essentially material.[9] Naturalistic accounts of how the world works have come to be privileged over theological explanations, at least in significant swathes of society. The gradual creation of a "buffered," autonomous individual has eroded the idea of the self as normatively embedded in a relational, narrative cosmos.[10] Comenius stands closer to the outset of this cultural journey, and there are aspects of its development that he would likely not have applauded. Although he has been lauded for his educational turn to the real, he also maintained[11] that "real things should be looked at individually and in their own context as arranged with divine skill in the fabric of the world, the structure of the human Mind, and the eloquence of the word of God." Since his view of reality was centered on the idea of a fundamental cosmic harmony holding together the realm of the senses, that of the intellect, and that of divine revelation, patterns of thought that sought to sever one of these from the others seemed to him unrealistic and unwise. His "syncritic" method focused on honoring the connections and helped tether the empirical to faith and virtue.[12] A move toward straightforward naturalism was, to him, unrealistic.[13] The degree to which his ideas may be taken to be "realistic" is connected in some measure to the degree to which a reader of his work finds naturalism plausible as an account of what is real.

This pushes us into related difficulties with "universally valid," because questions about what is fundamentally real are not ones about which all agree. Imagine a city council in a modern, secular state entertaining Comenius's proposal discussed above. It might, of course, still be felt that parks and museums are a good thing, that health and recreation matter, and even that such provision might help societal health. It is harder to imagine a call to reflect on Christ's securing of an earthly and heavenly paradise being taken up as the basis for inviting the public to partake of the new resource. The last element in Comenius's rationale intensifies the tension. When referring to his proposed gardens as a "test," he retains the Greek word δοκιμασία in his Latin text, apparently wishing to draw attention to its specific force. A δοκιμασία, in ancient Athens, denoted a public process for ascertaining the suitability of citizens for public rights and duties based on their lineage,

9. Taylor, *Secular Age*.

10. Taylor, *Secular Age*.

11. Comenius, *Universal Reform*, 49.

12. Woldring, "Syncritic Method"; Schaller, "Panharmonia."

13. Comenius, *Way of Light*.

life, and character.[14] The suggestion that provision of public parks should serve as a test of the public's capacity to grow in virtue in interaction with the Christian narrative of redemption raises evident difficulties for secular and/or pluralist democracies. Modern societies have moved away from the idea that shared faith in revelation should be the basis for belonging to and participating in society and its amenities.[15] Comenius certainly hoped that his proposals would be universally valid, but he also grounded that hope in a Christian faith taken as the horizon within which all things might hold together. Today, this move evokes the specter of coercion.

The very coherence of Comenius's thinking thus creates a challenge. On the one hand we may seek to extricate some practical, "realistic" suggestions from his framework and leave the theology behind on the assumption that it is either inessential to the practicalities of his project or incapable of transfer to present realities. Hábl, for instance, traces instances of this strategy.[16] Given Comenius's own insistence on understanding things in wholes, this risks ending up with something that is in the end not really Comenius's idea. Creative borrowing may be fine as long as we do not decorate it too enthusiastically with his name. Yet in the case of Comenius, removing the theological frame moves in a direction at odds with his basic intentions. On the other hand, we may work harder to get at the coherence of what Comenius was saying and end at the realization that his account is not quite as easy to appropriate for our own agendas as we might have wished. For myself, I take the most interesting challenge to be seeking pathways of reflection that might allow Comenius's thought in its own integrity to provoke ours, helping us to discover the historically parochial nature of our own assumptions in our encounter with his. Perhaps in place of the universally valid we should be accepting particularity (his and ours) as having its own claim on being real and useful.

## Schools

What Comenius wrote about municipal gardens is of a piece with what he wrote about schools. He even used the same imagery, urging in the *Pampaedia* that if schools are to be reformed, "we require an imitation of the School of Paradise, where God revealed the whole choir of His creatures for

14. Adeleye, "Purpose."

15. Taylor, *Secular Age*.

16. Hábl, *Lessons*.

man to behold, so that on finding nothing similar to himself, he might perchance learn that his own specific good was not to be found there and turn to the source of his own creation."[17] The goal of educational reform was that everyone should be taught to "know and understand things rightly," so that "paradise lost is regained, that is to say, that the entire world will be a garden of delight for God, for people, and for things."[18] The themes implicit in this talk of schools as gardens of delight should be familiar from our foray into the *Panorthosia*. Schools, like municipal parks, involve pleasure and delight, bodily health, spiritual discipline, virtuous character, social reform, harmony, and awareness of the larger story of redemption and reformation within which individual experience is to be embedded. Thus the three goals of education in the *Didactica Magna* were that learners should "(1) have knowledge of all things; (2) have power over things and over the self; (3) refer the self and all things to God, the source of everything,"[19] and these were not to be interpreted as discrete elements. Rather, "these three are so joined together that at no time can any separation between them be admitted."[20] The idea was not so much that rationality, virtuous action, and piety should each be given their space in the curriculum as that each should be understood in a way that fully implicated the others, and that education should unfold amid their interaction. Piety was not a curriculum component to be included, excluded, or distributed across faiths, but rather a structural feature of learning. Accordingly, the learning process (according to the *Pampaedia*) was to involve presenting "objects of perception for immediate sense experience," relating these to an intelligible schema "by some likeness or symbol," and encouraging integration of the named experience into a coherent picture of life, so that "the sense grasps the object of perception, the reason comprehends it, and faith accepts it in its own light."[21] Learning, it seems from this account, has a perceiving aspect, an understanding aspect, and a believing aspect, making interaction between sense experience and our beliefs an irreducible element in learning. Understanding was then to be articulated and made eloquent to bring it into the world of human interaction. The perceiving-understanding-believing account of cognition was itself in turn the substrate of another triad in which our thinking powers

17. Comenius, *Pampaedia*, 29.

18. Comenius, *Pampaedia*, 29.

19. Keatinge, *Great Didactic*, 37.

20. Keatinge, *Great Didactic*, 36.

21. Comenius, *Pampaedia*, 43.

were placed in the context of our ability to act virtuously and the larger horizon of faith that offered the possibility of meaning, joy, and *telos*. Cognition required virtue and piety to become education. As Comenius put it, "it is most important for all men that on their way through life their minds should be imbued with a sense of piety. . . . Otherwise in all our pursuits we shall be no better than squirrels imprisoned in our little cage of vanities; and the more we practice the material skills and business of life, the more we shall grow weary and fail to escape from the cage of the world."[22] Faith is not to be bracketed from sensory input or rational analysis, but rather provides their proper horizon, the hermeneutical condition of fragments becoming wholes and life finding its center. If this process can be directed in such a way as to simultaneously foster understanding, eloquence, skill, virtue, and piety, "schools will then be planned to such pleasant effect that they all become gardens of delight."[23] The celebrated *Orbis Sensualium Pictus* reflects this vision, joining language learning to conversation on care for creatures, bodily and spiritual health, vocation, virtue ethics, comparative religion, social structures, and an overarching frame stretching from creation to the day of judgment.[24]

In Comenius's educational writings, as in the *Panorthosia*, we see the recurring conviction that the growth of human society requires an understanding of human learning in which experience, understanding, virtue, and faith are intimately interwoven, and that this can be pictured as the effort to (re)establish a garden of delight as a foreshadowing of the eschatological restoration of the original paradise. Comenius's various exhortations on this topic are aesthetically and morally attractive, at least for anyone with half an ear for biblical imagery and a modicum of sympathy for grand idealism. And it is possible to overstate the difficulties; the present day is also inhabited by Christians, and educational provision around the world includes significant numbers of Christian schools that may well find a great deal about Comenius's narrative entirely congenial. As Charles Taylor has indicated at length, secularization has not brought about the demise of faith but rather its fragilization, a situation in which all belief patterns, religious and secular, have lost the privilege of society-wide, self-evident validity.[25] Yet if we are looking for something more universal, the challenges in

22. Comenius, *Pampaedia*, 38.

23. Comenius, *Pampaedia*, 56.

24. Comenius, *Orbis*.

25. Taylor, *Secular Age*.

Comenius's account of schooling seem similar to those at the municipal park. Can an impressively coherent account of education grounded in a narrative of cosmic harmony and in a Christian narrative of redemption and holistic growth offer "realistic" and "universally valid" pointers for schools in our more fragmented, plural, and secular settings?

## Learners

Resolving these questions might entail resolving the questions besetting modern societies about how religious commitment should relate to schooling, to pluralist democracy, and to advocacy in the public square, matters well beyond my scope or ability. Instead of further pursuing such grand themes, I propose instead to zoom in on the question of how we think of the predicament of learners in schools. My suggestion is simply that Comenius's holistic account of the growth of persons-in-the-world might help us see learners well. Perhaps that leads to larger ideas about schooling, but I focus here on what we see happening as students try to learn.

Modern attempts to separate learning from belief require us to approach the actions of teachers and learners in a manner insulated from their framing context of narratives and assumptions.[26] Yet as Comenius saw, pedagogical actions occur in belief-rich contexts and affect believing learners. Christian Smith notes that all social institutions, and this would include schools, are "morally animated enterprises," always "rooted in historical narratives, traditions, and worldviews that orient human actors to the good, the right, the true."[27] This remains true whether the narratives are religious or secular, cosmic or naturalist. Smith continues,

> Moral order embodies the sacred story of the society, however profane it appears, and the social actors are believers in social congregation. Together they remember, recite, represent, and reaffirm the normative structure of their moral order. All of the routines, habits, and conventions of micro interaction ritualize what they know about the good, the right, the true, the just.[28]

If this account holds true, then Comenius's account of pedagogical actions as always faith-involving remains relevant. Perhaps it is precisely at

26. Pinches, *Theology*.

27. Smith, *Moral*, 22–23; cf. Smith, *What Is a Person?*

28. Smith, *Moral*, 16.

the moment of refusal to separate learning from faith that Comenius can push us to attend to realistic possibilities that modern education has been tempted to neglect.

Consider the experience of one group of learners in a physical education class. Trevor Cooling and Elizabeth Green discuss the case of a physical education teacher planning a class on how to execute the push pass in field hockey at an Anglican school.[29] The push pass is a skill that, if we think atomistically, may well be viewed as a discrete element of the curriculum largely focused on bodily training. After the teacher in question was challenged to think about how the moral, the spiritual, and the bodily might interconnect in his teaching, he revised his plan away from his earlier practice of demonstration followed by individual practice. Instead, he assigned students to practice in pairs, alternating roles as one practiced the new skill and the other functioned as a peer coach. His prior demonstration also included an emphasis on thinking about how to encourage one's partner when the task did not initially go well, and the debrief afterwards focused on whether students felt they had offered encouragement effectively. Following this sequence, the students played a short game of field hockey, during which the researchers noted students voluntarily stopping play and raising their hand if they committed an infraction that the referee did not notice. In focus group conversation after the game the students articulated connections between their behavior during the game and the lesson's focus on considering the wellbeing of others, and volunteered that this was connected to the Christian ethical theme of loving one's neighbor. The teacher reported that he and his colleagues had been working at being consistent in practicing the same ethos in their own sporting activity in local adult leagues, and that the theme had also been taken up as part of the school's collective worship. The simple act of pushing a hockey ball took place within, and its experienced contours were shaped by, a complex relational context that included physical activity, interpersonal ethics, social responsibility, community connection, and theological narrative. Comenius might have glimpsed a garden.

Consider another set of learner experiences, this time drawn from the reflections of two students interviewed during a current research project on digital technology use in Christian schools.[30] Thinking aloud about a

29. Cooling and Green, "Competing Imaginations"; Cooling et al., *Christian Faith*.

30. Smith et al., *Digital Life*.

teacher's decision to insist on using paper Bibles within a school context highly invested in digitally mediated learning, one student mused:

> I kind of like it because I like . . . how he forces us to use paper, because now it's just not on the computer and it's not one-dimensional. It's actually in your hands and you are actually reading it on paper. Sometimes I think there's stuff that a computer can't really replicate. For me, reading it on paper, in your hand, is a lot more spiritual than actually just reading it on a screen. Well, I kind of feel like on a computer you have all these distractions and you get pop-ups and all that stuff and it kind of disrupts you and it's very easy to lose your focus whereas when you have a book, it's in your hands, you feel it, and you actually go and open it up and be, like, this is God's word and it's actually in your presence, not just on a computer screen.

A second student agreed:

> What I would probably say is that using a computer feels very high tech and new, and when you think about the Bible stories, you don't always think about them as super new. So when you get out a real book, a huge textbook kind of, you look at it—you feel like, you get the sense of this is God's word that someone wrote down specifically for me to read, like this is a big deal that it's sitting in front of me right now because these are God-breathed words. . . . It's no less important when you read it on a screen, but you don't get the same . . . there's been generations and generations of believers before me and this is an older way of doing things, but a way we should preserve.

I draw upon these examples here not to make a point against digital technology or in favor of print media—that question is far too complex for such a quick conclusion. Rather, I am interested in the awareness evident in these students' reflections of the complex relational context of learning. Tactile, physical experience is directly connected to the sense of possibilities for spiritual growth, and the distinction between digitally mediated and tactile objects is connected to the question of God's presence in the world. The choice of physical medium is not only a matter of negotiation between teacher and student, but is connected to how the past is experienced, including the larger human past and the more immediate question of how to inhabit a tradition and relate to one's forebears. The physical presence of the paper Bible is experienced as carrying within it a call to respond that tastes of the presence of forebears. Again, the point here is not whether these students are correct in their assessments, but rather to note that their experience of learning connects the physical, relational, spiritual, technological, and temporal/traditioned facets of experience in a cohesive pattern. Implicit in their comments is a seeking of personal congruence and relational integrity of the kind implicit in Comenius's quest for gardens of delight.

The positivistic approaches to education that have done much to shape the present educational landscape in the modern West have encouraged teachers and learners alike to think of curriculum as a collection of discrete, testable packets of knowledge. They encourage the perception that teaching English is just teaching English, that teaching sport is just teaching sport. Comenius insisted that learning is to be understood as nested within a relational nexus of bodily experience, cognitive activity, moral responsibility, and faith formation. These things are to be thought together as interconnected and mutually influencing. Perhaps the faith-based school context of the students just described does not make them anomalous, but rather brings normal features of all learning more explicitly to the surface. On this point I find Comenius more convincing, more realistic, than many manifestations of present-day educational practice.[31] I suggest that the provocation to think about learners, learning, and teaching within this complex relational context should be seen as one of the most enduringly valuable parts of his legacy. It might just help us to gain a realistic understanding of students' experience.

## Conclusion

I began this essay with a brief description of a recent visit to a history class in which information was transmitted in a manner insulated from its web of relationships. I will end with another school visit.[32] Like the school in the first vignette, this school was a private Christian school. A teacher at the school took the time to give me a tour of the school's new garden. A significant section of the school grounds had been set aside for landscaping and was in the process of transformation, inspired in part by conversations about Comenius that I had led during an earlier visit to the school. The newly redesigned areas included horticultural areas, where children were engaged in researching and growing vegetables, which they then sold to the school community; this involved learning about agriculture, biology,

31. Smith, "Schools."

32. Smith, "Schools."

economics, and healthy eating. Nearby a collection of artistically designed labels created by students named the plants in a native plant area that was alive with insect life. A little further on came a series of themed miniature landscapes evoking rocky country, sandy wilderness, and the vegetation of the Middle East; these were intended as experiential settings for learning about Bible stories. A xylophone, available for students to play at any time, stood at the lip of a small open-air amphitheater which offered space for outdoor prayer and song. Some students rushed up to us, concerned about the health of one of the chickens in their care, then returned to the sheds where chickens and goats were housed with the assurance that the teacher would check in a little later. Teachers were working to create connections between various facets of this environment and the more formal academic curriculum. The whole installation seemed quite reminiscent of what Comenius apparently intended, not only in its literal components, but in its implicit idea that all of these things are not just nature, but part of a connected whole binding together learning, care, responsibility, and spiritual growth. It did not seem dated, and the particularity of its theological and cultural frame of reference did not seem an obstacle to creating an enriching learning experience. In fact, it invited the imagination beyond the literal question of whether every school should have a garden to the underlying question of how we might grow in faith/joy/health/hope/virtue in our minds/spirits/bodies/cultures/societies in the context of school curriculum. On that topic, dialogue with Comenius in all his scandalous particularity still seems worthwhile.

## Bibliography


Adeleye, Gabriel. "The Purpose of the Dokimasia." *Greek, Roman & Byzantine Studies* 24 (1983) 295–306.

Comenius, J. A. *Comenius's Pampaedia, or, Universal Education*. Translated by A. M. O. Dobbie. Dover: Buckland, 1986.

———. *Orbis sensualium pictus* [Visible World]. Translated by Charles Hoole. London: Printed for John and Benjamin Sprint, 1728.

———. *Panorthosia*. In vol. 2 of *De rerum humanorum emendatione consultatio catholica*. Prague: Academia Scientiarum Bohemoslavica, 1966.

———. *Panorthosia or Universal Reform: Chapters 19–26*. Translated by A. M. O. Dobbie. Sheffield: Sheffield Academic Press, 1993.

———. *The Way of Light*. Translated by E. T. Campagnac. London: Hodder & Stoughton, 1938.

Cooling, Trevor, and Elizabeth H. Green. "Competing Imaginations for Teaching and Learning: The Findings of Research into a Christian Approach to Teaching and Learning Called 'What If Learning.'" *International Journal of Christianity and Education* 19.2 (2015) 96–107.

Cooling, Trevor, et al. *Christian Faith in English Church Schools: Research Conversations with Classroom Teachers*. Bern: Peter Lang, 2016.

Eagleton, Terry. *The Idea of Culture*. Oxford: Wiley-Blackwell, 2000.

Green, Rosalie, et al. *The Hortus Deliciarum of Herrad of Hohenbourg (Landsberg)*. London: Warburg Institute, 1979.

Hábl, Jan. *Lessons in Humanity from the Life and Work of John Amos Comenius*. Bonn: Verlag für Kultur und Wissenschaft, 2011.

———. *On Being Human(e): Comenius's Pedagogical Humanization as an Anthropological Problem*. Eugene, OR: Pickwick, 2017.

Keatinge, M. W. *The Great Didactic of John Amos Comenius*. Translated by M. W. Keatinge. London: Adam and Charles Black, 1907.

Pinches, Charles R. *Theology and Action: After Theory in Christian Ethics*. Grand Rapids: Eerdmans, 2002.

Schaller, Klaus. "Panharmonia und Panchresia: J. A. Komenský's Antwort auf die alte Frage nach der Lehrbarkeit der Tugend." *Acta Comeniana* 22–23 (2009) 133–47.

Smith, Christian. *Moral, Believing Animals: Human Personhood and Culture*. Oxford: Oxford University Press, 2009.

———. *What Is a Person? Rethinking Humanity, Social Life, and the Moral Good from the Person Up*. Chicago: University of Chicago Press, 2010.

Smith, David I. "Biblical Imagery and Educational Imagination: Comenius and the Garden of Delight." In *The Bible and the University*, edited by David Lyle Jeffrey and C. Stephen Evans, 188–215. Milton Keynes: Paternoster, 2007.

———. "Schools, Ideals, Gardens." *International Journal of Christianity & Education* 22.1 (2018) 3–7.

Smith, David I., and Susan M. Felch. *Teaching and Christian Imagination*. Grand Rapids: Eerdmans, 2016.

Smith, David I., et al. *Digital Life Together: The Changing Landscape of Christian Schools*. Grand Rapids: Eerdmans, forthcoming.

Staniforth, Maxwell. *Early Christian Writings: The Apostolic Fathers*. Harmondsworth: Penguin, 1968.

Taylor, Charles. *A Secular Age*. Cambridge: Belknap, 2007.

Woldring, Henk E. S. "Comenius's Syncritic Method of Pansophic Research between Utopia and Rationalism." In *Gewalt sei ferne den Dingen! Contemporary Perspectives on the Works of John Amos Comenius*, edited by Wouter Goris et al., 23–43. Wiesbaden: Springer, 2016.

# PART 2

## *Pedagogical-Psychological Perspective*

# Only an Educated Person Can Change the World in the Spirit of Humanization

Karel Rýdl

## To Understand the Universal Reform Efforts of J. A. Comenius from the Perspective of the Category of Time

I came to Comenius's pedagogical views from the perspective of the category of time and its influence on the organization of pedagogical processes. This led me to read several generally philosophically- and sociologically-tuned works, whose common theme was their attempts to understand the function of time in the coordination and integration of social processes.[1]

The developing modern industrialized society was also characterized by the fact that it drew more and more people into a dense network of clearly defined (timewise) structures of rationalized behavior. Most authors interested in analyzing the socio-genesis of time as a social category have come to very similar conclusions, that all social conduct in modern society is conditioned by the imperative of a pattern of behavior dependent on the logical use of infinite time.[2] The demand for a continual reduction of time while maintaining steady growth in production has, over the course of a few decades, been transformed into a generally valid rational principle, which still has both positive and negative affects on all areas of human activity. The economic use of time (in the sense of the phrase: time is money)

1. Cf. Elias, *Über*.
2. Rinderspacher, *Gesellschaft*, 57–58.

has become a key concept for understanding progress from mercantilism in the second half of the eighteenth century to contemporary society.

The basis of the modern concept of time became "linear time," which is constant, irreducible, and unlimited for rational planning in the areas of economics, politics, technology, and the military. With further economic development, however, another system of understanding temporal relationships emerged, which we can call "abstract time." This could allow a qualitative leap in terms of time as an economic resource.[3] The penetration of time-economic rationality has been increasingly promoted even in non-commercial areas of social life. The operating speed of machines and factories has been increasingly translated into the speed of action in the everyday lives of most people. The "phasing" of the rhythm of human activity according to the time scales of machines seems to be an irreversible phenomenon; as a trivial example, the artificially created time impulses of a telephone connection. In the following text I would like to focus on the influences and effects of structural forms of abstract time, promoted by ever more sophisticated information technologies, on the practices of social behavior of adults as well as children. Specific attention will be given to its influence in the areas of education and child-rearing.

## The Concept of Time in Pedagogical Thinking

On the basis of existing knowledge of the historical development of education and training, it can be said that pedagogy played a very significant role in shaping and promoting the modern awareness of time as a content-neutral framework of a certain order. The crucial and decisive importance of pedagogical institutions for the creation of new societal elites together with the formation of new forms of awareness of time has been observed here in Europe since the Middle Ages. In the monastery schools, later the church-influenced city schools, there developed a tendency to organize daily teaching by the hour. From this perspective, the gradual secularization of the educational system was one of the steps toward the modern age, expressed, for example, in the introduction of compulsory school attendance. It would be extremely difficult to overestimate its contribution to the universalization of the social application of linear time. The rapidly advancing orientation to linear time, structuring activity according to temporal units and norms, is the mark not only of the world of work, but it is also

3. Rinderspacher, *Wege*, 27.

becoming a mark of every other area of social life. One of the most important prerequisites for this society-wide phenomenon was the generalization and internalization of temporal norms in schools, and from there into the lives of new generations. The implementation of fixed temporal norms for the beginning and ending of processes, the organization of educational processes in fixed time units, harsh punishments for school children, the construction of classroom teaching in age-homogenous grades, all created a framework of institutional conditions that allowed no other choice than to submit to the discipline of time units, and to increase one's integration into society by submitting as best one could to the standards of linearly usable time throughout one's life. In the course of its historical development, the educational system, under the influence of the accepted rules of time-structured classifications, reached a state in which the educational process equally affected all members of the created group in the same place and at the same time.

## The Concept of Time in Comenius's *Pansophy*

Even in Comenius, a theological-pedagogical "pansophic" mediator at the crossroads between the Middle Ages and the Modern Age,[4] it is possible to show the insertion, from the beginning, of linear time structures of order as the framing conditions for learning processes and social behavior in the area of existing societal, especially pedagogical, institutions.

As early as his first pedagogical-didactic work "Grammaticae facilioris praecepta" (1614), written at the urging of Wolfgang Ratke (1571–1635), common requirements emerge as educational principles of his time: *cito, tuto, et jucunde* (quickly, safely, and enjoyably) the teaching process must take place; that is, as Klaus Schaller writes, "the teacher must quickly reach the set goal, the knowledge must become the pupil's security, and the effort of learning must be as pleasant as possible in order to handle the new learning tasks with pleasure."[5] Also, the *Great Didactic* (1632) is introduced with the motto "briefly, pleasantly, and thoroughly."[6] Comenius continued, "The art of teaching asks for nothing other than the artificial division of time, things, and methods. And if we can determine them precisely, teaching all teenaged students in any number will be as easy as daily printing thousands

4. Schaller, *Comenius*, 26.

5. Schaller, *Comenius*, 227.

6. Patočka, *Vybrané spisy* 1:41.

of sheets of the most beautiful lettering with the help of printing presses. . . . And all will be no less easy than how effortlessly a clock is controlled by its counterweight. And it is so nice and peaceful to watch such a self-propelled device. Finally it will go with such reliability as can be achieved only with any such artificial instrument."[7]

The pedagogical time structures developed in chapter 19 of the *Great Didactic*, "Principles of Cost-Effective Speed in Teaching," are exemplary.[8] The possibilities of time improvement and time rationalization are systematically discussed here. Comenius's proposed rules for speeding up learning remind us, from today's perspective, of the example of tailoring industrial production processes. Comenius dealt with, for example, these themes:

- How can one teacher be enough for one hundred students?
- Control by the teacher and the oldest students, mutual control of students.
- How is it possible to teach everything from the same textbook?
- How can everyone in the school follow the same material at the same time?
- How is it possible to teach everything to everyone by the same method?
- How can two or three tasks be dealt with in one working process?

With this Comenius became one of the main creators of modern curriculum scheduling. In the *Great Didactic* he wrote, "A natural day has twenty-four hours; when it is divided into three parts for the purposes of life, eight hours are for sleep, the same for external employment (namely health care, food, dressing and undressing, adequate recuperation, chatting with friends, etc.), and finally, eight hours for serious work, which we must then do diligently and without reluctance. Weekly, then, if we give the seventh day completely to rest, there will be forty-eight hours given to work; 2495 annually [the correct number is 2496, noted in Patočka's edition]; how many will there be in ten, twenty, or thirty years?"[9]

Likewise, the "school of early childhood" is subjected to the laws of a rational time scheme, not only in the *Pampaedia* (formulated in 1647),

7. Schaller, *Comenius*, 227.

8. Schaller, *Comenius*, 161–78.

9. Schaller, *Comenius*, 121–23.

but also in the *Kindergarten Informatorium* (1633):[10] in order to achieve as much as possible in the natural flow of time. Comenius was actually thinking about eliminating laziness, idleness, and loafing, which he probably observed himself during his active teaching experience in Leszno, as well as among the students at his pansophic school in Blatný Potoc, Hungary. In his pedagogical work at the school in Blatný Potoc, John Amos Comenius recognized that students are lazy and have bad morals. He wrote a booklet, "Resurrected Fortius," hoping that after reading it, the students would give up the laziness that polluted the school, but it never happened. Comenius realized that the teachers had little knowledge, didn't want to be educated, and would rather celebrate the various holidays; students were content with an incomplete education, they were apathetic, didn't read, would rather drink or sleep, or waste time with trivial amusements and empty gossip. The school administrators (that is, the founders) did not take care of the school and allowed everything to run as it would. It is still interesting today that Comenius tried to turn the students away from laziness and how he wanted to rectify the moral failure of the school. In a booklet called "How to Banish Laziness from Schools" he addressed several ideas and suggestions which I present in the following outline:

1. School is the workshop of humanity, a workshop of enlightenment in which people are brought up to be suited for the building of society.
2. The predominant characteristics of the student as well as the teacher and school principal must be eagerness and cheerfulness.
3. Reform can begin with the teachers, fighting against the laziness of the students can only be done by the example of a diligent teacher. The teacher must not be unapproachable or throw out questions in the way bones are thrown to a dog.
4. School administrators must supervise adherence to the rules, select hardworking teachers, and be interested in the life of the school.
5. Parents must not let their children be idle at home, but lead them to small duties so they do not grow into "lazy scoundrels."
6. The rulers [of nations] must set a good example by their own zeal and establish good schools to maintain their esteem.
7. As long as the above listed sentences are fulfilled, the students will have no choice but to become diligent at school.

10. *Informatorium školy mateřské.*

8. Work belongs to the young, advice to the old.

But John Amos Comenius went even further and proposed a set of School Rules in his book *Laws of a Well-organized School*, which is still relevant today in many points (regardless of the development of society, unfortunately).[11]

## Comenius's Purpose in Reforming the World from a Pedagogical Perspective

When we think about the legacy of J. A. Comenius, the influence of his ideas and thoughts in the present and into the near future, they all fall on us today like an attack of somewhat trite sentences about school games, school as the workshop of humanity, kind yet strict teachers, the meaning of a mother's parenting, and practical education in nature, which is the best school. I think that such an attitude not only demotivates us to have a deeper interest in Comenius's thoughts and ideas, but greatly oversimplifies his real legacy for today, and of course, the future as well.

Many schools have been named after Comenius, but which of them truly worked, or works, in the spirit of his ideas and didactics? Is it even possible for his didactic and methodological techniques to be applicable today? What is still viable and stimulating, and what was cast aside by the promotion of more effective teaching and learning methods which are child-centered and trending towards the strongly individualized?

If the theme of this reflection is the search for the spirit of Comenius's ideas and their usefulness in the theory and practice of today's schools which individualize their own educational and training methods, then it is impossible to not mention three of Comenius's ideas. They are the notion of school as the workshop of humanity, the notion of each person as a responsible and active individual, and the notion of lifelong learning for teachers. I will discuss in more detail these three principal aspects of Comenius's ideas about the spirit of schooling.

## The Notion of School as the Workshop of Humanity

Comenius's idea of school as the workshop of humanity was, in his day, very timeless and arose from the overall concept of the function and role

11. See Potočka, *Vybrané spisy* 2:228–52.

of education in Comenius's notion of the behavior of human society in the world. Schools should not only educate by mediating systematically classified knowledge and an understanding of the world around us, but should also provide an orientation of values by promoting a certain individual and social morality. Without ethics, there is no education, only knowledge. A person who knows a lot and has a lot of information but does not naturally behave ethically, is not educated and has only knowledge. In recent decades, European education, marked by Herbartism, has tried to break free from the preference for didactic materialism and to give at least the same weight of emphasis to ethical approaches. For this to be effective, situations must be created which children can experience together with their teachers; the transfer of mere information has just as little effect as teaching ethical concepts by precise definitions. For example, teachers in the city of Zlín, led by the headmaster Stanislav Vrána, understood this important function of schools as early as the 1930s, and their annual reports are a rich well of specific illustrations of the experiential educational activities offered.[12] Their activities and focus were very close to today's efforts to promote the targeted key skills of communicativeness, mutual tolerance, reverence, respect, self-respect, environmental sensitivity, mutual support and protection of ones own personality, gifts, and health. I think that it would be only with great difficulty that one could think up something new in the field of pedagogy; it is rather about finding appropriate combinations of already known (maybe half-forgotten) methods and ideas—always with consideration for the specific person. Nowadays the concept of schools as the workshops of humanity cannot function without socially motivated educational and training programs, which can be used to further develop the ready knowledge, and, above all, experientially strengthen it in a thematized curriculum which gradually, over time, relinquishes the primary goal of cultivating the personality of the student by teaching by subject. It will gain its primary meaning in the period of specialized training after the end of compulsory general education.

12. The complete collection of the Annual Reports of the Zlín Reformatory public and city schools is owned by the State District Archives of Zlín, headquartered in Klečůvka.

## The Notion of a Person as a Responsible and Active Individual

Comenius's notion of the goal and meaning of education was constantly changing and developing throughout his life. The meaning from his first period, known as the great "encyclopedic period," was the elevation of the Czech language and nation among other nations through education brought in from abroad. The goal of his second major creative period, the "didactic period," was the creation of the concept of their own Czech schools with original textbooks and methodologies. His unplanned emigration forced Comenius to think about his "Czech Paradise" concept much more extensively, and use it as the "Paradise of the Church" in the largest possible territory: the world. His last creative period, the "pansophic period," was devoted to thinking about effective pedagogical methods, especially in the teaching of languages,[13] and towards the end of his life his thoughts were also about the integration of education and his universal reform efforts for the improvement of the world and society. Not to be overlooked in his seven-volume work *General Consultation on the Restoration of Human Affairs*, is the fact that "Universal Education" is placed in the middle of the work and forms the heart of all his emendatory efforts. In this work Comenius formulated what is even today a very modern conception of the active person who lives on this earth and has a duty and responsibility to God as the Creator, to constantly improve it and not destroy it. In order to do this reasonably, we must understand our surroundings. This requires a school that gradually acquaints each person not only with individuals, but also with the relationships between them. And we also do this, in our efforts today to thematize the curriculum, to move away from the transmission of ready-made, isolated pieces of knowledge, and to promote an understanding of mutual relationships and influences—precisely in the division of the subject matter of schools with the goal of understanding (not just have knowledge of) the world and society. Comenius appreciated the active person more than all other human activity. His group of open souls,[14] who need new knowledge of the world around them and of themselves for their life, are able to ask questions of their surroundings, and from the answers they get, broaden their own cognitive horizons with

13. The titles of books Comenius wrote in this period often began with the Latin words *Vestibule*, *Ianua*, or *Atrium*, which all mean "way."

14. Comenius divided people into two groups that he called the "open souls" and the "closed souls," according to their interest in getting to know the world around them.

respect to other people and objects in the known environment. In contrast, Patočka interprets Comenius's ideas in the spirit of the principle of open and closed souls.[15] The concept of the "closed soul," which needs only itself to live, is preoccupied with itself and does not need anything more for its "development" than itself, does not respect other people or objects, and sees only itself everywhere. For the development of society and its general cultivation, closed souls are only an unpleasant and meaningless burden. Such souls despise education, because for their own small-minded lives themselves, it is not needed.

## The Notion of Lifelong Learning for Teachers

The teacher is for the children, not the children for the teacher. This approach requires from each teacher what Comenius considered a given: Teachers must continue their education throughout their lives, they cannot become stunted, or unknowing, or not have access to knowledge, information, aids, and resources. If they are denied this, that society is against its own self, because it is doing something very unwise and punishing its current and future generations with its own stupidity and short-sightedness. What form did continuing education take in, for example, the reform schools in Zlín? Primarily, it went in two directions. The first was in having events to support their own teachers in the form of field-trips, lectures, seminars, their own magazines, joint activities, etc. The second direction was represented by the activities of the teachers towards other teachers and interested parties. Teachers from Zlín promoted their own pedagogical methods, toured the country, traveled abroad (to the Balkans and Poland), wrote their own textbooks and professional articles in methodological and pedagogical journals, published their own magazine "The Creative School," and with their experience participated in local and national educational policies. This is slowly beginning to reawaken thanks to the activities of numerous pedagogical and teacher associations and groups.

## Conclusion

Although I read all the annual reports of the Zlín Reform School, their preserved archival documentation, and became acquainted with various

15. Cf. Schifferová, "Patočka."

speeches by representatives of the school and the city of Zlín from the period under review, I found only one direct reference to Comenius, in Stanislav Vrána's book *The Idea of a Free School*. The author mentioned Comenius in the sentence: "the education and teaching of young people should follow the natural paths of human development, as our J. A. Comenius entreated."[16] It was not a matter of having pedagogical writings and documentation interspersed with quotations and references to Comenius, but of understanding the meaning of his thinking and fulfilling it in their own work. And the teachers in Zlín did so to a great extent, even though many of them may not have even known they were working in accordance with Comenius's ideas. For that matter, even today we can see it in the series of current teachers and pedagogues who, at least intuitively, have felt the need for a pedagogical change. They have understood that the discipline of forming humanity merely on the basis of other disciplines will no longer be enough, but the real meaning of humanizing people and society is based on openness of the soul. This is because, "when Europe has already failed with a closed soul, . . . there are far sharper contrasts lurking in the post-European period, which could be fatal in today's heightened, destructive techniques based on the self-centered life, which probably belongs to the blossoming of the closed soul. Thus, a new spirituality is needed."[17] Education for a new age cannot be built where a person is seen as a thing among things, as a force among forces; in short, it cannot be carried out by a closed soul.

16. Vrána, *Idea*, 5.

17. Patočka, *Komenský*, 414.

## Bibliography

Elias, Norbert. *Über die Zeit* [An Essay on Time]. Frankfurt am Main: Suhrkamp, 1988.

Komenský, Jan Amos. *Informatorium školy mateřské.* Praha: Academia, 2007.

Patočka, Jan. *Jan Amos Komenský: Gesammelte Schriften zur Comeniusforschung* [John Amos Comenius: Collected Writings on Comeniological Research]. Bochum: Comeniusforschungstelle der Ruhr-Universität Bochum, 1981.

———. *Vybrané spisy Jana Amose Komenského* [Selected Works of John Amos Comenius]. Vol. I. Praha: SPN, 1958.

———. *Vybrané spisy Jana Amose Komenského* [Selected Works of John Amos Comenius]. vol. II. Praha: SPN, 1960.

Rinderspacher, Jürgen P. *Gesellschaft ohne Zeit* [Society without Time]. Frankfurt am Main: Campus, 1985.

———. *Wege der Verzeitlichung* [Ways of Temporalization]. Stuttgart: Kohlhammer, 1988.

Schaller, Klaus. *Comenius: Erkennen, Glauben, Handeln.* Schriften zur Comeniusforschung 16. Sankt Augustin: Richarz, 1985.

Schifferová, Věra. "Patočka a Komenský." *Literární noviny* 25 (2012).

Vrána, Stanislav. *Idea volné školy a její vývoj za posledních 30 let* [The Idea of a Free School and Its Development over the Last 30 Years]. Brno: Vydavatelský odbor Ústředního spolku jednot učitelských, 1936.

# Comenius's Notion of the Educational Reform of Society in the Context of His Social and Pedagogical Thinking

Miroslav Procházka and Miluše Vítečková

## The Labyrinth of Today and That of the Time of the Pilgrims

Comenius's work is being opened today in a number of current contexts. The change in the paradigm of education in connection with the reliving of a society-wide crisis is the impetus forcing us to think about the topicality of his work. Today's society, with its crisis phenomena, opens a new look at the perspectives of humanity in the twenty-first century, and Bauman and Donskis characterize it as the infiltration of fear and hatred into a glorious new world.[1] Intellectual disillusionment, which comes after an era of growth and peace, is characterized by dismay from new forms of fear, stemming from one's own doubts and uncertainties. The shared feeling calls into question the age-old idea that things must only get better, and admits a growing fear that in fact they will be worse. The current concerns about the "culture of illiteracy," fed by feelings of danger and the perceived anomic condition, call for a way out of the crisis as soon as possible.[2] This is not possible without an honest answer to the question of the nature of the situation we are experiencing. In our mediated world, a whole series of

1. Bauman and Donskis, *Tekuté zlo*.
2. Giroux, "Anti-public Intellectuals."

attributes are devoted to the crisis. There is talk of a financial, economic, political, or ecological crisis. However, in order to understand the essence of the problems of our day, a certain time lag is necessary, an interval in which we can detach ourselves from the pressure of political populism, reconstruct the historical memory, and establish critical thinking.

The first such thought excursion might be the situation of the 1930s. At the time, Karl Jaspers, the outstanding thinker of his day, called it an anthropological crisis. Jaspers pointed out that we lived in a grand time that was rich in material gains, yet was also the poorest time for failing humanity.[3] The important work of pedagogy would then be to reveal what people were failing in, and to strengthen those competencies that are a sign of a mature society. In this context, Jaspers spoke about a return to humanity, thus re-establishing the work of the restoration of humanity through education.[4] Zakaria raised an interesting question in this sense when he asked whether the current liberal system of education was changing young people for the better. In his book, *In Defense of a Liberal Education*,[5] he defended young people, but recalled an interesting study by the Higher Education Research Institute of the University of California. The study stated that, in contrast to the mid-twentieth-century, the number of students who considered developing a meaningful life philosophy as something fundamental had dropped significantly (from 86 percent in 1967 to 45 percent in 2013). As if the skepticism of postmodern society and nonresistance to "big ideas" led the younger generation to new idols, including influential entrepreneurs, technicians, businessmen. But the turn to everyday life and the goals associated with economic growth and maintaining the competitiveness of the individual and society, has its pitfalls. It is the risk of the orientation of education, that is, only having the power to emancipate humanity to its functionalistic-reductionistic meaning. In this respect Helus warns about the loss of originality, autonomy, resignation from the search for the meaning of life.[6] Palouš warns about people surrendering their ability to "see beyond the horizon," to being overwhelmed by life's everyday "errands."[7] Thus education, which should be the solution to the situation of humanity within a society in crisis, is itself, as a human creation, threatened by the

3. Jaspers, *Die geistige*.
4. Jaspers, *Die geistige*.
5. Zakaria, *Obrana*.
6. Helus, "Edukace."
7. Palouš, *Čas výchovy*, 267–70.

crisis. So is it possible to break free from the "Labyrinth" of this world by education, and does education have a chance to remain that power of universal reformation even today? We believe so. It was Comenius's rationale for orienting education toward the restoration of all the human affairs of his day, which we could not call idyllic. Thus, our second excursion is a search for a connection between the current situation in the world and the crisis Comenius lived through in his day.

Living in a time of social and political upheaval brings with it the tragedy of personal destinies of individuals thrown on the chessboard of political games and the indiscriminate cruelty of wars. In a situation where every certainty is called into question and even the opportunities of life find themselves in the hand of chance, a person's view of the world and its values is worsened. It is a time when the weak, in their numbness, depart, and the strong often doubt and lose their way. The period at the end of the sixteenth century and the start of the seventeenth century was just such a time. Masaryk characterized this reality as a time "when the old order had broken down and the new, half-built, caused the desire to have a view of the world as a whole, to have a view of life and death which every person could accept and which could lead and guide them through their whole life, everywhere and always."[8] The emergent modern society created a confusing labyrinth for its contemporaries, in which economic, cultural, political power and spiritual tensions were vented. The social pressure to change the status quo, in which the Middle Ages lingered with its old form of social division of power, led to the widening of the gaps between the individual social classes. This condition escalated the disagreements and intolerances which had, until then, been hidden beneath the surface of the "happy" years of the late sixteenth century. The currents of reform in the church and politics, which rose up with the notion of achieving a new unity of the world and faith, met with resistance from the representatives of the traditions. Thus, even then there was a general human experience that showed how difficult it is to resist frustration in a situation where you come full of enthusiasm, leaning on the certainty of new truths and better "tomorrows," and encounter rejection and condemnation. Comenius identified the human dimension of this problem of the world that comes from the inability of the individual to engage in dialogue. It is the lack of ability to put up with non-acceptance, in the spirit of his saying, "Stop attacking, and the other will stop defending";[9]

8. Masaryk, *O Škole*, 39.

9. Komenský, *Všenáprava*, 91.

it is the pathological cause of the lack of the art of listening and formulating one's thoughts.

Comenius was born into that crumbling system. The ever-present chaos became the foundation for the formulation of his life credo, based on the pursuit for harmony and unification, moral awareness, and human understanding. However, Comenius's vision was limited beforehand by the Habsburg expansion, which in symbiosis with the Catholic Counter-Reformation shaped a new form of political absolutism. The drama of these conflicts was not just the backdrop of human destinies, but struck at their everyday lives with the full force of its antagonisms, going even into the innermost moments of life. The loss of property, the threat to the security of one's home, the death of loved ones, the ever-present feeling of the possibility of the end of one's own life—Comenius did not escape any of this, and it gradually led him away from the role of a passive spectator, astonished by the corruption of this labyrinth. But that allegorically scathing initial critique of the world in the *Labyrinth* was also the germ of the *Consultation*.[10] The moment we realize a problem exists and reveal it, when we take off the glasses of deception and see the nature of the manipulative lies, we have already embarked on the path of change. Comenius called the main character (a personification) Pilgrim, thus fulfilling each person's natural need for direction. Because of this need, each of us has a chance to find our goal, for only a pilgrimage has a goal: the goal in the journey from childhood to the fulfillment of the adult life of the individual, from Creation to the Last Judgment of the life of society. Each one is to gradually reach their self-identity and come into their own on this path. It should progressively clarify the meaning of life, which would gradually, as in the last act of a theater play, be untangled and made clear. It should be a pilgrimage for building relationships and finding one's life goals, the meaning of life. "It is the path of Peace, that we are all looking for."[11] This path is natural, but challenging because we all want to reach that state in which we are satisfied with our way of life and can live it freely and safely. Anyone who sets out on a journey for satisfaction will encounter many snares, which can turn a pilgrimage into a mere wandering, and the life of the pilgrim into that of a wanderer, a kind of vagabond. Comenius saw the problem here as being in the means we choose to achieve our goals.[12] The important thing

10. Komenský, *Labyrint*.

11. Komenský, *Cesta Pokoje*, 457.

12. Komenský, *Cesta Pokoje*, 457.

is that Comenius's personal tragedies did not lead him away from his path, as Popelová put it, "the loss of his wife and children, along with his home in the turmoil of war, led to a desperate reflection on the most intimate things. But even this personal grief was, in Comenius's thoughtful spirit, transformed to a philosophical level."[13] Patočka suggested that Comenius managed his life crisis not only because of his great energy for life and work, but mainly because of the new idea that gave all his efforts thus far a new unity. It was the idea that education "is a means of real reform, of all human activities it is the one which is not in vain."[14]

## Comenius's Path to Universal Reform

The universality of Comenius's work and the focus of his intellectual views, of course, touch on the formation of the idea of the general influence of education on society. Can education be granted an emancipatory significance through changing the negative societal reality founded in the imperfection of human relationships, dominance of human misunderstanding, and victory of fear and cruelty? Comenius gave an unequivocal and widely substantiated answer. It came naturally from his primarily theological notion of the relationship between the world and God. Comenius the theologian, with his idea, is included in the stream of thinkers who have perceived history as the history of salvation, where God, as the "supreme pedagogue," brings to humans the impulse for change. Comenius sensitively perceived the situation that the first evangelists faced. After Christ's sacrifice, they expected the end of the age and the beginning of a new kingdom; for examples, see Luke's Gospel (17:20–37) or The Acts of the Apostles (2:14–34). In the end, they had to become reconciled to the situation when a new view of the fulfillment of the future was opened to them, in, for example, Paul's Letter to the Thessalonians (ch. 5). At that time, part of the church realized that the task which lay before them was the education of Christian civilization.[15] It opened the place for centuries of effort which had a pedagogical base, and which was to lead to the transformation of human beings in the spirit of Christ's message. Comenius diligently followed that moment in his supreme work, *General Consultation on the Restoration of Human Affairs* (*De rerum humanarum emendatione consultatio catholica*). Interpreting the

13. Popelová, *Filozofie*, 33.

14. Patočka, "Základní filozofické myšlenky," 9:262.

15. Funda, *De Profundís*.

*Consultation* and its significance is very demanding, as the work touches on the entire complex of social reality and concerns every area of human activity. Comenius created a book, as is more and more clearly shown, that will always be current, for at every moment we can find inspiration for the most current questions in it.

In the introduction to the *Consultation* itself, he spoke of the work of renewal and saw Jesus Christ as its bearer: "he is the new Adam, determined by God's eternal decision as the blessed restorer of all that the old Adam corrupted."[16] But this plan was to be carried out only in connection with people: "God requires the cooperation of his faithful," or "God does not want to do anything without man."[17] Comenius thus consistently placed people and education side by side, as instruments of the restoration of the world, as implementers of the historical mission revealed in the Gospels. Comenius, as Popelová noted, extensively relied on the religious foundation of his philosophy before rolling out his plan of universal restoration.[18] This rhetoric, in which rationalism was mixed with chiliasm, made sense. It gave Comenius an argument for the historical dimension of his work, and oriented the work towards the future. Patočka emphasized exactly this empowering by Comenius of the person who "actively cooperates in completing the plan of the universe and the fulfilling of its meaning."[19] Comenius's people, with their active roles, were to fortify, strengthen, and humanize their lives and the world.

The deep faith in human beings that Comenius expressed underwent a series of tests. As a man of deep faith, in the cruel times of war he had to cope with difficult tests of his faith in people and humanity. God created the world as perfect, and then created man in his own image, that is, essentially good. Although in practice we encounter much evidence of the corruption of the world and human nature, it cannot be due to an imperfect work by the Creator. It is the result of independent human action. The bloody conflict at the end of the era of humanism was, despite the religious rhetoric of both sides of the war, a work motivated by human wickedness. In the *Labyrinth* he had already colorfully described how Death itself shoots his arrows of death only because the people themselves give them to him. They do this by their bad human qualities, their lack of morality, which become

16. Komenský, *Obecná porada*, 25.
17. Komenský, *Obecná porada*, 25.
18. Popelová, *Filozofie*.
19. Patočka, "Základní filozofické myšlenky," 11:188.

deadly arrows that destroy human lives. Is it possible, then, to expect God to use his creativity again to make things right? But the responsibility for the world, its social and moral development, lies with the ones who corrupted it, that is, humanity. Only humanity can fix it again. Each one only needs to purify the image of the Creator which they carry inside.[20] Education should be this tool of cleansing, education should help a person to continue to find and develop that inner picture of love and the desire for good. Comenius emphasized that this cleansing is a natural tendency for people. In his reflection on discipline he reminds us that education must respect the person's own direction. Human nature, as a reflection of God, heads freely towards improvement.[21] Long before Rousseau and his celebration of natural education,[22] Comenius showed how forced discipline, the violence in education, destroys human nature. In this context, Hábl added that Comenius's view of human nature was more complicated than Rousseau's preromantic idea that the nature of humans is always good.[23] If each of us has been endowed with both good and evil, then humanism is not able to save in itself. Perhaps even in this plasticity and hidden doubt about humanity we can see the impulse that led Comenius again and again to a thorough justification of his pedagogical thesis and didactic principles, as well as to a reflection on the broader social perspectives of education.

The fourth and sixth parts of the *Consultation* have the most significance for pedagogy—Universal Education (*Pampaedia*) and Universal Reform (*Panorthosia*). Included here are ideas that put into a clear context the further development of society and the creation of a social (human) environment in which education towards tolerance, peace, and mutual communication between individuals and nations would find a use. Comenius's views on the proper organization of society and the nature of relations between the various social classes are very interesting. In the first area mentioned, in light of the importance and character of education, Comenius's *Consultation* is a kind of challenge and a plan for the social and spiritual transformation of the world. For in the Introduction the author called everyone to a consultation about the way, the strategy, for restoration. He was well aware that no change could be dictated "from above," but had to be discussed and convincingly explained from all levels of human society.

20. Cf. Funda, *De Profundís*.

21. Komenský, *Didaktika*.

22. Rousseau, *Emil*.

23. Hábl, *Aby člověk*.

At the same time, he perceived the reform as a completely human work and not a divine work. For human beings it was both their highest task (to restore what they have themselves corrupted), and their potential, their chance. People combine in themselves everything that other beings have only in part; they are endowed with reason, free will, and the determination to act. Thus, the removal of maladies had to take place in all the analogous pillars of social coexistence and order—in knowledge (philosophy), in faith (theology), and in government (politics). In this context, Somr commented on Comenius's vision of society and people in connection with Plato's conception of the soul.[24] One example could be the following thought from the *Consultation*: "Philosophy, which is the pursuit of wisdom, comes from the thirst for truth. Piety, which is the concern for the highest good and its use, is born out of the desire for the good. From the will to organize things according to their quality comes, ultimately, Politics, which is the leadership of people who are doing business according to rules, so that they don't interfere with each other, but help."[25] The strength of Comenius's plan for the transformation of society lay precisely in that combination of the development of education, spiritual purity, and political (social) justice.

Let us return once again to the metaphysical nature of Comenius's thinking about education. If Comenius wanted to defend the creative role of education in society, he had to deal with the idea of the fatal influence of inherited sin and give human beings a chance to reform. In his thoughts on the nature of humanity and society, Comenius was, of course, coming from his vision of the primary dominance of God and his creative role in shaping the essence of social relations. So God and his plan take first place in the restoration of the world, for in the beginning He was the perfect Creator of the perfect world. He handed over his work to humanity, for "the world was created for us."[26] Everything was entrusted to us, but not as superior administrators, but as the last created (and therefore the most perfect) beings, which ourselves were created for God and his glory. The fact that humanity "corrupted" the world was not, for Comenius, a reason for skepticism. Human nature has given us the ability to cooperate in the restorative "work" inherent in the educational return to the substance of our own creation. Human beings, whose archetype was the Creator himself, have within them the imprint of part of God's wisdom and goodness.

24. Somr, *Jan Amos*.

25. Komenský, *Obecná porada*, 81–82.

26. Komenský, *Theatrum*, 116.

Their upbringing and development through education has given them a chance to revive and open those hidden capacities.

But what is the place, the role, the importance of education in a world built on God's plan; is there still a big enough space for it, does humanity have a real chance to repair the corrupt work? Comenius had no doubt about it: "Man is everything and nothing. When he is born, he is, in and of himself, nothing. Everything he is comes from the mind of God, who created him in His image, and from a good upbringing, which further completes him."[27] Moving towards the essence of God's nature and at the same time submitting an educational plan is what, in human society, teaches a person about that relationship in order to be able to act like a human being. In everything, Comenius affirmed his great belief in simplicity, the simple transparency of education: "Thus, to teach a person to act as a human being needs nothing more than to educate him to adapt his natural knowledge, impulses and abilities to the given instances in harmony with nature."[28]

## Comenius's Pedagogic Accents in Scholastic Education

Comenius's pedagogical thinking was closely tied to his social feelings which, as Kraus emphasized, came to fruition in the thinker's efforts to promote the right to education for all people, regardless of status, property or gender.[29] According to Comenius, if education is the universal path to humanity, then it is in the best interest of society to provide everyone, without distinction, access to this path. Comenius's view of the social function of education has a very current connection even to this day. Aptly, Comenius included educational work in a model of the social behavior of all human society: "We, all of humanity, are one generation, one blood, one family, one home. Therefore, just as the right hand helps the left, as one limb helps every other limb in the body, as one member of a family helps the whole family, we should also help our species.[30]

To put into practice the idea of equality in education was, of course, extremely difficult in that society, ravaged by war and ideological conflicts. In general, Comenius was concerned with the spiritual, organizational, and economic provision of schools as public institutions. Scholastic education

27. Komenský, *Obecná porada*, 46.

28. Komenský, *Obecná porada*, 46.

29. Kraus, *Základy*.

30. Komenský, *Unum necessarium*, 110.

should be "mass" in the sense of communal work, natural social learning, and also by utilizing the effect of a well-managed school education, which created the possibility "to put into the head more teaching, instill better morals, eradicate more defects (over time) and finally save more money and time."[31] Comenius also saw the influence of the social role of the school environment in its support of the mutual harmony of the children, in competition, and in the liberation of piety.

If we wanted to point to a practical example of Comenius's socially-oriented schools, we would find perhaps the most comprehensive model in his pansophical school project. In his tumultuous life, Comenius was given few real opportunities to fully implement his pedagogical views on upbringing and education in practice. One opportunity to carry out a socially and didactically oriented reform school was his work in Blatný Potok (Sarospatak). The motives for Comenius's trip to Hungary (then Transylvania) were primarily political. Prince Sigismund Rakoczi was to become the new hope of the anti-Habsburg opposition and reopen the post-White Mountain exiles' hopes for a way back to Bohemia. After arriving in Hungary in 1650, Comenius also received the promise of generous support for the establishment of "pansophic schools." However, we must note that, as so often happened to Comenius, misfortune manifested itself here again. The generous patron, Prince Sigismund Rakoczi, died on April 2, 1650 and the new ruler, George II Rakoczi, had no understanding of Comenius's political plans. Also, the willingness of the new prince of Transylvania to support the concept of the school did not last long; his treasury, exhausted by the war, soon closed to Comenius. In his letters to friends, Comenius complained about the lack of understanding, the unwillingness of the nobility to truly support him, and also the unwillingness of the teachers to invest their efforts and creativity into the school "project."[32] Comenius documented the importance of his project in its plan, which he presented in the booklet "Idea illustris scholae patakianae." Here he spoke about a "bright" school—inside full of light and spreading light outside. The education provided by the school was democratic, general: "it is necessary to educate everyone who was born as a human being."[33] The social aspects of the Transylvanian school also included specific requirements to ensure equality of students in access to education. Comenius required his patrons to invest financially in

31. Komenský, *Obecná porada*, 46.

32. Komenský, *Škola vševědná*.

33. Komenský, *Idea*, 37.

school furnishings for the benefit of all—the provision of textbooks to all children, food and accommodations for the poor ones, etc.

The educational goal of his school was to mold the students towards humanity and thus bring them closer to the image of God which is hidden in each of us. After all, people are born capable of everything, but in reality their capabilities are tied only to those things they are used to, which have been shown to them and in which they have had experience. Therefore, Comenius understood the significance of school as that of a "workshop" into which everyone must be ushered in order to be shown things and to try them.[34] To Comenius, school was thus a workshop, a place where three essential areas were developed: reason, because the mind should be filled with the light of knowledge; the hands, which should acquire the ability to do every job well; and language, which enables understanding between people. Comenius himself realized that he would be thrown into doubt about whether it would be possible to manage such complex school goals. At the same time, he saw three elements as key to whether his model of school would be viable. The first element was quality textbooks, which, according to the ideas of the time could be a summary, or literature search, of accessible knowledge. The next was quality teachers, who would be able to use these books to give the students knowledge, and would use an appropriate method to lighten the effort of teaching and learning. In this sense, Bendl recalled that Comenius's emphasis on the social role of the school environment was directed towards its democratic spirit, accessibility, and freedom.[35] The goal of a school education, for Comenius, was to achieve the unity of the children, positive support of competitiveness, and the freeing of the children's religious (moral) feelings.

If we look for ways to apply Comenius's educational view of the role of school today, we meet with a whole series of problems. One special characteristic of school education is that it intersects with a sensitive period in a child's life. Especially in puberty and adolescence, the child's personality matures in social roles, which the child tests and changes in the social environment of the school. But the microcosm of the school classroom is open to changes in social reality as well as the microcosm of the family. Social changes affect the functioning of the family, but the medicine that society offers in the form of institutional education, is a relative solution. After all, the school, as a generally human creation, is affected by the same

34. Komenský, *Idea*, 37.

35. Bendl, *Základy*.

critical manifestations as all of society. Helus warned about reductionistic and hedonistic pressures, which force the role of school into economic-managerial models of efficiency.[36] Today's society—with its characteristics of the "fluidity of the period" of postmodernism,[37] with its global openness, information interconnectedness, growing individualism and intolerance—seeps into social relations in children's groups and transforms the social world of school. There is, therefore, a growing need to define new school goals, to orient the school towards education for humanity in its complex understanding and ethical dimension.[38] Today's school needs teachers who will be able to bring initiatives containing ethical and educational accents. Then the school can offer the children stories that will orient them towards values and stabilize their attitudes.[39] Only through these lessons in humanity will children be able to cope with the complex labyrinth of this world.

"For we must consider it certain that human affairs will do better only when we all recognize each other as classmates in the same school, as brothers in the same house of God, and as fellow citizens in the same community of God, and when we all begin to consult together for the common good, well-being, and security in order that no one is left who has not been invited, admitted, heard and who could not use the common goods of light, peace, and life.[40]

## Comenius from the Perspective of Future Teachers

If we want to think about the stories that teachers can bring to their students and thus contribute in the above-mentioned sense to their interest in the key themes of humanity, the character of Comenius is an excellent example. Laying aside how Comenius as a person is part of the primary and secondary school curricula, it is fascinating to us how this "compulsory" theme of school education programs has been preserved and handed down in the memories of students over time. Regardless of the scientific accuracy of the information appropriated, for us it is important how colorfully the personality of Comenius has been remembered and what categories it is associated with. After all, a personality is not a marble statue or bust, and a

36. Helus, "Edukace."
37. Bauman, *Tekuté časy*.
38. Lorenzová, *Kontexty*.
39. Hábl, *Učit*.
40. Komenský, *Obecná porada*, 323.

story only works as long as it is alive. The aim of our research was to determine how the students perceive Comenius, what they associate his name with, what "fragments of knowledge" become representative knowledge, as the residuals of the complex information acquired during their school education. The sample of respondents were students in university teacher preparation programs, at the start of their studies. The research took place in the first semester of study, in the first lecture of Introduction to Pedagogy. We based it on written statements of the students at a time in their studies when they could not yet have encountered J. A. Comenius in the formal curriculum of the university's study program.

A survey questionnaire was used to collect the data from 200 students—158 women (79 percent) and 42 men (21 percent)—in the Schools of Education, Science, and Philosophy at the University of South Bohemia in České Budějovice. Specifically, some were students in the field of Teacher Training for Kindergartens (and in the field of Special Education for Preschoolers—teachers at Nursery School)—38 students (19 percent). The questionnaire was also filled out by 17 students (8.5 percent) who will be primary school teachers, 98 students (49 percent) are preparing to teach at the middle school level, and 11 students (5.5 percent) will be high school teachers. Another part of the sample of respondents consisted of 32 students (16 percent), who will be teachers of information science, teachers at an arts school, or are studying Health Education. Four students did not respond to the question about their field of study

The students were asked to write five expressions, phrases, or sentences expressing who, according to them, J. A. Comenius was, or what came to their mind when hearing his name. The answers were coded and evaluated using IBM SPPS Statistics 21. A total of 1162 statements were obtained. The most frequent reactions were connected with the teaching legacy of Comenius, and also with his works, or with the titles of his works. The dominant answer was that J. A. Comenius was a teacher of nations (mentioned 117 times); students also remembered the titles of two of his books, *The Labyrinth of the World and the Paradise of the Heart* (102 times), and *The Great Didactic* (96 times). The specific results, with codes, are presented below in Table 1.

*Table 1: When the name Comenius is spoken, what comes into our—the people of Comenius—minds?*

| Code | absolute frequency | relative frequency |
|---|---|---|
| Teacher of Nations | 117 | 58.5 |
| *Labyrinth of the World and Paradise . . .* | 102 | 51 |
| *The Great Didactic* | 96 | 48 |
| School as play | 91 | 45.5 |
| Educator/teacher | 61 | 30.5 |
| *Orbis pictus* [*Visible World in Pictures*] | 58 | 29 |
| The Netherlands | 44 | 22 |
| Exile/emigration/banishment | 44 | 22 |
| Priest and preacher | 43 | 21.5 |
| Unity of Brethren | 42 | 21 |
| Reformer/revolution | 36 | 18 |
| Bank note | 32 | 16 |
| Philosopher | 29 | 14.5 |
| Author | 29 | 14.5 |
| Education/teaching/school | 27 | 13.5 |
| Leszno | 25 | 12.5 |
| Educational system | 25 | 12.5 |
| Library fire | 22 | 11 |
| Didactics | 19 | 9.5 |
| Greatest Czech thinker/persona of the Czech nation/recognized worldwide | 16 | 8 |
| Education/educator | 16 | 8 |
| Kindergarten Informatorium | 12 | 6 |
| Thinker | 12 | 6 |
| External description—beard, long coat | 12 | 6 |
| Calendar | 11 | 5.5 |
| Family | 10 | 5 |
| Pansophist | 9 | 4.5 |
| Relationship to children | 8 | 4 |
| "He jumped from the window to the woman" | 8 | 4 |

| Code | absolute frequency | relative frequency |
|---|---|---|
| Bishop | 7 | 3.5 |
| Nivnice | 7 | 3.5 |
| *Gate of Languages Unlocked* | 7 | 3.5 |
| *The Dying Mother of the Unity of Brethren* | 6 | 3 |
| Map of Moravia | 6 | 3 |
| Meeting with Descartes | 6 | 3 |
| Other codes with fewer than five occurrences | 73 | 43.5 |

If we compare the codes created by the analysis of the responses according to the order they were given by the students, we can see the primary focus of the students on J. A. Comenius as a teacher of nations whose basic philosophy was school as play. Even through the last of the five phrases given by each student, they put his role as author of important pedagogical works (although not all appeared in the responses) into the context of his life.

*Table 2: Comparison of the first phrase given with the last (fifth)*

| Code | Total | first phrase | fifth phrase |
|---|---|---|---|
| Teacher of nations | 117 | 71 | 4 |
| *Labyrinth of the World and Paradise . . .* | 102 | 14 | 13 |
| *Great Didactic* | 96 | 6 | 56 |
| School as play | 91 | 32 | 13 |
| Educator/teacher | 61 | 18 | 11 |
| *Orbis pictus [Visible World in Pictures]* | 58 | 5 | 4 |
| The Netherlands | 44 | 2 | 15 |
| Exile/emigration/banishment | 44 | 2 | 8 |
| Priest and preacher | 43 | 1 | 1 |
| Unity of Brethren | 42 | 5 | 6 |
| Reformer/revolution | 36 | 6 | 3 |
| Bank note | 32 | 5 | 7 |
| Philosopher | 29 | 13 | 6 |
| Author | 29 | 3 | 7 |

| Code | Total | first phrase | fifth phrase |
|---|---|---|---|
| Education/teaching/school | 27 | 14 | 0 |
| Leszno | 25 | 1 | 8 |
| Educational system | 25 | 0 | 5 |
| Library fire | 22 | 0 | 5 |
| Didactics | 19 | 0 | 3 |
| Greatest Czech thinker/persona of the Czech nation/recognized worldwide | 16 | 2 | 3 |
| Education/educator | 16 | 0 | 3 |
| Kindergarten Informatorium | 12 | 4 | 2 |
| Thinker | 12 | 3 | 2 |
| External description—beard, long coat | 12 | 1 | 1 |
| Calendar | 11 | 2 | 0 |
| Family | 10 | 0 | 2 |
| Pansophist | 9 | 2 | 2 |
| Relationship to children | 8 | 4 | 0 |
| "He jumped from the window to the woman" | 8 | 2 | 1 |
| Bishop | 7 | 2 | 2 |
| Nivnice | 7 | 0 | 0 |
| *Gate of Languages Unlocked* | 7 | 0 | 1 |
| *The Dying Mother of the Unity of Brethren* | 6 | 1 | 1 |
| Map of Moravia | 6 | 2 | 2 |
| Meeting with Descartes | 6 | 0 | 1 |
| Other codes with fewer than five occurrences | 62 | 7 | 19 |

It is possible to indirectly derive from the responses the factual focus of Czech schools, when the predominating entries had the character of mere information (e.g., the name of the work, place, date), and only secondarily suggested an interpretation of work and ideas (e.g., reformer, thinker, greatest teacher, persona of the nation). One respondent admitted the influence of the high school graduation exam on his knowledge of J. A. Comenius: "I will also remember the *Labyrinth of the World and the Paradise of the Heart*, but only because of the Maturita exam in Czech." We can only speak of surface knowledge, as follows from one of the responses mentioning the relationship to literature: "almost no one reads it, but everyone quotes it." According to the students, J. A. Comenius was "a teacher of body and soul." But he was also "a little unlucky, everything he had burned up."

Among the responses that appeared fewer than five times, some were mistakes, some sympathetically original, and only sporadically mentioned. Some of the erroneous ones were students confusing Comenius with other people, such as John Hus, "7/6/1415 burned for heresy," and "removal of the rabble;" with Joseph Dobrovský, "gave rise to the rules of Czech orthography;" with Charles IV, "he founded Charles University;" or with Albert Einstein's thought, "a joke with a fish—if you tell it to climb a tree it will feel stupid." There were also wrong connections, such as "the father of the nation." Among the original statements from the category of student humor was, for example, the idea that J. A. Comenius was a "great guy," and another connected him with "respect." The perception of Comenius as a source of inspiration was sympathetic, as it illustrated to some students how today's education does not function: "the opposite of today's schools (in most cases)," or "a model for teachers." In the context of the present, J. A. Comenius is recalled with competitions for the best teacher, with streets and schools, script, and magazines named after him, with pictures in staff rooms, with a statue in one of the buildings of the schools visited; even with the façade of a particular primary school, built at the beginning of the twentieth century and decorated with excellent frescoes of Czech personalities. Last but not least, one student mentioned the theatrical performance in the Žižkov Theater of "The Czech Sky." We did not want to close our reflection on the importance of Comenius with this connection of Comenius with the legacy of Jára Cimrman, the fictitious genius of the Czech people. Nevertheless, we can conclude that the young generation has not forgotten his legacy. The fact that it is associated with information rather than with its interpretation is, ultimately, also part of his legacy. Nothing is alive except what has been experienced. Leading teachers to work with living contexts, to lead them to critical thinking, to search for connections and formulate opinions, can be one of the ways out of the labyrinth of our time, drowning in the information jungle. Finding connections and opinions, then, will be the children's *Consultation* and security.

## *Bibliography*


Bauman, Zygmunt. *Tekuté časy: Život ve věku nejistoty* [Liquid Times: Life in an Age of Uncertainty]. Praha: Academia, 2008.

Bauman, Zygmunt, and Leonidas Donskis. *Tekuté zlo, život bez alternativ* [Liquid Evil, Life without Alternatives]. Praha: Pulchra, 2018.

Bendl, Stanislav. *Základy sociální pedagogiky* [Fundamentals of Social Pedagogy]. Praha: Univerzita Karlova v Praze, 2018.

Funda, Otakar A. *De Profundis* [From the Depths]. Praha: Pedagogická fakulta UK v Praze, 1997.

Giroux, Henry A. "Anti-public Intellectuals and the Tyranny of Manufactured Forgetting." https://philosophersforchange.org/2014/07/01/anti-public-intellectuals-and-the-tyranny-of-manufactured-forgetting/.

Hábl, Jan. *Aby člověk neupadal v nečlověka: Komenského pedagogická humanizace jako antropologický problém.* [On Being Human(e): Comenius's Pedagogical Humanization as an Anthropological Problem]. Praha: Mervart, 2015.

———. *Učit (se) příběhem: Komenského Labyrint a didaktické možnosti narativní alegorie* [Teaching and Learning through Story: Comenius' "Labyrinth" and the Didactic Possibilities of Narrative Allegory]. Brno: Host, 2013.

Helus, Zdeněk. "Edukace jako projev starosti o člověka: Příspěvek k osobnostně rozvíjejícímu pojetí výchovy" [Education as a Manifestation of Concern for Man: Contribution to the Individually Developing Concept of Education]. In *Teorie výchovy—tradice, současnost, perspektivy*, edited by Richard Jedlička, 13–34. Praha: Karolinum, 2014.

Jaspers, Karl. *Die geistige Situation der Zeit* [The Spiritual Condition of the Age]. 9th ed. Berlín: de Gruyter, 2010.

Komenský, Jan Amos. *Cesta pokoje* [The Way of Peace].Veškerých spisů Jana Amosa Komenského 17. Brno: Ústřední spolek Jednot učitelských na Moravě, 1912.

———. *Didaktika analytická: Nejnovější methody jazykové kapitola X* [Analytic Didactic: Newest Methods of Language, chapter 10]. Vybrané spisy Jana Amose Komenského, 2. Praha: Dědictví Komenského, 1908.

———. "Idea skvelej školy v Potoce" [Idea for a Great School in Potok]. In *Výbor z potockých spisů a reči*, 35–40. Bratislava: SPN, 1992.

———. *Labyrint světa a ráj srdce* [The Labyrinth of the World and the Paradise of the Heart]. Praha: Svobodné slovo/Melantrich, 1958.

———. *Obecná porada o nápravě věcí lidských* [General Consultation on the Restoration of Human Affairs]. Praha: Svoboda, 1992.

———. "Škola vševědná to jest dielňa všeobecnej múdrosti" [The School of All Knowledge Is the Workshop of Universal Wisdom]. In *Výbor z potockých spisů a reči.* Bratislava: SPN, 1992.

———. *Theatrum universitis rerum* [Theater of the Universe]. Veškerých spisů Jana Amosa Komenského 1. Brno: Ústřední spolek Jednot učitelských na Moravě, 1914.

———. "Unum necessarium" [The One Thing Necessary]. In *Apoštol míru J. A. Komenský*, edited by Radovan Krátký and Václav Stejskal. Praha: Československý spisovatel, 1949.

———. *Všenáprava (Panorthosie), Všeobecné porady o nápravě věcí lidských část šestá* [Universal Reform, General Consultation on the Restoration of Human Affairs, Part 6]. Brno: Soliton CZ, 2008.

Kraus, Blahoslav. *Základy sociální pedagogiky* [Fundamentals of Social Pedagogy]. Praha: Portál, 2008.

Lorenzová, Jitka. *Kontexty vzdělávání* v *postmoderní situaci* [Contexts of Education in the Postmodern Situation]. Praha: Karolinum, 2016.

Masaryk, Tomáš Garrigue. *O škole a vzdělání* [On School and Education]. Edited by Josef Cach. Praha: Státní pedagogické nakladatelství, 1990.

Palouš, Radim. *Čas výchovy* [Time for Education]. Praha: Státní Pedagogické Nakladatelství, 1991.

Patočka, Jan. "Základní filozofické myšlenky J. A. Komenského v souvislosti se základy jeho soustavného vychovatelství" [Basic Philosophical Ideas of J. A. Comenius in Connection with the Foundations of His Systematic Education]. In *Komeniologické studie I: Sebrané spisy Jana Patočky*, vol. 9. Praha: Oikoymenh, 1997.

———. "Základní filosofické myšlenky J. A. Komenského v souvislosti se základy jeho soustavného vychovatelství." In *Komeniologické studie III. Sebrané spisy Jana Patočky*, vol. 11. Praha: Oikoymenh, 2003.

Popelová, Jiřina. *Filozofie Jana Amosa Komenského* [Philosophy of Jan Amos Comenius]. Bratislava: Pravda, 1986.

Rousseau, Jean-Jacques. *Emil čili o vychování* [Emil, or, On Upbringing]. Part 1. Praha: Dědictví Komenského, 1910.

Somr, Miroslav. *Jan Amos Komenský: Poutník na cestách naděje* [Jan Amos Comenius: Pilgrim on the Path of Hope]. České Budějovice: Vlastimil Johanus Tiskárna, 2007.

Zakaria, Fareed. *Obrana liberálního vzdělávání* [Defense of Liberal Education]. Praha: Academia, 2017.

# "Preventing Humans from Becoming Unhuman"

## *Comenius's Restoration from the Perspective of a Contemporary Educator*

Dana Hanesová

### Introduction

A holistic grasp of Comenius's pedagogical system in order to fulfill his vision to help humanity fulfill the meaning of its existence can, for a teacher today, snowed under by the amount of emerging tasks and practical problems, present a very difficult challenge—which, if it is not to be only a subjective pinpointing of partial thoughts, demands scholarly Comeniological study. Therefore, we want to note at the outset that this study does not come from the pen of a Comeniologist. It came about as a reflection of the author—a present-day teacher—on Comenius's supreme pansophic work, *General Consultation on the Restoration of Human Affairs* (published in Czech in 1992). Although Comenius was not able to complete it, the pain that consumed him over the unhappy state of "human affairs" (the condition of piety, education, politics, culture, family and work life) is often heard in it. At the same time, as a theologian, philosopher, and teacher, his life's calling drove him to weigh in on this complex situation. It demanded the employment of education to prevent "anyone from falling into a non-human" and to open the way to the restoration of a "universal refinement" of the corruption of the whole of humanity.[1] The *Pampaedia* (Universal Education, part 4 of the *Consultation*) was his vision of the universal education of all, by every means available, so that all might gain the wisdom to understand everything and every idea, and to be able to "distinguish the essential from the secondary, the harmless from the harmful."[2]

The pedagogical ideas of Comenius are not unknown to teachers in Central Europe. Novice teachers at teaching schools have been led for decades to associate the name of Comenius with the emergence of pedagogy, or didactics. In this sense, Comenius has been a role model for teachers in several countries, even during the socialist era. Soviet authors praised not only his individual ideas, but the versatility of Comenius's pedagogy, considering him one of their pedagogical role models. On the other hand, however, his didactics were separated from his "metaphysical" beliefs about the meaning of life and education, under pressure from the demands of scientific atheism. Kairov assessed him this way: "Comenius's creative activity dates back to a time when theology had a significant influence on society. . . . Comenius paid the tax of his time when he explained his notion of education in a religious spirit. . . . Due to the conditions of his time he was unable to expose the problems of moral education and humanism."[3] The holistic picture of Comenius's contribution has thus remained misunderstood, even rejected, hidden behind "the biased emphasis on his indisputable importance for pedagogy."[4] After the revolution in 1989, some educators in Czechoslovakia began to uncover reductions in the understanding of Comenius. In some universities, parts of Comenius's works containing spiritual ideas became the subject of discussions with students.[5]

In this essay we wish to reflect on Comenius's vision for the restoration of humanity with an attitude of respect for its author—a personality inseparably linking pedagogical as well as theological and philosophical ideas on human beings and their world. What did Comenius think about humanity and education? What made him think that way? Could his vision truly contribute to the restoration of "human affairs" in the twenty-first century?

1. Komenský, *Obecná porada*, 798, 806.

2. Komenský, *Obecná porada*, 807. For the purposes of this essay, the term "education" will be used in its broader sense, and educology and pedagogy are synonymous.

3. Kairov, "Jan Amos," 186, 190.

4. Somr and Pavličíková, "Ethical Visions," 404.

5. Spilková and Hejlová, *Příprava učitelů*.

## Historical Context and Anthropological Starting Point of Comenius's Pedagogy

Understanding the historical circumstances at the emergence of the *Pampaedie* is not in the intentions or abilities of the author of this essay. Nevertheless, even at first glance it is clear that it is not possible to understand or compare the ideas of a more than three-hundred-year-old work with current pedagogy without suggesting, along with Helus in his reflection,[6] the need for smoothing the way into the historical context of Comenius's creation. It requires a certain pre-understanding and reflection on the circumstances of his life; there is not enough space here to write of them, but they are elaborated in detail elsewhere, for example, by Hábl.[7] For a postmodern educator today it is almost impossible, although necessary, to realize that the world of Comenius's time considered religion—faith in the divine nature, the human spirit, and life after death—to be an integral part of public and professional life. Comenius's opponents had other worries—they fought against the principle of educating everyone, for "Who would stay with the plow?"[8] An educator can easily imagine the indelible influence of Comenius's childhood and youth on his pedagogy. The tragic events of his personal, family, working, and social life (especially being orphaned at the age of twelve; postponement of the start of his systematic education until age sixteen; the loss of his most-loved ones, property, library, personal work; the Thirty Years War; repeatedly sent into exile; the disappointment of his own vision) never hinted at his becoming a man of "hope."

At the same time, it is necessary to take into account the influence of his education in a religious family of the Unity of Brethren. The church's teachings could have been the impetus for the development of Comenius's love for God and people, and unwavering faith—verified in situations of huge loss—as well as his ideal of humanity, the source of his ethical evaluation of events, and positive approach to life.[9] He sealed his identification with this theology with his decision to take the position of clergyman, and later bishop.

Zealous for God's truth yet at the same time suffering emotionally and longing for change, the exiled Comenius was several times subject to

6. Helus, "Učitel."
7. Hábl, *Aby Člověk*.
8. Komenský, *Obecná porada*, 808.
9. Somr and Pavličíková, "Ethical Visions."

various eschatological apocalypses. Yet his idea of the universal restoration of society reflected the contemporary tendency to solve social problems by means of utopias (as did More, Campanella, and Bacon). Therefore it is not surprising that his vision was also classified as a utopia, although it was not a utopia in the original sense of the word. Comenius did not specify what society would look like, he left that question open.[10] He focused on the description of the method—universal education, by which it would be possible to repair all human affairs across the board. His vision reflected the understanding of unified science of his time. That perspective gave Comenius the sense of, and hope for, the real existence of a universal, perhaps instrumental-sounding, way of teaching everyone, everything, by all possible means.

Comenius's attraction to pedagogy, encyclopedism, and pansophy was probably influenced by the schools from which he graduated. For example, the University of Herborn, one of the centers of encyclopedic Ramism and pansophism, which emphasized the requirement that a theory be able to function in its practical implementation. Among the teachers interested in pedagogy he was influenced by, for example, Ratke and Alsted—the "father of the encyclopedia." Comenius reworked the philosophical and theological education he acquired into his own writings; the influence of Bacon and Descartes was also reflected in his efforts to systematize knowledge and develop an inductive method.

Reflecting on the thinking of the seventeenth century opens the way to pay attention to the resources, and not only the fruit, of Comenius's work,[11] and thus gain a more realistic insight into the *Pampaedia's* contribution to current pedagogy. Its task was to find a way for all people to acquire pansophia—the universal wisdom of the world—by becoming wise "to eternity and unwise to the world."[12] Nourished by such transcendent roots the work matured, tenderly addressing all people, without regard to religion, "It is deplorable . . . that everyone is invited to heaven, but not everyone is taught the heavenly path!"[13] On the one hand Comenius's pedagogy was anchored with both feet on the ground in a real context, yet on the other hand his universal restoration demands super-human strength, and therefore a turning to God—to manage with his help "to create God's kingdom in this life and

10. Vliet, "Utopian Ideas."

11. Vliet, "Utopian Ideas."

12. Komenský, *Obecná porada*, 806.

13. Komenský, *Obecná porada*, 806.

not just someday."[14] Although in the *Pampaedia* Comenius implemented his "didactic" competency, other parts of the *Consultation* undoubtedly reveal his inability to separate the *Pampaedia* from the consistent whole and attempt to explain it purely didactically.

## On What Anthropological Starting Points Did Comenius Base His Universal Education?

### *The ontological nobility of human beings: They have an inner life*

According to Comenius, humanity is created by God in the image of God, differing from other beings in their "noble nature." The goal of their will and actions is to rise to the "majesty of God,"[15] to know and live consistently with the real, everlasting Good, dissatisfied with any substitutes.

The uniqueness of the human spirit is manifested in its natural intellectual abilities (to truly understand the complexity of life), freedom (to distinguish and choose the good), and ability to act (to actively assert the choice of the good, to be proactive, to intentionally work on their surroundings). People were created with a desire to not remain in ignorance or mere introduction. In their being they desire to truly know the world. Their conscience—inner light—enables them to immerse themselves "in things, from within and without", exploring, "measuring and knowing" the world.[16] From these three "roots" of human nobility grow their "fruit," namely knowledge (philosophy as a result of the pursuit of wisdom), religion (piety—the desire for and care of the highest good), and politics as the manager of public affairs.[17]

### *The moral corruption of man: He enjoys the shadows more*

"According to God's purpose, this world to which we are sent by birth should be a school of God, full of light."[18] But instead of a record of the most fundamental relationship for life, humanity chose their own "self-sufficient" way of knowing the world, even though "under our own guidance we can

14. Palouš, *Paradoxy*, 15.
15. Komenský, *Obecná porada*, 35–36.
16. Komenský, *Obecná porada*, 182.
17. Komenský, *Obecná porada*, 36.
18. Komenský, *Obecná porada*, 39.

go nowhere but towards destruction."[19] Comenius quoted Seneca, who was ashamed of the way people equate themselves with God and prefer unstable values: "People seek themselves outside themselves, things above them and God beneath them."[20] People choose a different direction for all three of the sources of the image of God in them: the direction of their power, knowledge, and piety is not towards "service to the Father of light,"[21] but towards self-satisfaction, self-enrichment. The result of their decision is a life not rooted in God, people would rather live in the shadows. Comenius cried from his grief over the fact that people, despite the nobility they are endowed with, do not pursue the goal of their existence and "therefore no human affairs are in order."[22]

The most shameful thing is that expressions of hatred and superficiality come to the forefront in religious matters. Faith in imaginary gods and unbelief are spreading, even though "God is a universal concept, implanted in the heart of every person so deeply that Cicero said of those who refute God, they can hardly be judged to be mentally healthy."[23] Many believers in God live as if eternity doesn't matter, or they fight for their religion with weapons. If people would control their reason and conscience, they would be able to rule themselves and others, and there would be peace and order in society. What broke Comenius's heart the most was that humanity rushes to perdition by blindly surrendering to the "will of God" without making an effort to know what God's will is.

Comenius's view of humanity—God's noble creation, behaving inhumanely, Hábl calls "realistic."[24] Humanity is ontologically noble, but morally corrupt. "Comenius's distinction between the ontological and moral nature of man realistically captured the complexity and ambivalence of humanity. . . . A person is capable of both humanity and inhumanity."[25]

19. Komenský, *Obecná porada*, 831.
20. Komenský, *Obecná porada*, 40.
21. Komenský, *Obecná porada*, 41.
22. Komenský, *Obecná porada*, 45, 48.
23. Komenský, *Obecná porada*, 42.
24. Hábl, *Aby Člověk*, 13.
25. Hábl, *Aby Člověk*, 146.

### *Hope for man: Restoration through the re-acceptance of the light*

Comenius saw a possible remedy for such a state of "human affairs" in a change of thinking—an awareness of one's condition and desire for God as the source of light.[26] However, in light of God's nature itself, it was necessary to look to him as higher and accept the non-self-governing path of change in accepting the redemption of Christ. For Comenius, Christ was always the permanent, global *centrum securitatis*.[27]

Everyone must have the freedom to choose this solution, "lest the image of God be violated in man, at least in those things where it is brought to completion the most, in freedom of choice. If this freedom is taken away, . . . the will becomes a non-will and the person a non-person."[28] A person can renew the *nexus hypostaticus*[29] only by the educational "attraction of everyone to the smell of true good," so that "they gain an interest in and time to transfer to more noble endeavors and do throughout mortal life what contributes to immortal life."[30] He praised the forerunners of "didactics," who longed "with tremendous effort . . . to show others a way to remove ignorance from uneducated minds."[31] He put his efforts into the detailed elaboration of a system of pan-education, overcoming the human "tendency to live life only for ourselves," which leads "people away from the twisted self-centeredness."[32]

Comenius's pedagogical optimism manifested itself in the hope that if schools would offer (a) to human reason "a true basis for reasoning," people would learn to think well; (b) to the human will "that which is truly good," it would attract them to the good; and (c) "the love of harmony," it would motivate them to "behave rather nobly." After all, "everyone rejoices that the deity is favorably inclined towards them and that they can be blissful in his favor now and in eternity." That is why Comenius thought that if "it were possible to show people what is beneficial for them, they would

26. Komenský, *Obecná porada*, 28.
27. Burton, "Jan Amos."
28. Komenský, *Obecná porada*, 818.
29. Hábl, *Aby Člověk*, 145.
30. Komenský, *Obecná porada*, 1181.
31. Komenský, *Obecná porada*, 52.
32. Hábl, *Aby Člověk*, 146.

necessarily reach for it, or even grab it."[33] The reason they don't do that is that they do not have enough education.

Thus, "in addition to grace and prayer," people also need the necessary education. Comenius thought of education as a much more serious activity than just a simple transfer of information and training in craftsmanship. He believed that by restoring human nature and developing its possibilities, it would be a true "creation." People become human by their own human effort.[34] Comenius's call for the restoration of humanity through universal education gives the impression that Comenius, as a theologian, overestimated the educational method, because he reckoned that a relationship to God could be resolved through education (despite what 1 Cor 2:12 says about the limitations of human wisdom).

It is clear from the *Consultation* that Comenius perceived the meaning of his "earthly" life to be consistent with his faith in the "afterlife." It did not deter him, and even gave him strength to fight for changes to life "on earth" by means of universal education, for the benefit of all people, not only Christians. He had an unshakeable hope that restoration of things was possible before the end of this material world, and it was this hope that determined how he valued the "current moment":[35] "So even Jews, Turks, pagans (not to mention us Christians) can enter this work without hindrance and proceed through it until each one has been moved to where he feels that he is surrounded by rays of light."[36] Education matters to God (so that one could rejoice in the glory of God), people (so they could live wisely and attain the meaning of human existence), and it is good for the world too (e.g., nature).

## The Spirit of the Time and the Starting Point of Contemporary Pedagogy

Pedagogy has been growing for 350 years since Comenius's death, influenced by developments in the natural sciences, psychology, as well as in philosophy itself, which has paid more attention to epistemology from the time of Kant.[37] The result is an explanation of the whole of reality on the basis of its sensory cognition. The concept of education has been gradually

33. Komenský, *Obecná porada*, 56–58.
34. Dobinson, *Comenius*.
35. Dodd, "Hope."
36. Komenský, *Obecná porada*, 27.
37. Kant, "Über Pädagogik," in *Ausgewählte schriften*.

penetrated by the ideas of the Enlightenment (emphasis on reason, rejection of revelation), romanticism, existentialism, structuralism, postmodernism, and finally, transhumanism, seeking to "improve humanity by means of modern technology."[38] The fundamental difference between thinking in the seventeenth and twentieth centuries lies in the method of knowing reality. Unlike Comenius, "today we no longer believe that metaphysics allows us to understand the development of the child or adult in society . . . [or] says anything about the laws of nature."[39] Contemporary science is compartmentalized, that is, competing scientific theories coexist.[40]

The *Zeitgeist* of contemporary pedagogy is radically different from that of Comenius's time. The world is under serious threat to the balance of the ecosystem, increasing addictions, aggressivity, egocentrism, social inequalities, moral hedonism.[41] More and more people tolerate amoral behavior, manifested in wrong attitudes towards property and power.[42] When, in 1999, Fukyama predicted a great upheaval as a result of such morality, he had hope that humanity could reconstruct the perversion in current society on the basis of innate abilities.[43] But the situation has only worsened, as evidenced by more intense natural disasters, the growth of criminality, wars, terrorism, the refugee and economic crises, the breakdown of families, and the weakening of social capital and trust among people.

In contrast to Comenius, the current postmodern age has no aspiration to find one complex solution to the accumulating problems. The globalized society expects pedagogy to respect the mega-trends of society's development, safeguard the entrance of the status of a knowledgeable society, and increase its ability to compete. Current "pedagogy is experiencing a general decline,"[44] hit by the harsh pressure of neoliberalism[45]—the dominance of economic interests in setting and evaluating pedagogic goals to prepare for the labor market.[46] The "current industrialization of knowledge has changed the meaning of education, it has become a commodity. In-depth

38. Kosová, "Quo vadis," 24.
39. Piaget, "Jan Amos," 177.
40. Schubert, *Teoretické*.
41. Turek, *Inovácie*; Helus, "Společenská krize."
42. Jablonský et al., *European Values*.
43. Fukyama, *Velký rozvrat*.
44. Porubský, "Inštitúcia," 8.
45. Kosová, "Quo vadis."
46. Turek, *Inovácie*.

and multi-dimensional reflection on social reality is not supported."[47] According to Helus, this has weakened the moral, aesthetic, and spiritual values of humanity. Society more or less resigned from education and educational institutions, ceasing to fulfill its "basic formative function."[48]

On the other hand, proactive educators are drawing attention to the problems and seeking their educational solutions. In the educational practice of developed countries, the emphasis is on an individualized approach to the needs and abilities of each learner. The teachers only facilitate the learning process and their activity is not superior to the learning of the individuals. However, this has also led to the relativization of a selection of reliable models of teaching, which are "markedly socially determined."[49]

The traditional, Judeo-Christian starting point set up "education focused on the cultivation of humanity mediating ontological meaning and basic values."[50] Religiosity underwent a phase of strong displacement from public places in the twentieth century. At present, the persistent human desire for spirituality resonates in the politically correct educational goals of spiritual development.

The current state of society in developed countries is this unflattering, despite the compulsory schooling of all children. As early as 1961 Rogers stated, "we are educated, but we are evil,"[51] and Fromm said, "We reason in the twenty-first century, but our hearts are in the Stone Age."[52] The dependence of educational attainment on social origins persists. It has been confirmed that "socio-political measures . . . have no significant effect on this fact. Therefore the educational system is not able to eliminate social inequalities."[53] In addition to ineffective external conditions, Spilková also saw the internal causes of the school crisis, in particular, the insufficient internal acceptance of change, inertia, and unpreparedness of the teachers.[54]

Many educators are calling for a serious solution to the state of society and education. Helus encouraged a search for the anthropological causes of the current crisis in the long-term failing lifestyle. He proposed a so-called educational turn "respecting the anthropological constants,

47. Kosová, "Quo vadis," 65.

48. Helus, "Společenská krize."

49. Beneš, *Andragogika*, 81.

50. Kosová, "Výzvy súčasného sveta," 18.

51. Rogers, *Ako byť*. Not translated to Slovak until 1996.

52. Fromm, *Escape*, xiv.

53. Beneš, *Andragogika*, 66.

54. Spilková, "Výzvy."

that is, the quality of the personalities, forming an essential part of its full development, but the possibility of its actualization was weakened by the current social determination."[55] It emphasized the so-called turn to the child, morality, a broader context, and transcendence in education. The goal was that people would be able to resist the pressure of reductionism and individualistic hedonism because they would know themselves, know how to come out of themselves and integrate into their life mission, and consciously participate in their transformation. They would be essentially free, wise and responsible, able to pay attention their inner selves. Kosová called for the need to create a new, holistic, humanistic pedagogical theory, able to deal with the disagreements and contradictions at "the level of an in-depth justification of their complementarity."[56]

Thus, a solution is still being sought, which is why we have decided to analyze Comenius's potential benefits for today's society and the education of the new generation. As we have shown, efforts to apply only his practical solutions, such as the requirement of comprehensive education, have failed. A holistic remedy, as Comenius really did present in the *Consultation*, would require a much more radical change and we will characterize that in the next section.

## The Search for Overlaps and Intersections in the Starting Points of the Pampaedia and Current Pedagogy

We will now try to compare Comenius's starting points in the *Pampaedia* with those of current pedagogy. We realize this is risky because the danger of a superficial evaluation of the work of such a historic figure living three hundred years ago, by selecting only certain elements from his work and deciding to look in them for the foundations of current trends of thought, is considerable. As Piaget evaluated Comenius, it is one thing to find current ideas in his work and to ignore the rest.[57] But it is most difficult to understand the principles of the internal coherence of his work. Piaget perceived the tension between Comenius's didactic need to write a philosophy for everyone, and his desire to, at the same time, construct pansophy itself; this led him to various simplifications of ideas, and with that, a lack of understanding by his contemporaries. On the other hand, Piaget did not consider

55. Helus, "Učitel," 24.
56. Kosová, "Výzvy súčasného sveta," 28.
57. Piaget, "Jan Amos."

it important to address Comenius's metaphysical starting points. He regarded Comenius's contribution to be the idea of integrating natural processes with the educational system, the requirement of international educational systems, and especially Comenius's naming of the whole range of problems related to education, and with that also, the acceleration of the emergence of new sciences (pedagogy, as well as developmental psychology).

The complexity of this comparison is also connected to some terminological ambiguities in Comenius[58] and ambiguities in understanding the subject of current educology, similar to the case in other synchronous multi-paradigmatic sciences.[59]

At the moment there exist many educational concepts and paradigms, either objective-subjective (neofunctionalism, radical structuralism) or conservative-activist (interactive or radically humanistic). We consider it most logical to compare Comenius with current pedagogy in the Czech Republic and Slovakia. Post-revolutionary pedagogy in this region underwent a transformation from traditional education to humanistic, personally-oriented education, based on personalistic and constructivist concepts.[60] Although traditional education claimed as its goal a well-rounded, highly developed individual, in reality it placed primary emphasis on the transmissive acquisition of knowledge with an emphasis on memorization. The efforts of teaching colleges since the early 1990s have been aimed at having the teachers, especially at the primary level, master the practical starting points of humanistic education, ensuring a holistic, balanced person (cognitively, emotionally, volitionally, morally), and the social- and self-development of each child.[61] A superficial look at the occurrences of concepts of humanistic education[62] in Comenius's *Pampaedia* confirms an analogous focus on the holistic education of each individual (the term "freedom" occurred 382 times, and an emphasis on experience 100 times, plus tolerance, respect for the freedom of others, motivation, self-confidence, cooperation, independence, learning through the acquisition of knowledge, evaluation and personal experience, choice, emphasis on communication, and conative learning).

58. Čížek, *Conception of Man*, 182.

59. Průcha, *Moderní pedagogika*, 30.

60. Spilková and Hejlová, *Příprava učitelů*; Kosová, *Vybrané kapitoly*.

61. Kosová, *Humanizačné premeny*; Kosová, *Vybrané kapitoly*; Helus, *Dítě v osobnostním pojetí*; Lukášová, *Učitelská profese*; Spilková, *Proměny primární školy*; Spilková et al., *Proměny primárního vydělávání*.

62. Švec, *Základné pojmy*.

The search for Comenius's intersection with humanistic pedagogy is essentially a willingness to understand each other without prejudice, including understanding the starting points of the Christian ethos. Since "an intersection of the Christian ethos is possible only where problems are discussed and processed conceptually and analytically,"[63] for our case we decided to use Schultze's own method of mediating categories, the "middle axioms," that is, specific "concepts that take part in both correlated dimensions."[64] First we examined both positions, and then chose the middle axiom—a generally plausible statement, anchored on both sides of our chosen dividing line, and thanks to which the values of Comenius's education can become understandable to twenty-first-century educators. A similar approach to dialogue has been proposed by Thielicke.[65]

The results of the search for middle axioms between the solutions in the *Pampaedia* and current pedagogy, following the example of the discussion between secular social ethics and theology,[66] could be the examples of terms given in Tables 1–3, open to further discussion and correction.

*Table 1: Personal experience*[67]

| *Comenius's starting points* | *Middle axiom* | *Current pedagogy* |
|---|---|---|
| Individual religious experience | Plurality of individual experiences of being | Freedom |
| Direct action of the Spirit of God | Individual approach to truth | Tolerance |
| Inner word (*verbum interius*) | Universality of the affective | Meditative learning |
| Conviction of sin (repentance) | Experience of conscience | Responsibility |
| Turning to God, seeking salvation in God | Personal crisis, personal development | Human rights |
| Spiritual presence of God, transformation, good deeds | Authenticity of the experience of the saint | Religious attitudes |
| Spiritual freedom | Relationship in otherness | Ethical creativity |

63. Schultze, *Theologische Sozialethik*, 117.

64. Schultze, *Theologische Sozialethik*, 133–4.

65. Thielicke, *Theological Ethics*, xv.

66. Hanes, *Duchovné prebudenia*.

67. Compiled according to Hanes, *Duchovné prebudenia*, 161.

*Table 2: Pragmatism*[68]

| *Comenius's starting points* | *Middle axiom* | *Current pedagogy* |
|---|---|---|
| Practical Christian life as a norm of the importance of theological doctrines | Experience as a criterion of the meaning of ideas | New, global problems require the addition of theory through practical experience |
| Moral behavior—a form of the existence of faith | Behavior as a criterion of the distinctiveness of ideas | Change social behavior through learning ethical values |
| Naive realism | Epistemological optimism | Hope that they find a solution to "unsolvable" problems |
| Willingness to risk one's life in the desire to live according to God's will | Risk of abuse of pragmatism for unethical behavior | Risk of failure of attempts to find non-traditional answers in education |

*Table 3: Moral education*[69]

| *Comenius's starting points* | *Middle axiom* | *Current pedagogy* |
|---|---|---|
| Evil as a demonic principle, rebellion against God, sin | Radical evil (Kant, "Über Pädagogik") | Injustice, inequality, violence, abuse |
| Repentance, change of thinking | Purification, catharsis | Education towards ethical change |
| Gospel perfection: perfect submission to God's will | Definition of the good life | Prescribed ideal of ethical management |
| Perfection as the process of sanctification | Fulfilling the goals of education/Perfection as fulfilling its purpose | Human development as an ethical value |
| Value of the person as the *imago dei* | Determination of individuality by community | Community of people—a value balancing individual freedom |
| Love of God and love of neighbor | Love of the virtues[70] | Social good |

68. Compiled according to Hanes, *Duchovné prebudenia*, 183.

69. Compiled according to Hanes, *Duchovné prebudenia*, 206.

70. "For what constitutes the good for man is a complete human life at its best, and the exercise of the virtues is a necessary and central part of such a life, not a mere preparatory exercise to secure such a life" (Maclntyre, *After Virtue*, 149).

Finally, we will consider the possible overlaps of Comenius's universal education into current pedagogy, thanks here to the thought-provoking works of Palouš, Ries, Helus, and Spilková mentioned above, following the ideas of Comenius, emphasizing the need to search for new, deeper values in education and the teaching profession, especially "the value of humanity, humaneness, and the spiritual dimension of teaching."[71] According to Ries, pedagogy should integrate three aspects: philosophy, science, and art, including the spiritual aspect of education and pedagogy, and artistic intuition, which includes the creation of textbooks—the art of pedagogy so inherent in Comenius."[72]

One of the most significant overlaps is the placement of the *Pampaedia* as the most important idea of the restoration of human affairs. Behind it is the full-fledged, reality-based yet at the same time reality-exceeding, pedagogical optimism of Comenius—the hope of positive change for society and lifelong effort to contribute to it. Let us now focus on a few more ideas:

### *The transcendent view of Comenius's view of the multi-dimensionality of human existence*

As follows from the summary of Comenius's anthropology, Comenius—in contrast to the pedagogy of his time—considered people to be not only physical and thinking beings, able to feel, decide, and act, but ones that also live spiritually, that is, truly drawing strength, love, and joy from their personal relationship with transcendent, yet physically unknowable, God. The spirituality of a person has its needs, and without fulfilling them the person cannot be happy. It is fundamentally integrated with the other areas of life, it is a source of living strength when other dimensions of the person have lost the reason for optimism. Palouš stated that Comenius's piety was an "immensely public" matter, inseparable from his other personal and social practice.[73]

In our context, the spiritual dimension of education was, until recently, marked as unscientific, that is, inappropriate. This was also reflected in the intentional non-observance of the internal system of Comenius's starting points. "If we do not reduce the work of Comenius to mainly didactic

71. Spilková and Hejlová, *Příprava učitelů*, 11.

72. Ries, *Člověk a výchovy*, 8.

73. Palouš, *Paradoxy výchovy*, 14–15.

knowledge, there is no doubt that his own root, the basis of his pedagogical work, is deeply philosophical and religious."[74]

Research on the thinking of children at the end of the twentieth century revealed that the naturalistic worldview did not correspond with the results found. During a thirty-year research study, secular psychiatrist Coles found that children naturally extend their faculties towards the transcendent.[75] Together with Anna Freud, they recognized the existence of the spiritual world in children, even those from a non-religious background, and thus too, the existence of spiritual phenomena, until then classified in psychopathology. Internalized religiosity correlates with improved mental health and intellectual performance.[76]

Regarding the question of spirituality, current mainstream pedagogy can be based on (a) a naturalistic worldview of the non-existence of the spirituality of the person, (b) the belief that it is one of the alternative approaches to life and thus a completely private matter, potentially causing a threat of quarrels in the public sphere, or (c) allowing it and deliberately guiding it by more or less directive educational measures. For example, the subject of religious education as a requirement or an option—a specific example is the National Curriculum of England. (It should be noted that, like every other ability, a person's spiritual capacity can also be abused; it needs to be identified—superstitions, indoctrination, manipulation, or mental disorders.) Ries and Lukášová pay special attention to the spiritual side of education because they consider it neglected.[77]

In moral education Comenius (1992), in accordance with the ethical education of this time, emphasizes the harmony of human conduct with one's moral conscience. However, being aware of the violations of self-centered humanity, he regarded his relationship with God as the focus of his morality. Comenius went beyond education towards pro-sociality with his demand for education towards agape love—the self-transcendental love for God and for people, that excludes hatred: "One would be a non-human, who would not feel love for people, who would not seek the common good of humanity."[78]

74. Ries, *Člověk a výchovy*, 10.
75. Coles, *Spiritual Life*.
76. Stríženec, *Súčasná psychológia*; Říčan, "Spiritualita jako základ."
77. Ries, "Humánní pedagogika"; Lukášová and Ries, "Pedagogická fakulta," 199.
78. Komenský, *Obecná porada*, 1190.

*Comenius's transcendent view of the triadic structure of human relations*

Humanistic education is about developing one's relationships with oneself, other people, and the world. The relationship to God, so essential for Comenius, is no longer part of pedagogical anthropology. "The phenomenon of lover, with its vertical relationship to divinity, has somehow disappeared from the current pedagogical discourse."[79]

From observing the functioning of postmodern society it is possible to make the hypothetical statement that today's society increasingly prioritizes the relationships to oneself over relationships to other people and the world (these becoming horizontally equal—e.g. relationships to children, to pets, to whales, to robots). All of these shifts in relationships have their reasons, for example, reactions to corporal punishment, authoritarian education, abuse, manipulation, failure to exercise power, etc. At the same time, however, it must be stated that in real life it is not feasible to be consistently guided by them, because at every step one must question whether someone has the right to have authority, a dominant position, the responsibility to manage others, the final word in serious questions, etc. American psychiatrists have found that education for the self did not objectively increase the well-being or inner self-acceptance of individuals, on the contrary it encouraged the development of narcissism and arrogance.[80]

Comenius's structure of human relations thus agrees in some respects and in some respects overlaps current pedagogical anthropology. Comenius spoke of an education as successful, on the condition that the created people accept their natural place in the triadic structure of relationships—in the vertical relationship subordinate to the transcendent, higher authority, and in the horizontal relationships to themselves and others, to nature and to the state.[81] Their relationships to others and to themselves they regulate by the biblical principle: "Love your neighbor as yourself." Comenius viewed both relationships positively: "I must love myself as God's most preeminent gift, to respect myself as a true image of God. The same is true in relation to my neighbor."[82] The people are aware of their dignity, for which they don't have to wage a religious war. At the same time, humankind has been entrusted since Creation with the oversight of public

79. Ries, *Člověk a výchovy*, 49, 51.

80. Harrison, *Big Ego Trip*.

81. Bravená, "Symboly štěstí," 420.

82. Komenský, *Obecná porada*, 564.

affairs, common property, and the environment. This structure does not limit human dignity in any way, but ensures it without supporting them in their egocentrism or narcissism, and does not lead them to abuse nature, but to treat it responsibly.

### *The transencent impact of educational efforts on the future*

In his *Consultation*, Comenius synthesized in a special way two, if we may call them thus, complementary eschatological positions. The first was faith in the biblical account of spiritual life after death. He considered it his duty to teach everyone about this doctrine so that no one would remain blind in ignorance, but could freely decide to reject it or give it appropriate attention. This challenge is particularly provocative and limiting for today's scientifically-based person. C. S. Lewis also addressed its barbs: "The people who try to hold an optimistic view of this world would become pessimists: the people who hold a stern view of it become optimists."[83]

Comenius's second position was the realization of the need for every person, regardless of worldview, to be able to transcend the boundaries of their life here on earth for the future good of human society. "Let us all work for eternity, which is approaching. . . . Let us all begin to long for better things. . . . Let us all do this, that it may go well for everyone."[84] Comenius's *Pampaedia* had a bold goal that extended beyond the end of the world—to serve "to restore and save the sick world."[85] These days we do not normally encounter such ambitious projects in pedagogy, only to a limited extent (for example, from Freire,[86] who sought a path of radical educational transformation of society after the Civil War). We do, however, encounter challenges from dissatisfied pedagogues to reform the school system. If the "cessation of entropy, fragmentation and individualism" is to occur, it is necessary to reflect on the need for a "holistic change of thought and action."[87] Comenius's attitude, applied to our present time which is full of egocentrism and the loss of not only eschatological hope, but also of the ability to make a personal sacrifice for society or nature, we consider to be extremely stimulating also with regard to the current crisis in education.

83. Lewis, *God in the Dock*, 41.

84. Komenský, *Obecná porada*, 1192.

85. Beneš, *Andragogika*, 14.

86. Freire, *Pedagogy of the Oppressed*.

87. Kosová, "Quo vadis," 25.

## Conclusion

Comenius's universal education could have a double effect on today's pedagogy. First are the practical-didactic solutions, proclaimed in our schools for decades. If they were actually put into effect, we would consider it a significant contribution to the education of future generations.

Our contribution, however, focused on a more fundamental, complex dimension of Comenius's influence—the effort to help today's society deal with the deep crisis of values in its people. In order to be able to understand the holistic intent and specific ideas of this project of the restoration of "human affairs," we looked at Comenius's anthropological starting points. His work created the space that would allow, from these "roots," the growth of a tree of philosophic and concrete didactic stimuli for the education of all people, reflecting the spirit of his time, but also extending to current pedagogy. Unfortunately, one of the marks of our day is the *a priori* rejection of traditional values and ways to adopt them. We tried to point out specific examples of such extensions with the intention that, if current educators are open to them, they can apply them as a stimulus to their own reflections about solutions to current educational problems.

In order to not fall into non-humanness, people should live for higher values that go beyond their current knowledge, and at the same time, want to function with respect and love in the triadic structure of their transcendent horizontal and vertical relationships. Although from a theological perspective, as well as the perspective of our current multi-cultural age, it is unrealistic to expect the fulfillment of Comenius's vision of a unified, religiously-oriented society, his call for the common good and peace with people of other faiths is valuable. Knowing that God is the God of all people, he challenges all scholars, rulers, clergy, and thoughtful people to engage in the restoration of "human affairs."[88]

88. Komenský, *Obecná porada*.

## Bibliography


Beneš, Milan. *Andragogika* [Andragogy]. Praha: Grada, 2014.

Bravená, N. "Symboly štěstí otevírající svět dětí" [Symbols of Happiness Unlocking the World of Children]. In *Nahlížení do světa dětí*, edited by Helena Hejlová et al., 41–44. Praha: Pedagogická Fakulta Univerzita Karlova, 2013.

Burton, Simon J. G. "Jan Amos Comenius's Trinitarian and Conciliar Vision of a United Europe." *Reformation & Renaissance Review* 19.2 (2017) 104–21.

Čížek, Jan. *The Conception of Man in the Works of John Amos Comenius*. European Studies in Theology, Philosophy and History of Religions 15. New York: Peter Lang, 2016.

Coles, Robert. *The Spiritual Life of Children: The Inner Lives of Children*. Boston: Houghton Mifflin, 1990.

Dobinson, C. H., ed. *Comenius and Contemporary Education*. Hamburg: UNESCO, 1970.

Dodd, J. "Philosophical Significance of Hope." *The Review of Metaphysics* 58.1 (2004) 117–46.

Freire, Paulo. *Pedagogy of the Oppressed*. New York: Continuum, 2000.

Fromm, Erich. *Escape from Freedom*. New York: Avon, 1969.

Fukuyama, Francis. *Velký rozvrat* [The Great Decline]. Praha: Academia, 2006.

Hábl, Jan. *Aby člověk neupadal* v *nečlověka* [So That Man Would Not Fall into a Non-human]. Červený Kostelec: Pavel Mervart, 2017.

Hanes, Pavel. *Duchovné prebudenia a spoločnosť* [Spiritual Awakenings and Society]. Banská Bystrica: Pedagogická Fakulta, Matej Bel University, 2013.

Harrison, Glynn. *The Big Ego Trip*. Nottingham: InterVarsity, 2013.

Helus, Zdeněk. *Dítě v osobnostním pojetí* [The Child in the Concept of Personality]. Praha: Portál, 2004.

———. "Společenská krize—důsledky pro pojetí edukace jakožto starosti o člověka" [Social Crisis—Implications for the Concept of Education as the Concern for People]. In *Proměny pojetí vzdělávání a školního hodnocení*, 8–27. Praha: Asociace waldorfských škol ČR, 2012.

———. "Učitel, vůdčí aktér osobnostně rozvíjející výuky" [The Teacher, Leading Actor in Individually Developing Instruction]. In *Perspektivy učitelství*, edited by Zdeněk Helus et al., 7–47. Praha: Pedagogická Fakulta Univerzita Karlova, 2012.

Jablonský, Tomáš, et al. *European Values and Cultural Heritage*. Debrecen: Center for Higher Educational Research and Development, 2012.

Kairov, Ivan Andrejevič. "Jan Amos Komenský." *Pedagogika* 21.2 (1971) 185–92.

Kant, Immanuel. *Ausgewählte schriften zur Pädagogik und ihrer Begrundung*. Paderborn: Schoningh, 1963.

Komenský, Jan Amos. *Obecná porada o nápravě věcí lidských* [General Consultation on the Restoration of Human Affairs]. Vols. I–III. Praha: Nakladatelství Svoboda, 1992.

Kosová, Beata. *Humanizačné premeny výchovy a vzdelávania na 1.stupni ZŠ* [Humanizational Changes to Education and Upbringing at the Elementary School Level]. Banská Bystrica: Metodické Centrum, 1996.

———. "Quo vadis doktorandské štúdium (nielen) v pedagogických vedách" [Quo Vadis Doctoral Study (Not Only) in the Pedagogical Sciences]. In *Pedagogická profesia z aspektu vedy, výskumu a praxe*, edited by I. Ištvan, et al., 11–35. Prešov: University of Prešov, 2017.

———. *Vybrané kapitoly z teórie personálnej a sociálnej výchovy* [Selected Chapters from the Theory of Personnel and Social Education]. Banská Bystrica: Matej Bel University, 2005.

———. "Výzvy súčasného sveta pre premeny školy a edukácie" [Current World Challenges for Transformations of Schools and Education]. In *Perspektivy výchovy a vzdělávání v podmínkach současného světa*, edited by Miriam Prokešová, 63–74. Praha: Česká pedagogická společnost, 2017.

Lewis, C. S. *God in the Dock*. Grand Rapids: Eerdmans, 1970.

Lukášová, Hana. *Učitelská profese v primárním vzdělávání a pedagogická příprava učitelů* [The Teaching Profession in Primary Education and Teacher Training]. Ostrava: University of Ostrava, 2003.

Lukášová, Hana, and Lumir Ries. "Pedagogická fakulta Ostravské univerzity v Ostravě" [Faculty of Education, University of Ostrava]. In *Příprava učitelů pro primární a preprimární vzdělávání v Česku a na Slovensku*, edited by Vladimíra Spilková and Helena Hejlová, 195–214. Praha: Charles University Press, 2010.

Maclntyre, Alasdair. *After Virtue*. Notre Dame: University of Notre Dame Press, 2007.

Palouš, Radim. *Paradoxy výchovy* [Paradoxes of Education]. Praha: Karolinum, 2009.

Piaget, Jean. "Jan Amos Comenius." In *Prospects (UNESCO, International Bureau of Education)* 23.1–2 (1993) 173–96.

Porubský, Štefan. "Inštitúcia školy na rázcestí" [The School as an Institution at the Crossroads]. In *Premeny spoločnosti a perspektívy školy*, by Štefan Porubský et al., 8–21. Banská Bystrica: Matej Bel University, 2013.

Průcha, Jan. *Moderní pedagogika*. 1st ed. Praha: Portál, 1997.

Říčan, Pavel. "Spiritualita jako základ mravní výchovy" [Spirituality as a Basis of Moral Education]. *Pedagogika* 56.2 (2006) 119–31.

Ries, Lumir. *Člověk a výchovy II* [Man and Education]. Ostrava: Universita Ostraviensis, 2011.

———. "Humánní pedagogika Šalvy Amonašviliho" [Human Pedagogy of Shalva Amonashvili]. *Pedagogická orientace* 19.4 (2009) 5–21.

Rogers, Carl. R. *Ako byť sám sebou* [How to Be Yourself]. Bratislava: IRIS, 1996.

Schubert, Martin. *Teoretické koncepcie andragogiky* [Theoretical Concepts of Andragogy]. Banská Bystrica: Belianum, 2017.

Schultze, Hermann. *Theologische Sozialethik* [Theological Social Ethics]. Gütersloh: Gütersloher Verlagshaus Mohn, 1979.

Somr, Miroslav, and Helena Pavličíková. "Comenius' Ethical Visions of the Improvement of Human Things." *Studia Edukacyjne* 35 (2015) 395–404.

Spilková, Vladimíra. *Proměny primární školy a vzdělávání učitelů v historicko-srovnávací perspektivě* [Changes in Primary School and Teacher Education in a Historical-Comparative Perspective]. Praha: Charles University Press, 1997.

———. "Výzvy, které přínáší osobnostne rozvíjející pojetí vzdělávaní pro školu, učitele a vzdelávací politiku" [Challenges Posed by the Personally Developing Concept of Education for the School, Teachers, and Educational Policy]. In *Proměny pojetí vzdělávání a školního hodnocení*, 27–42. Praha: Asociace waldorfských škol ČR, 2012.

Spilková, Vladimíra, and Helena Hejlová, eds. *Příprava učitelů pro primární a preprimární vzdělávání v Česku a na Slovensku: Vývoj po roce 1989 a perspektivy* [Teacher Training for Primary and Pre-Primary Education in the Czech Republic and Slovakia: Developments after 1989 and Perspectives]. Praha: Charles University Press, 2010.

Spilková, Vladimíra, et al. *Proměny primárního vzdělávání v ČR* [Changes in Primary Education in the Czech Republic]. Praha: Portál, 2005.

Stríženec, Michal. *Súčasná psychológia náboženstva* [Contemporary Psychology of Religion]. Bratislava: IRIS, 2001.

Švec, Štefan. *Základné pojmy v pedagogike a andragogike* [Basic Concepts in Pedagogy and Andragogy]. Bratislava: IRIS, 2005.

Thielicke, Helmut. *Theological Ethics*. 2 vols. Philadelphia: Fortress, 1966.

Turek, Ivan. *Inovácie v didaktike* [Innovations in Didactics]. Bratislava: MPC, 2005.

Vliet, P. van. "The Utopian Ideas of Comenius and the Dutch Republic: An Uneasy Relation." In *The Utopian Ideas of Comenius*, 85–92. http://www.dwc.knaw.nl/DL/publications/PU00010518.pdf.

# Comenius's Educational Plans from the Perspective of Developmental and Social Psychology

Radka Skorunková

## Introduction

J. A. Comenius's educational plans included one to teach everyone for the good of the whole. If everyone is brought up to look for the benefit of the whole society, it will be possible to maintain the order of the world: "If we consider what it is that keeps our universe and every single thing about ourselves in proper condition, we find that it isn't anything, absolutely nothing other than order. . . . For all that is well-ordered remains intact in its state as long as order is maintained; when order is forsaken, it withers, vacillates, falls, breaks down."[1]

Comenius considered the source of all the problems of human society to be that people are guided in their lives mainly by what is to their own benefit. "We don't exert ourselves for the common good, but each one is only out for themselves."[2] By the urgency with which Comenius expressed himself on the issue of education oriented towards the common good, it can be concluded that the negative manifestations of human behavior that he noticed were not exceptional phenomena. Since the beginning of the history of school reform, there have undoubtedly been many advances in

1. Komenský, "Velká didaktika," 112.
2. Komenský, *Obecná porada*, 112.

favor of general education and the humanization of society. Nevertheless, even today criticism of the development of human society appears in works of philosophers, psychologists, sociologists, educators, and other thinkers. This criticism has reached an urgency comparable to the rhetoric of Comenius, and in many respects has even surpassed it: "At the end of the twentieth century the whole human community is faced with the problem of how to solve the series of connected crisis phenomena, most global in nature. . . . Humanity is in a new, unknown, unprecedented situation in which the whole living world is in jeopardy."[3] "Society is fast approaching the limits of industrial growth and the next generation will have to pay the price for the unsustainable practices of preceding generations."[4] What is to blame for the critical state of a world heading for extinction? It is, in parallel with the thoughts of Comenius, the widespread and ubiquitous selfishness of humanity. "The ruling egocentrism (instead of sociocentrism) and the idea that one should acquire as many material goods as possible and enjoy bodily well-being as much as possible, portrays a wrong approach."[5]

Selfishness (or egotism) manifests itself in various forms of behavior, whose common feature is that the individual prioritizes their own interests and acts for their own benefit, often thoughtlessly and to the detriment of other members of society.

## Innate Sources of Selfishness

Human selfishness is formed, as are other personal traits, by the action of innate dispositions, environmental influences, and their mutual interaction. Selfish behavior can be completely conscious and planned, or completely unconscious or impulsive. Innate dispositions to selfish behavior lie in the biological determination of the human psyche.

### Intraspecific Aggression

Ethology and comparative psychology provide the knowledge that intraspecific aggression is a common part of life in communities of different animal species. Konrad Lorenz defined intraspecific aggression as "the

3. Horká and Hrdličková, *Výchova*, 9.
4. Winter and Koger, *Psychologie enviromentálních problémů.*
5. Horká and Hrdličková, *Výchova*, 9.

aggressiveness of an animal or a human being, which is aimed at a member of their own species."[6] This behavior includes fighting for prey, food sources, territory, status in the hierarchy of society, obtaining a sexual partner, and intimidation of rivals. Through aggressive behavior individuals strive to reach their goals, that is, aggression can be considered as one of the manifestations of selfishness. Aggressive behavior has a negative impact at the level of individual relationships (for example, wounding or killing an individual from the same species), but according to the conclusions of ethologists it has an important function in terms of the whole ecosystem. Zdeněk Veselovský stated that mutual intraspecific conflicts lead to the stabilization of the social hierarchy, which represents a favorable model of coexistence, ensuring the survival of the entire animal community. Aggressive behavior ensures that members of the community are evenly distributed throughout the biotope.[7] Wild ducks and geese, for example, which remain in one large flock throughout the winter, disperse to smaller areas inhabited by individual pairs in early spring due to mutual conflicts, thus gaining the necessary living space for reproduction. Individuals also defend their living space by pushing out their adult young or weak individuals from their own territory. These have no choice but to look for new territory, and fight for it with other members of their kind.

Comenius, who asked that people strive to find order in the world, drew attention to the importance of the laws of nature: "Each creature is kept very carefully within its limits according to the rules of nature; this maintains the order of the universe."[8] The conclusions of the comparative psychologists reveal a fundamental biological source of the difficult fate of every living individual. Natural laws force living organisms to behave selfishly towards individuals of their species, including their own offspring. To be capable of this necessary evil, they are equipped with innate instincts which are the driving force of aggressive behavior. If they did not fulfill the innate pattern of behavior, it would disrupt the "order of the world." This conflict also shows how difficult it is to answer the question, "What is the good?" If we accept Comenius's view that the good is that which is beneficial for the whole society, and compare it with the knowledge about the positive benefits of intraspecific aggression, then we have to state that

6. Lorenz, *Takzvané zlo*, 5.

7. Veselovský, *Etologie*.

8. Komenský, "Velká didaktika," 112.

to completely eradicate the selfish behavior of individuals would not be desirable from the point of view of the whole.

## The Moral Degeneration of Humankind in Terms of Phylogenetic Development

The biological nature of living organisms is a constant source of selfish behavior that ensures balance in their communal coexistence. But why, unlike other animal species, has selfishness in people risen to such an extent that its negative effects fundamentally disrupt the original function of selfishness, to maintain the balance of life? Lorenz explained the causes of the moral decline of human society by the Darwinian principle of phylogenetic development, which reaches a dead end when development is determined only by competition between members of the same species.[9] For the development of a species to be successful, individuals striving for dominance must always be exposed to the need to deal with the external influences of the broad interspecific environment. Dominant individuals must be able to help their community withstand the threats posed by the surrounding environment. If the rivals who are fighting are both lacking a functional relationship to some problem in the external environment, then an individual may become dominant who passes to his offspring unfavorable genes for the survival of the species, thus leading to the degeneration of the whole animal species. Lorenz believed that the phylogenetic decline of human beings began in the Stone Age, when they used their weapons, clothing, and social organization to mitigate the external dangers threatening them, such as starvation, freezing, or large carnivores. When those dangers were eliminated, it began to be that only intraspecific selection affected development. The alpha individuals determining the course of society could be the ones who were the most successful fighters in comparison with their rivals, and it was no longer necessary that they could protect their society from external threats. Victory over rivals enabled them to dominate society, and there came to be an extreme cultivation of intraspecific militancy. Humans ensure their survival only through intraspecific fighting and have forgotten that attention must also be paid to external dangers that threaten the whole species, and which the whole society should face.

Comenius considered the process of moral degeneration to be a consequence of turning away from God and usurping his self-determination.

9. Lorenz, *Takzvané zlo.*

Nothing stands above humanity, every person is the creator of their world.[10] Here we find the same principle as in the discoveries of Lorenz. As long as people live as if they are the fearless lords of the world, their development will rightfully continue on the path to extinction.

## Acquired Sources of Selfishness

Lorenz described innate instincts that influence human nature, but he also discovered that an individual's behavior is determined by learning at an early age. Imprinting is set during a short, critical period in the life cycle; it is a supra-individual learning and it influences patterns of behavior which are not innate and without learning would not appear in an animal's repertoire of behavior.

In humans the learning experience is permanently retained and influences the maturation process of the central nervous system, for the maturation processes are carried on intensively throughout the first year of life and affect the following developmental stages. Ivo Čermák reviewed the findings of longitudinal research, according to which individual difference in the manifestations of aggression were displayed in children up to three years of age, and then the level of aggressive behavior stabilized and remained steady until adolescence.[11]

The incompleteness of a newborn's innate faculties allow human beings to acquire a much larger repertoire of behavior during ontogenetic development than any other species can. The readiness to gain learned patterns of behavior is both advantageous and risky, because the influences of the environment can enrich the human psyche as well as corrupt and destroy it.

### Emotional Deprivation

The term imprinting has taken on a more general meaning in psychology and refers to any process in early learning which relates to the manifestation of an emotional bond in a young individual that is directed preferentially and stably to one figure. Research in emotional attachments shows that the formation of early emotional attachment is essential for healthy

10. Komenský, *Obecná porada*.

11. Čermák et al., *Agrese*.

personal development and has lifelong impacts on an individual's behavior and experience.[12]

A longitudinal study by a Czech-American team led by Zdeněk Dytrych and Zdeněk Matějček showed that children born from an unwanted pregnancy and rejected by their parents had more problems later in life than children received positively. Children born from a demonstrably unwanted pregnancy were followed into adulthood and compared with a group of children born to mothers who accepted pregnancy and childbirth. Unwanted children had a higher frequency of minor injuries and illnesses at age nine compared to the control group, were overweight, underperformed at school, their diligence and behavior were negatively evaluated by both their teachers and their mothers, and they were less popular in the classroom. At ages fourteen to sixteen, these differences not only persisted, but substantially deepened. At ages twenty-one to twenty-three, they appeared more often in the records of anti-alcohol counseling centers and also in the criminal record, and they had a marked tendency to create social problems. Overall, they experienced less satisfaction with their own lives, in their work, in their partnerships, as well as with their mental state.[13]

Forming an emotional bond at an early age has an impact on an individual's behavior toward society as a whole. A child's deficit in the area of emotional attachments brings negative consequences for the whole society, for an emotionally deprived individual is more often prone to egotism, ruthlessness, and anti-social behavior. These individuals lack empathy for other people and have no interest in contributing to the benefit of society as a whole. A pioneer in the study of emotional attachment, John Bowlby, compared a group of delinquent juveniles with a group of non-delinquent juveniles. Disturbed emotional relationships in childhood were found in the case histories of the group of delinquents (in contrast to the control group). To verify the theory that emotional deprivation in childhood later leads to delinquent behavior, he conducted a catamnestic study in which he followed the development of a group of children who were placed in a medical sanatorium at an early age, and compared them with a group of children without this psychologically deprived experience.[14]

It is more difficult for children and adolescents with behavioral disorders to change if they have not formed an emotional attachment to anyone,

12. Cassidy and Shaver, *Handbook of Attachment*.

13. David et al., "Born Unwanted."

14. Bowlby, *Vazba*.

which occurs primarily in the conditions of institutional education. Children who have formed an emotional bond at an early age have a greater chance of correcting their behavior. This basic emotional connection can become the motivation and an effective factor in the treatment of behavioral disorders.[15]

In response to the knowledge about the importance of early emotional attachment, psychology focused on the study of the processes of forming relationships between parents and children. The mechanism of imprinting applies in early childhood in the context of communication. In the healthy formation of relationships, parents intuitively set up a "biological mirror" or make a "biological echo" in response to a young child's mimicry and voice signals. On the basis of the intuitive emotionally oriented responses of the parents, the children are increasingly aware of themselves, their own behavior, and their emotional states.[16] Intuitive parental communication sets the basis for the child's socialization and its application in society. It is a recurring scenario of sharing experiences from these early relationships, as children who have been emotionally received by their parents and have received emotional responses from them are able to provide the same in adulthood to their own children.

## Dysfunctional Education

An understanding of the importance of early learning provides an answer to the question of what it is necessary to do to humanize society. School education is one of the important sources of humanization, but it is not the main factor in determining the process. Achieving the desired state of humanization of a society is complicated by the fact that the formation of an individual's personality starts at birth—that is, long before the child enters school. In addition to education reform, which could ensure the desired education of all members of society, there is also a need for society to take an interest in raising children within families, and in helping those families in which the child's development is disrupted by various adverse factors. More severe and long-lasting behavioral disorders occur in 5 to 10 percent of children and adolescents in the Czech Republic. The issue of domestic violence, which, according to Marie Vágnerová "has always occurred,"[17]

15. Hort et al., *Dětská a adolescentní psychiatrie*.
16. Dittrichová et al., *Chování dítěte raného věku*.
17. Vágnerová, *Současná psychopatologie*, 578.

currently happens in nearly one in ten partner relationships in our country. Domestic violence occurs regardless of the level of education or professional affiliation. The aggressivity of the perpetrator of domestic violence is often generalized, with 80 percent of beaten women saying their partners treated their children and parents the same way. At least 5 percent of children currently suffer from CAN syndrome; 5 to 10 percent of children suffer physical abuse, according to estimates from various studies, and 6 to 10 percent of the child population suffers from neglect and psychological abuse.

Not only the reform of education, but also universal education is still relevant. Children come to school at an age when they have already had a major period of development in which the school cannot intervene. Ideally, the indirect effect of school on children could be evaluated if their parents would achieve wisdom and virtue through education. In his writings on educational deficiencies in the family, Comenius mentioned, "There are few among parents who could teach their children anything good, either because they have not learned anything like it themselves, or because, in the midst of their other tasks, they neglect these things."[18] In addition to the parents' education, a child's upbringing within a family is influenced by many other circumstances, for example, the current situation (poverty, unemployment, divorce) or the personal problems of the parents arising in the course of life, such as alcoholism, depression, or other mental disorders. Ensuring functional educational activity in every family is an important, yet today unfulfilled, task of human society.

## Frustration

Dissatisfaction with an individual's emotional needs and dysfunctional upbringing are not the only negative influences of the environment from which actions directed against society originate. Other important factors are stressful situations, feelings of danger, dissatisfaction or discomfort. If individuals are frustrated, that is, there is a certain obstacle between that person and their goal so their needs are not met, tendency to behave aggressively. Dollard et al. formulated a theory about the connection between frustration and aggression as early as the 1930s.[19]

18. Komenský, *Velká didaktika*, 55.

19. Dollard et al., *Frustration and Aggression*.

People are easily frustrated, given that they are equipped with a large number of needs, not only innate, but also those shaped by the social environment. Abraham Maslow classified human needs into a hierarchy from basic biological needs to the highest, in this order: (1) physiological needs, (2) need for security, (3) need for belonging and love, (4) need for approval, (5) need for self-actualization (personality growth).[20] The mental balance of a person is threatened by many other psychological needs, an outline of which is based on a study of various theories by Pavel Říčan: the need to join together, the need for autonomy, the need for love, the need for protection and help, the need for approval, the need for aggression, the need to defend oneself, the need to care for another, the need to court someone, the need to excel in high performance, the need to submit, the need to challenge, the need to control, the need to show off, the need to worship, the need for order, the need to play, the need to condemn, the need for privacy, the need for superiority, the need to know, the need to understand intellectually, the need to avoid shame, the need to save things, the need to laugh.[21]

The complexity of the human psyche brings specific sources of frustration that other animal species do not have. For example, frustration caused by social exclusion is one of the common motives for acts of violence against society as a form of revenge for the injustice it inflicted on the frustrated individual. Overall, life in modern society and in the environment built by human beings, is a source of everyday psychological stress. Aggressive behavior manifests itself more often in a noisy environment or one crowded with people,[22] which are features of environments typical of urban areas, shopping malls, public transportation, and large schools, in which a large part of the population moves.

Opportunities for frustration also increase with the rising number of modern achievements and possibilities for people, who perceive all they do not yet have compared to all that the market offers and compared to their peers. Erich Fromm raised the classic question, "To have, or to be?" in the context of human life in modern times; he pointed out that focusing on the consumerist way of life does not lead to a desirable state of satisfaction.[23] Tim Kasser and Allen Kanner summarized the findings concerning the consumer lifestyle and confirmed that efforts to fulfill a person's

20. Maslow, *Theory of Human Motivation.*

21. Říčan, *Psychologie osobnosti.*

22. Hayesová, *Základy sociální psychologie.*

23. Fromm, *Mít nebo být?*

psychological needs through excessive consumption endanger both the environment and human mental health.[24]

## Social Influence

How is it possible the people can hold onto a certain lifestyle for a long time, even though they have been informed about its negative consequences? Social psychology studies the mechanisms of how the wider society affects the behavior of people and how individuals adapt to social norms established by society. Social learning takes place both by imitating the model of someone close to us or admired by us, and by imitating people with whom we have no personal relationship. Robert Zajonc showed that what people perceive often, they like more, because the experience of having already met that thing invokes positive emotions in them.[25] On this principle, people quickly become accustomed to behavior that is common in society, even though that behavior may have negative consequences. Behavior that is often repeated becomes a habit, and then the individual acts automatically, without realizing the consequences. The individual is only doing what everyone else is doing, and with this all members of society mutually affirm that their selfish behavior is completely legitimate and acceptable. Ways of behaving formed by the social mainstream include many detrimental habits, among them selfishness in the form of over-consumption or wasting resources. Information about the negative consequences of that behavior are ignored or downplayed. This is the mechanism that causes cognitive dissonance, described by Leon Festinger. When people find themselves in a situation where their opinion or behavior is in conflict with objective reality, they reduce the anxiety and tension arising from the conflict so as to continue to appear to themselves and the outside environment to be acting consistently. Instead of changing their opinions or behavior, they twist, deny or denigrate objective reality with various distorted arguments.[26]

People behave differently when they are anonymous and can hide in a crowd. This de-individuation reduces the sense of responsibility for their actions and at the same time allows them to keep their self-image acceptable. Social influence plays a big role in the formation of aggressive behavior, as demonstrated, for example, by Stanley Milgram's experiment,

24. Kasser and Kanner, *Psychology and Consumer Culture.*

25. Zajonc, "Feeling and Thinking."

26. Festinger, *Theory of Cognitive Dissonance.*

which examined obedience to authority,[27] or the prison experiment of Philip Zimbardo, which proved the influence of assigned social roles and adaptation to pathological social situations are significant.[28] Modern times have expanded the sources of social learning with media-mediated models. Albert Bandura began his work researching the influence of media on the occurrence of aggressive behavior.[29] According to Vagnerová, the risk factor is the predominance of negative information in the media, which leads to a reduction in sensitivity to various manifestations of aggression.[30] Violence contained in film or PC games can stimulate aggression, especially in children and immature individuals who are less able to distinguish the symbolic level from reality, and can more easily identify with the aggressor and consider his behavior as normal. Social influence and its mechanisms lead to the fact that an individual growing up in an inhumane society naturally adopts inhumane behavior and becomes its carrier to future generations.

## Knowledge and Virtue

Lorenz believed that if we understand the causes of our own behavior, we can give our reason and morals the power to decisively intervene in the development of society.[31] Thanks to knowledge, one can become better. The development of science in various areas of human life and school education have created the conditions, in modern times, for Comenius's prediction to be fulfilled: "The time will surely come when all people will learn not to guess, but to know, and to not be satisfied with foreign opinions, but to verify everything by their own senses and retain it in their minds."[32]

Have there been changes in the human psyche due to the development of knowledge and education? It has been proven that the emphasis in school education on the development of scientific (or theoretical) thinking had a positive influence on the development of the intellectual capabilities of the populace during the twentieth century. James Flynn analyzed the results of measurements of intelligence taken over the last century and found that the results of intelligence tests gradually improved by an average of 3.3

27. Milgram, "Behavioral Study of Obedience."

28. Zimbardo, *Moc a zlo.*

29. Bandura, *Aggression*

30. Vágnerová, *Současná psychopatologie.*

31. Lorenz, *Takzvané zlo.*

32. Komenský, *Obecná porada*, 233.

points per decade. In connection with the modernization of society and a generally higher level of education, people began to look at the world through "scientific glasses." Today, people are better than their ancestors of a hundred years ago at classifying information into abstract categories and applying logical thought to hypothetical situations. It could be further stated that they can use reason more than previous generations. However, Flynn points out that this does not automatically guarantee a more developed ability to solve problems in practical life.[33]

Nor can the development of human cognitive abilities in itself guarantee that people will use the acquired knowledge for the benefit of the whole society. It does not prevent the "confusion of the senses and the mind as a result of selfishness," which also affects educated individuals: "Philosophers want to understand everything themselves, better than others, and in contrast to others, and thus drive themselves into contradictions."[34] The current struggles for power, the promotion of one's "truth" or the gaining of an advantage in the community of scientists shows that Comenius's wish: "Then let selfishness perish everywhere and in everything, and the universe will return to everything everywhere"[35] has not been fulfilled even in the educated strata of society after long centuries.

Individual scientific disciplines have set their own codes of ethics, because each one's needs have only become apparent gradually, over the course of their existence. With the accumulating knowledge that enables people to intervene more and more in various areas of human life, the number of ethical questions and dilemmas are increasing. In the field of psychology, the Code of the American Psychological Association (APA) was first established in 1953, more than half a century after the founding of the professional organization of psychologists. The ethical aspects of professional activity are usually complex. In an effort to establish ethical guidelines for psychology, it has already proven difficult to define what a "profession" is, and even harder to define the "profession of the psychologist." Discussions have been sparked by many aspects of the psychologist's work, for example, whether the terms "confidentiality of information" and "professional secrecy" have the same meaning.[36] The code of ethics makes it easier for psychologists to orient themselves in the requirements of their

33. Flynn, *What Is Intelligence?*

34. Komenský, *Obecná porada*, 115.

35. Komenský, *Obecná porada*.

36. Lindsay et al., *Etika pro evropské psychology*.

profession, but it also often lays on them conflicting requirements. Alena Plháková stated that compliance with the code of ethics is not easy at all, because its application in specific practical situations brings psychologists many dilemmas. In their work psychologists must consider what is good for whom, who will benefit from their actions, and, conversely, to whom it can bring negative consequences.[37]

It is clear from the previous paragraphs that connected to education is the need to deal intensively with ethical questions, not marginally or only formally. Comenius emphasized that "piety and morals" should particularly be implanted in human minds, and they should also be the pinnacle of education in the academies.[38]

## What Are the Sources of Virtue?

Comenius noted that people are endowed with both positive and negative potential, and believed that people are "by nature born with the seeds of leadership, morality, and piety," so "nothing is needed but a little inducement and some reasonable guidance."[39] The results of research on comparative psychology, developmental psychology, and social psychology confirm this assumption.

### The Biological Basis of Prosocial Behavior

In the same way that living beings have an innate drive for aggression, they are also biologically predetermined to develop prosocial behavior. Durkin stated that infants already show an innate empathetic reaction to stress. In a group of children, if one cries the others react by also crying. Toddlers tend to share their toys, or bring their mother to a crying peer to help him.[40]

Ethologists in animal behavior have described the mechanisms that lead to the mitigation of the consequences of aggression. In order to preserve the family it is important that intraspecific rivalry does not have destructive consequences, and that leads to the establishment of functioning rules of coexistence that ensure the survival of all member of the community. If the

37. Plháková, *Učebnice obecné psychologie*.
38. Komenský, *Obecná porada*, 115.
39. Komenský, *Velká didaktika*, 106.
40. Durkin, *Developmental Social Psychology*.

defeated individual were physically killed in a fight, it would mean loss for the whole community in which each member plays an important role. It is advantageous for the whole community if the fight takes the form of a ritual in which impressive behavior, intimidation of the opponent, threat, repulsive behavior, and behavior that appeals or subordinates are applied. Lorenz looked for the path to the common good in the laws he observed in the realm of various animal species: "During phylogenesis, when many animals had to moderate aggression to allow the peaceful coexistence of two or more individuals, there arose bonds of personal love and friendship. . . . The life situation of humanity unquestionably calls for some mechanism of restraint that would prevent real aggression not only towards personal enemies, but towards all people in general. From that would come a natural, direct-from-nature requirement to love all of one's neighbors, regardless of the person. . . . I believe that in the not too distant future, our descendants will be given the ability to meet this greatest and most beautiful requirement of true humanity."[41] Lorenz believed that people would be able to use scientific knowledge to benefit society as a whole, and that the biological preconditions for the development of positive qualities would be fulfilled in humans thanks to the development of knowledge. Without connecting knowledge to virtue, however, that cannot happen. Jan Hábl pointed out that knowledge does not, in itself, guarantee humanity—education should be closely linked to moral education, because "a person who is educated but immoral is a threat to themself and others."[42]

## Learning Prosocial Behavior

Social psychology has provided much insight into how aggressive and reckless behavior is maintained in society through the influence of social groups and social learning. On the other hand, these same principles of learning can be used to shape prosocial behavior. Positive patterns of behavior can spread in society on the principle of imitation and social empowerment.

The opinions and behaviors of individuals can be influenced by building social groups that achieve cohesion and integrity. If the group is cohesive and each of its members feels accepted by the group, the conditions are created for the individual to form opinions and behaviors that take into account the interests of the whole group. Solomon Asch examined conformity

41. Lorenz, *Takzvané zlo*, 230.

42. Hábl, *Lekce z lidskosti*, 102.

and looked for reasons why people in a group would adapt their view to the majority opinion.[43] Helus mentioned that the tendency to conform is high in strongly cohesive groups, because members consider it important to give up their personal views if it is for the good of the group and will maintain its cohesion.[44] Accommodation to the views is motivated by the individual's interest in being accepted by the group. The dynamics of social groups also allow the acting minority to be able to change the opinions of the majority of group members. A minority can convince a majority of its opinion if it is put forward consistently, without displays of inflexibility, dogmatism or arrogance.[45] A persistent minority can change the attitudes of the majority if it has the courage to hold its own opinion and withstand the disagreement of the majority.[46] School education has an impact on the formation of pupils' attitudes, and this also happens at the level of higher education. According to Atkinson, university students often deviate from the views of their family reference group and accept the views of the academic reference group. Newly accepted views usually persist even into later life, thanks to them being internalized and confirmed by new reference groups, which the young person chooses because they share common opinions.

The mechanisms of social groups acting on individuals as described above demonstrate that the school environment, where pupils congregate and form small social groups, presents an opportunity for using group processes to develop prosocial behavior. Appropriate leadership in the school classroom can develop empathy, respect for other people, personal responsibility, etc. It also shows that enforcing rules and regulations is effective for achieving changes in behavior,[47] which adds importance to the need for legislative changes in education aimed at, for example, the introduction of ethical education, global education, and other parts of humanizing pedagogical aims.

## Conclusion

The educational plans of Jan Amos Comenius, whose goal was the achievement of the "common good," are utopian from the perspective of

43. Asch, "Effects of Group Pressure."
44. Helus, *Sociální psychologie pro pedagogy.*
45. Atkinsonová, *Psychologie.*
46. Baron and Bellman, "No Guts, No Glory."
47. Winter and Koger, *Psychologie enviromentálních problémů.*

psychological knowledge, if we take into account the innate and acquired psychological sources of the selfish human behavior. In order for human society to reach the ideal state of humanization, it would have to be able to ensure optimal educational activities for every child from the beginning of their lives. It would also have to provide necessary social, health and psychological care to everyone who needed it. No one in society should be able to get in the position of being an outsider or experience long-term frustration. Every social group emerging in society, especially families, school classes, work teams and professional associations would have to achieve the necessary degree of cohesion and integrity. In the practice of everyday life in a complex human society these conditions are hard to fulfill, therefore the question of humanization and the search for ways to achieve it will be eternal. We can consider the success of humanization to be the fact that efforts to achieve it still persist. The teachings of Comenius are of primary motivational importance for the maintaining of these efforts: "Let us be consumed by the terrible, over and over again incoming and almost constant ruin of everything. Or, rather let us discuss how to help, if possible."[48]

48. Komenský, *Obecná porada*, 78.

## Bibliography

Asch, Solomon E. "Effects of Group Pressure Upon the Modification and Distortion of Judgments." In *Groups, Leadership, and Men: Research in Human Relations*, edited by Harold Guetzkow, 177–90. Oxford: Carnegie, 1951.

Atkinsonová, Rita L. *Psychologie*. Praha: Portál, 2012.

Bandura, Albert. *Aggression: A Social Learning Analysis*. Englewood Cliffs, NJ: Prentice-Hall, 1973.

Baron, Robert, and S. Beth Bellman. "No Guts, No Glory: Courage, Harassment, and Minority Influence." *European Journal of Social Psychology* 37.1 (2007) 101–24.

Bowlby, John. *Vazba: teorie kvality raných vztahů mezi matkou a dítětem* [Bond: Theory of the Quality of Early Relationships between Mother and Child]. Praha: Portál, 2010.

Cassidy, Jude, and Phillip R. Shaver, eds. *Handbook of Attachment: Theory, Research, and Clinical Applications*. New York: Guilford, 2016.

Čermák, Ivo, et al. *Agrese, identita, osobnost* [Aggression, Identity, Personhood]. Brno: SCAN, 2003.

David, Henry P., et al. "Born Unwanted: Observations from the Prague Study." *American Psychologist* 58.3 (2003) 224–29.

Dittrichová, Jaroslava, et al. *Chování dítěte raného věku a rodičovská péče* [Early Childhood Behavior and Parental Care]. Praha: Grada, 2004.

Dollard, John, et al. *Frustration and Aggression*. New Haven: Yale University Press, 1939.

Durkin, Kevin. *Developmental Social Psychology: From Infancy to Old Age*. Oxford: Blackwell, 1995.

Festinger, Leon. *A Theory of Cognitive Dissonance*. Evanston, Ill: Row, Peterson, 1957.

Flynn, James R. *What Is Intelligence? Beyond the Flynn Effect*. New York: Cambridge University Press, 2007.

Fromm, Eric. *Mít nebo být?* [To Have or To Be?] Praha: Naše vojsko, 1992.

Hábl, Jan. *Lekce z lidskosti v životě a díle Jana Amose Komenského* [Lessons in Humanity: From the Life and Work of Jan Amos Comenius]. Hradec Králové: Gaudeamus, 2010.

Hayesová, Nicky. *Základy sociální psychologie* [Principles of Social Psychology]. Praha: Portál, 1998.

Helus, Zdeněk. *Sociální psychologie pro pedagogy* [Social Psychology for Teachers]. Praha: Grada, 2015.

Horká, Hana, and Alena Hrdličková. *Výchova pro 21. století. Koncepce globální výchovy v podmínkách české školy* [Education for the 21st Century: The Concept of Global Education in the Conditions of the Czech Schools]. Brno: Paido, 1998.

Hort, Vladimír, et al. *Dětská a adolescentní psychiatrie* [Child and Adolescent Psychiatry]. Praha: Portál, 2000.

Kasser, Tim, and Allen D. Kanner. *Psychology and Consumer Culture*. Washington: APA, 2004.

Komenský, Jan Amos. *Obecná porada o nápravě věcí lidských* [General Consultation on the Restoration of Human Affairs]. Vol. I. Praha: Nakladatelství Svoboda, 1992.

———. "Velká didaktika" [Great Didactic]. In *Vybrané spisy J. A. Komenského*, vol. I. Praha: Státní pedagogické nakladatelství, 1958.

Lindsay, Geoff, et al. *Etika pro evropské psychology* [Ethics for European Psychologists]. Praha: Triton, 2010.

Lorenz, Konrad. *Takzvané zlo* [So-called Evil]. Praha: Mladá Fronta, 1992.

Maslow, Abraham. H. *A Theory of Human Motivation*. Seaside, OR: Rough Draft, 2013.

Milgram, Stanley. "Behavioral Study of Obedience." *Journal of Abnormal and Social Psychology* 67 (1963) 371–78.

Plháková, Alena. *Učebnice obecné psychologie* [Textbook of General Psychology]. Praha: Academia, 2003.

Říčan, Pavel. *Psychologie osobnosti* [Psychology of Personality]. Praha: Grada, 2010.

Vágnerová, Marie. *Současná psychopatologie pro pomáhající profese* [Contemporary Psychopathology for Helping Professions]. Praha: Portál, 2014.

Veselovský, Zdeněk. *Etologie* [Ethology]. Praha: Academia, 2005.

Winter, Deborah Du Nann, and Susan M. Koger. *Psychologie enviromentálních problémů* [The Psychology of Environmental Problems]. Praha: Portál, 2009.

Zajonc, Robert B. "Feeling and Thinking: Preferences Need No Inferences." *American Psychologist* 35.2 (1980) 151–75.

Zimbardo, Philip G. *Moc a zlo: sociálně psychologický pohled na svět* [Power and Evil: A Socio-psychological View of the World]. Břeclav: Moraviapress, 2005.

# PART 3

## *Philosophical-Theological Perspective*

# On the Philosophical Foundations of Comenius's Emendatory Work

Pavel Floss

Some historians of philosophy have in the past spoken of specific features of the philosophical thinking of the authors from Romanesque, Germanic, or Slavic nations, pointing out, for example, that Slavic thinkers mainly cultivated areas of practical philosophy, while German authors gravitated towards highly sophisticated speculation and philosophical systems. This approach combines the attitude of František Xavera Šalda, whose wording from his text *Treatises and Dictations* I find to be a controversial introduction to my subsequent interpretations: "A strange and yet understandable thing: in Bohemia we did not and do not have creator-metaphysicians; in Bohemia people directly avoid metaphysical speculation as impiety, audacity, devilish temptation. The greatest thinkers of our past, Chelčický and Comenius, are practitioners and empiricists; not with eagle-like thoughts that are aimed absolutely towards the sun, but useful and valuable stewards of the human family, the family of God."[1] Although the whole of Comenius's work was oriented "praxeologically" (as pointed out primarily by Robert Kalivoda), Comenius's concept of fundamental reform of the sphere of education and knowledge, politics and religion, was built on certain metaphysical foundations. From the Czech thinkers, Tomáš Garrigue Masaryk pointed out the essential connection of Comenius's philosophical-theological vision of the world with his program of education and emendation of human affairs, i.e., the inner connection of Comenius the pedagogue and social reformer with Comenius the philosopher. This

1. Šalda, *Časové i nadčasové*, 434.

way of interpreting Comenius's work was also followed later by such prominent Czech thinkers as Jan Patočka[2] and the above-mentioned Robert Kalivoda.[3] I do not intend to develop new, detailed analyses of the alleged problems, but I will attempt to show how Comenius's ideological foundation of the emendational concept was connected with key events in the history of European thought.

If we think about metaphysics, or the onto-theological foundations of Comenius's universal program for the restoration of human affairs, then we must not miss the fact that they were built on the cornerstones of representative structures of European philosophy.

1. One of its most powerful shrines was the emanationist concept of the origin of everything from the absolute One, standing outside all that exists, and from it flowing less and less perfect ontological forms—from the absolute emanation of the intellect (*nous*) to matter (*hýlé*) on the border of nothingness. In the third to the sixth centuries the emanationist understanding of the origin and nature of the universe underwent remarkable development and the work of Prokov was of fundamental importance for the Christian phase of the development of Neoplatonism. His Christian reinterpretation has been considered to be the texts of the mysterious (because still unidentified) Pseudo-Dionysius the Areopagite, who was still worshiped as an extraordinary, even divine, author by the great systematists of the Middle Ages and beginning Renaissance (Albert the Great, Thomas Aquinas, Nicholas of Cusa). The emanationist concept underwent various transformations—not only in medieval and renaissance Christian philosophy, but also in Arabic philosophy (for example, in Avicenna)—and its important forms include Campanella's system in his work *Universalis philosophia seu metaphysica* and Comenius's system of pansophic worlds in his emendational work *De rerum humanarum emendatione consultatio catholica*. Comenius's urgent call for the execution of thorough reform as the culmination of human history, and associated doctrine of "Elijah-ness,"[4] as offered in the spiritual diary *Clamores Eliae*, cannot be understood without including humans and their world in the grand concept of pansophic worlds (shaped by emanationist tradition) as Jan Amos explained them primarily in the book *Pansofie* in his *General Consultation*.

2. Patočka, *Komeniologické studie* I, II, and III.

3. Kalivoda, *Husitská epocha*.

4. This refers to the prophetic attitude, or nature, of the Old Testament prophet Elijah.

While Plotinus's conception had the ontologically descendent rhythm outlined above, Proklus's system of interconnection represented both descendant and, partly, ascendant ontological processuality, which Christian authors were always interested in, for the biblical conception of the origin of the world represented God's creation as acts within which were created always higher levels of beings, and the apex of God's creativity was the creation of humans. In this study I cannot deal with the various forms of combinations of descendant and ascendant processuality that we encounter in European philosophy from the early Middle Ages to modern times, and therefore I will only state that Comenius occupies a very important position among those authors. Let us at least recall the basic ontological picture of reality that we encounter in Comenius.

A series of four pansophic worlds proceed from God as an absolute unity in descending order: the possible, the archetypical, the angelic, and as the ontologically lowest world, the material. Although this world represents the most distant phase of ontological processuality from divine perfection, it is at the same time a kind of turning point, for in other pansophic worlds everything gradually returns to the divine original, and here the descending line of the first four worlds is replaced by the ascending line of the world of human creations (i.e., artificial), the moral world, the spiritual world, and finally the eternal world. Since I mentioned Proclus in connection with the development of Neoplatonism, I must say that his triadic scheme—*moné proodos epistrofé* (remaining, proceeding, reversing)—which is one of the most inspiring models of interpretation in the history of European thought, has its specific echo in Comenius's conception described above.

2. In connection with what has been said so far, let us ask ourselves what makes Comenius's position extraordinary not only in the history of Neoplatonically-oriented speculation, but in fact in the whole history of European thought.

The crucial moment in Comenius's conception is the fact that the actor in the ascendant phase of reality, the return of everything back to God, is the human race. They build the artificial world, the moral world, and the spiritual world. The first includes science and all human arts (including technology), the second includes the area of formation of social communities from families to countries, and the spiritual world concerns the spheres of human spiritual and religious life, and religious communities (churches).

I believe that this remarkable conception of the role of humanity manifests one of the constitutive features of the Renaissance era, at the end of which Comenius stands together with Campanella (and they opened the modern age). While for the Middle Ages humans were the *imago Dei* primarily because their souls were endowed with reason and free will (although the intelligence and freedom of God is unlimited in comparison with that of humans), in the Renaissance the idea caught on that the human likeness to God (as well as their ontological nobility) establishes to a greater degree their ability to create. Human creativity, which makes the human soul happy, is, as Cusanus emphasized at the beginning of the Renaissance, an act of participation in the creativity of God.[5] In this interpretive context, I must point out the high value of imagination, which is no longer understood as only the second stage of the human cognitional process between the first stage, which is sensory knowledge, and the third stage, which is intellectual knowledge, but it is often credited as another, and by its nature, sovereign activity. For the dawn of the Renaissance that heralded early humanism, it is arguably significant that Dante celebrated imagination, at the end of the *Divine Comedy*, as the greatest upsurge of the mind, illuminated by divine brightness which then possesses the power of wonderful imagery.[6] Paracelsus labeled the imagination, for example, as the most important spiritual activity of a person, and Campanella called it the spiritual imagination (*imaginatio mentalis*) which is the inventor of science (*inventrix scientiarum*). Campanella distinguished this imagination from sensual imagination, which is only a specific reproduction of things. Cusanus, who called humans the "second God" (*hominem esse secundum deum*),[7] assigned human beings a wide sphere of activity for their creativity (if we take into account his other writings, in essence, from the speech *Dies sanctificatus* to the *Compendium*) Basically, there are four types of human creations: the *entia rationalia*, which includes conjectures (in Cusanus's conception there were various cognitive forms of the interpretation of reality) and concepts; then, in the field of mathematics, primarily numbers; and finally, products of two types of "artificial forms," that is, man-made and things non-existent in nature, which are the material realizations of human ideas—both works of art and all technical works, thus all technical inventions (these included various mechanisms such as a tower clock or

5. Nicholas of Cusa, "Dialogus," 102:14–16, 128.

6. Dante, *Božská komedie*, 508–12.

7. Nicholas of Cusa, "De Beryllo," 7:1–2, 9.

astrolabe, which was a device for determining the coordinates of the stars).[8] Cusanus's contemporary, the Italian Renaissance philosopher Gianozzo Manetti, in his work *De dignitate et excellentia hominis* which was divided into four volumes, inserted reflections on human creative activities into the realm of reflections on the causes of human dignity and nobility. Manetti thus confronted the tradition of Christian anthropology, to which the most prominent patristic philosopher, Aurelius Augustinus, as well as a number of medieval theologians such as Lottario di Segni (later Pope Innocent III) also contributed. In it, humans were portrayed primarily as being characterized by attributes, rather than nobility and dignity.

The beauty of human creativity was seen in the Renaissance especially in the area of fine arts, in which men like Leonardo da Vinci and Michelangelo Buonarroti played important roles. In one of his sonnets, Michelangelo even expressed the view that art transcends nature and is not merely an imitation of it.[9]

It can further be said that Comenius completed the spiritual characteristic of the Renaissance thematized above, because he was convinced that humanity is a competitor of the Creator[10] and that, thanks to creativity,[11] by which they imitate God, they are destined to attain the highest degree of perfection possible under heaven.[12] In comparison to Cusanus, who created at the beginning of the Renaissance, Comenius, at the end of it, crossed the horizon of what had been considered as the place for human creativity, for humanity is an actor in the whole sphere of reality, not only in spiritual, artistic, or technical creations.

Humanity, to whom such extraordinary dignity is attributed, is in Comenius's view, however, part of that *mundus materialis*, which is ontologically the lowest level of all that comes from God. Isn't it ironic that humanity, as a member of the lowest sphere of being, becomes the actor in its ontological ascension through the creation of the new pansophic worlds? What's more, the urgency of this issue is underlined by the fact that ahead of the material world stands the higher angelic world, inhabited by more perfect beings than humans.

8. Nicholas of Cusa, "De Beryllo," 7:3–5, 9.

9. Buonarroti, *Podoba*, 108.

10. Comenius, *De rerum I*, 373 par. 588; cf. Floss, *Příroda*, 32.

11. For Comenius's relationship to artistic creation, see Urbánková, "Jan Amos Komenský," 59–76.

12. Comenius, *De rerum II*, 216 par. 370; cf. Floss, *Příroda*, 34.

It must first be said that in Comenius's conception, the material world has two positions. In view of the preceding pansophic worlds, it is admittedly the lowest ontologically, but in that very place is a fundamental turn. It is the last moment of descendance, but at the same time it is the first chord of the ascendance of reality. And that first chord isn't about humanity, but the very nature of nature, which Jan Amos presented as the gradual organizing of the whole from the elements through the vapors, minerals, plants, animals, and at the top of the pyramid, humanity. Comenius reasoned that this arrangement in steps follows from the order of nature itself (*ordo naturae*),[13] and that every form of degeneration which we may encounter in it always leads, ultimately, to the realization of its essentially ascending orientation. All stages of nature emerged by mutually connecting, and at the same time gradually transforming, the three basic principles from which everything was made. These are matter, spirit, and light (*materia, spiritus, lux*), which were created directly by God, while the stages of nature mentioned above, created by the increasingly intense interaction of those principles (which transform themselves in the structures of the things they create), have already been called the works of nature (*opera naturae*). Comenius's conception of the transformation of constitutive principles in the process of the stages being formed by them is the first appearance of his pro-structural thought. It eventually culminated in the *General Consultation* (or in the *Lexicon reale pansoficum*) and especially in the *Janua rerum* in an approach by which Comenius presented himself as an extraordinary European thinker.[14] Comenius presented the opportunity to understand things as structures, rather than as substances, defining them as a composition of some kinds of things where the parts forming the whole are not arranged confusingly, but according to order, and are connected by specific bonds. He was the first person in history to ontologize the concept of structure and place it on the level of the concept of substance that prevailed in his time. (He was thus a worthy forerunner of that remarkable stream of modern European thought called structuralism, which was formed in the Czech Republic in the 1920s and 1930s.)

As a result of this concept of reality, supremacy and subordination are not relevant on the level of social and community decision making, but what are relevant are the mutual relationships of the entities forming the whole. That is why Comenius's basic motto was *omnes omnia omneno*,

13. Comenius, *De rerum I*, 393 par. 626.

14. Komenský, *Dílo*, 181.

which in its application also means that students are the teachers of their teachers in certain ways, and that every citizen is a king in a certain context. The relevance of the relational and contextual sides of reality in Comenius hang on their connection to another serious current of European thought, which is trinitarianism, which seeks a parallel to the Triune God at various levels of the created world. Comenius, together with Augustine of Hippo, Joachim of Fiore, Nicholas of Cusa, Marsilio Ficino, and Paracelsus, was one of the most important representatives of this spiritual tradition.[15] In Cusanus's, and probably also Paracelsus's intentions, Comenius was a critic of all forms of dualism, which to him was also, among other things, the ideological basis of wars, which he wanted to definitively eliminate as part of his universal reform of human affairs. On the other hand, Trinitarianism is intrinsically irenic, because at all levels it inspires the search for the so-called third unifying principle, making it analogous to the third Divine person, i.e., the Holy Spirit, who is the union of God the Father and God the Son, and thus the apotheosis of the relationship, the *nexus*. The critique of dualism and the search for the third principle, overcoming the opposition of the two principles, which we encounter at a key point in Comenius's *Pansophy* in his *General Consultation*,[16] is a dignified continuation of Cusanus's critique in his work "De Beryllo," which was one of the key events in European philosophical spirituality.[17]

Jan Amos, however, did not work with the dynamic-ascendant conception only with nature, but he also understood human history in that way. There are, despite various reversals, processes in which humanity heads inevitably from original barbarianism to ever greater civilization and education. The fundamental reform of human affairs which he elaborated in the *General Consultation* (and also in *Via lucis*) is not a utopian dream without a real basis, but a real challenge that flows out of the course of history up to now. (Comenius said that it is the fruit of history.)

While in the early period of Comenius's work humans were understood as docile spectators in the theater of the world, and in the following tragic period as deceived pilgrims in the labyrinth of the world, his mature work asks that people become reformers of the world and follow the example given to them by the biblical prophet Elijah. In Comenius, fundamental

15. However, in modern times it also had a number of secularized forms, including Hegelian, or—for that matter, in connection with it—Marxist, etc.

16. Comenius, *De rerum I*, 211 par. 302.

17. Nicholas of Cusa, "De Beryllo," 40:3–10, 46.

reform merges with "Elijah-ness," and that is why in *Clamores Eliae* he asks that there be as many repairers of the world as possible.

3. Let us now ask ourselves which traditions in European philosophy inspired Comenius to, in his work, ascribe to humanity such a sovereign mission: to contribute to the creation of new pansophical worlds and the maximal improvement of what was created within these worlds, that is, knowledge, technology, and works in the first one, human society in the second one, and spiritual life and communion within the church in the third one.

First of all it is necessary to, at least briefly, introduce the framework in which the issue of the position of humanity in the universe was dealt with. For antiquity, partly the Middle Ages and mainly the Renaissance, humanity (or even the sphere of human activity) was understood as a microcosm which, in itself, in a specific way, brought to life all other beings (the macrocosm). Christian authors had certain problems accepting the micro-macrocosmic paradigm born in antiquity, as it competed with the Judeo-Christian notion of humans as an image of God. In the end both approaches were synthesized—on the basis of triadic thinking, because humans can be understood as images of nature as well as of God, since God is the originator of both.

The particular problem with this synthesis was, what is the basis for the uniqueness of humanity's position in the universe. In patristics, and then with new vigor in the Renaissance, the idea was born that humans are the only beings in the universe whose nature is not essentially anchored, but remains open and the final form of human existence depends on human decisions. To understand how Comenius approached this problem, we must take a brief look at history. In this context we must focus mainly on the ideas of the patristic author, Gregory of Nyssa, who saw in the never-closed earthly pilgrimage of humanity (which has a beginning but never an end), one of the images of God's infinity in creation. Gregory understood this human pilgrimage as a never-ending improvement of the human soul, which has an unlimited degree of "perfectionizational" elasticity. Humans can, on the basis of their free decisions, live in the dimension of their animality, or cultivate and develop their virtues in a field radiating the love of God. From this perspective, everyone is the "father" of their earthly existence, the nature of which is, in its own way, undetermined, unlike that of other beings.[18]

While Gregory of Nyssa saw the image of God's infinity in humanity, especially in their never-ending moral improvement, Jan Amos understood it as an endlessly implemented self-creation through free decision-making, into infinity. What was narrowed down to the moral realm in Gregory, became in Comenius the general designation of humanity as *creatura indeterminata*.

The patristic inspiration for Comenius's notion of humanity, to which Jan Amos himself referred, is then, in my judgment, completed by the stimuli he found in the work of Nicholas of Cusa. It particularly presents itself in a comparison of Cusanus's formulations found in one of the main works from the second period of his output, namely *Idiota de mente*. Cusanus, who in this dialogue transformed his doctrines of various forms of the mind (*mens*), that were contained in the extensive work *De conjecturis*, also discussed the difference between the angelic and the human mind. Although the human mind is an act of one's creation in relation to other minds at the lowest ontological level, it does not mean that this status is definitive for it, because if it is encouraged by its creator, it can continually improve itself and thus approach its divine image.[19]

Comenius, who in other moments of his philosophical thinking showed a tendency for impressive synthesis,[20] also manifested this habit of his spirit in solving research problems. He combined, from the patristics, emerging views on a certain indeterminacy, incompleteness, as well as the continuing movement to perfection of human nature, with Cusanus's permanent inclination to search for traces and images of God's infinity in creation. These are manifested especially in concepts of the world in *De docta ignorantia*, in *De venatione sapientiae*, and in the conception of humanity in *De coniecturis*.

Inspired by Cusanus's search for traces of God's infinity in God-produced reality, Jan Amos presented humans as beings which are manifested in a most significant way by the will (*voluntas*), or freedom of choice. Comenius's formulation is: *producenda fuit creatura indeterminata, in infinito*

18. Chvátal, "Der Mensch," 63–64.

19. Nicolas de Cusa, "Idiota," 148:5—149:12, 203–4.

20. See, for example, his synthesis of contemporary gnoseological concepts (cf. Floss, "Komenský's Erkenntnislehre," 83–91).

*infinite se ipsam agens.*[21] For Comenius, this conception of the human being is a necessary ontological consequence of the fact that God, as Creator, had to create a kind of his infinite image that would be a suitable object for God's wisdom. According to Comenius, all created things are subject to necessity except for humans, who escape the power of fate "*in infinito infinite se ipsam agens*," and this form of infinity is a prerequisite for their freedom. Because of this, humans are also beings who do not live only in the present, but transcend it, as they prepare and organize the future.

In conclusion to this passage it can be said that while Cusanus attributed it to the infinity of humanity as such,[22] Comenius considered each freely-acting and continually self-creating human individual as a specific image of God's infinity.

The form of infinity that Comenius attributed to humanity, in the intentions of the Cusanian search for forms of God's infinity in creation, is disposed so that being, in its traditional form (something unchangeable) is not attributed to humanity. All created things have a fixed essence, albeit on incomparably different ontological levels. Humanity, precisely in order to be like God, does not have such an essence.

The ideological moments that I have followed from patristics through Cusanus to Comenius (and in which other Renaissance thinkers, such as Giovanni Pico della Mirandola, also figured), co-created the preconditions for European thinking to give birth to existential philosophy, which John-Paul Sartre defined as the prioritization of existence over essence.[23]

We see that Comenius's concept of humanity, whose supreme activity is the fundamental and universal reform of human affairs, was born in Comenius's contemplations on key themes of European thought from antiquity until his day. At a time when our modern civilization is moving into an ever-increasing crisis (ecological, social, educational and moral), Comenius's indomitable, reformist activism is a challenge that is not only extremely topical, but also inspiring.

21. "The indeterminate creature was produced in infinite infinity by itself" (Comenius, *De rerum I*, 356 par. 553).

22. Nicholas of Cusa, "De coniecturis," 144:4–5, 14.

23. Sartre, *L'existentialisme*, 17.

## Bibliography


Buonarroti, Michelangelo. *Podoba živé tváře: básně, dopisy a dokumenty* [The Appearance of a Living Face: Poems, Letters and Documents]. Praha: SNKLU, 1964.

Chvátal, Ladislav. "Der Mensch als Mikrokosmos" [Man as a Microcosm]. *Byzantinoslavica—Revue internationale des études byzantines* 62 (2004) 63–64.

Comenius, Jan Amos. *De rerum humanarum emendatione consultatio catholica* [General Consultation Concerning the Restoration of Human Affairs]. Vol. I. Praha: Academia, 1966.

———. *De rerum humanarum emendatione consultatio catholica* [General Consultation Concerning the Restoration of Human Affairs]. Vol. II. Praha: Academia, 1966.

Dante. *Božská komedie* [Divine Comedy]. Praha: Vyšehrad, 1952.

Floss, Pavel. "Komenský's Erkenntnislehre und ein Einblick in seine Metaphysik" [Comenius's Theory of Knowledge and an Insight into His Metaphysics]. *Colloquia Comeniana* 2 (1969) 83–91.

———. *Příroda, člověk a společnost v díle J. A. Komenského* [Nature, Man, and Society in the Work of J. A. Comenius]. Přerov: Městský národní výbor, 1968.

Kalivoda, Robert. *Husitská epocha a J. A. Komenský* [The Hussite Epoch and J. A. Comenius]. Praha: Odeon, 1992.

Komenský, Jan Amos. *Dílo Jana Amose Komenského: Johannis Amos Comenii Opera omnia* [The Works of Jan Amos Comenius]. 9/II. Praha: Academia, 1974.

Masaryk, Tomáš G. *J. A. Komenský: přednáška T. G. Masaryka* [J. A. Comenius: Lecture by T. G. Masaryk]. Praha: Státní nakladatelství, 1920.

Nicolas of Cusa. "De Beryllo" [On the Beryl]. In *Nicolai de Cusa opera omnia XI*, edited by Hans Gerhard Senger and Karl Bormann. Hamburg: Felix Meiner, 1988.

———. "De coniecturis" [On Conjectures]. In *Nicolai de Cusa opera omnia III*, edited by Joseph Koch and Karl Bormann. Hamburg: Felix Meiner, 1972.

———. "Dialogus de ludo globi" [Dialogue on Group Play]. In *Nicolai de Cusa opera omnia IX*, edited by Hans Gerhard Senger. Hamburg: Felix Meiner, 1998.

———. "Idiota de mente" [The Layman on the Mind]. In *Nicolai de Cusa opera omnia V*, edited by Renate Steiger. Hamburg: Felix Meiner, 1983.

Patočka, Jan. *Komeniologické studie I: Texty publikované v letech 1941–1958* [Comenius Studies I: Texts published between 1941 and 1958]. Praha: Oikoymenh, 1997.

———. *Komeniologické studie II: Texty publikované v letech 1959–1977* [Comenius Studies II: Texts published between 1959 and 1977]. Praha: Oikoymenh, 1998.

———. *Komeniologické studie III: Nepublikované texty* [Comenius Studies III: Unpublished Texts]. Praha: Oikoymenh & Filosofia, 2003.

Sartre, Jean-Paul. *L'existentialisme est un humanism* [Existentialism Is a Humanism]. Paris: Editions Nagel, 1970.

Šalda, František X. *Časové i nadčasové* [The Temporal and the Timeless]. Praha: Melantrich, 1936.

Urbánková, Lucie. "Jan Amos Komenský a dobová teorie umění" [Jan Amos Comenius and the Contemporary Theory of Art ]. In *Ex definitione: Pansofické pojmy J. A. Komenského a jejich dobové kontexty: Studie Martinu Steinerovi*, edited by Lenka Řezníková and Vladimír Urbánek, 59–76. Praha: Filosofia, 2018.

# On Earth, as It Is in Heaven

## *The Theological Basis of Comenius's Universal Restoration*

Pavel Hošek

In his time, Comenius expressed a remarkably daring and surprisingly optimistic prophecy about the future of the human race. Some scholars of his work have explained Comenius's vision of the restoration of human affairs as one of the first plans for the enlightened emancipation of humanity, that is, as a progressive plan for freeing the human heart and mind from subjection to "obscurantism and superstition" in the name of the ideals of reason, progress, and enlightenment.

Because Comenius was a remarkably educated person and excellent observer, gifted with extraordinary pedagogical intuition, many of his pedagogical and reformative proposals proved successful in practice—regardless of the ideological starting points from which Comenius proceeded.

Examples include his proposals in the area of pedagogy, based on the methodological distinction of individual age brackets and developmental stages of childhood; his application of effective didactic methods (such as the "school through play" principle or the picture encyclopedia method); his suggestions concerning the teaching process from the simplest things to the most complex; his suggestions on the observation of nature as a starting point for teaching the natural sciences—all were truly proven to be worthy, and later were often confirmed by developmental psychology, anthropology, and theoretical education.

In addition, although many of his reformative proposals in the area of international relations and the organization of society were not implemented until much later, and often not by Comenius's initiatives but on the basis of favorable historic circumstances, they can be seen in retrospect as prophetically prescient, and in the emergence of institutions such as the United Nations, the International Red Cross, the International Court of Justice, the World Council of Churches, and the European Union, we can see the realization of Comenius's bold vision and proposals.

Within this indisputable "success" of Comenius's pedagogical and reformative proposals, however, lie certain difficulties for the interpreters of Comenius's work. His successful and effective pedagogical methods and his later-realized proposals for reform were often separated from the biblical and theological foundations of Comenius's thought, as if they were independent of them.[1] Comenius has been alternatively understood as an Enlightenment scholar, humanist, and reformer who used biblical and theological concepts as an "expression of his period," in which he "dressed" his progressive and humanistic enlightened program. Comenius's proposals for reform in the field of societal organization and international relations have been similarly classified.

The Communist ideology of the previous regime (in the Czech Republic) also worked very intentionally with Comenius's pedagogy and theory of society. To a large extent it stripped his ideas of their roots in the Christian worldview and placed them in the ideological framework of the Marxist conception of history. Comenius's *Letters to Heaven* and other appeals for solidarity between the rich and the poor were seen as progressive ideas aimed at the establishment of a just and classless society in accordance with the Marxist philosophy of history. This (mis)interpretation of Comenius was then, to some extent, opposed by some theologians, that is, those who were allowed to publish during the Communist regime.[2]

The history of the interpretation of Comenius's legacy is thus at the same time the history of the misinterpretation of the meaning of his most distinctive statements. They are in principle inseparable from the biblical and theological coordinates of thought, without which his pedagogical and reformative proposals fall apart. They would lack any kind of meaningful justification. That is, at least, in terms of how Comenius really thought.

Something similar can be stated about Comenius's monumental vision of the universal reform of human affairs.[3] In no way was there any kind

1. Molnár, "O Komenského," 3; Liguš, "Funktion und Bedeutung," 14.

2. Dobiáš, "Sociálně teologické motivy," 17.

3. Smolík, "Komenského přínos ekumenismu," 53; Kolesnyk, "Chiliasmus und Rationalismus," 121; Palouš, *Komenského Boží svět*, 88.

of enlightenment or progressive optimism. If Comenius was an optimist, it was because he believed in "God's optimism." If Comenius believed in the "reform" of humanity, it was because he believed that human beings are created in the image of God.[4] And yet, because God's image in humanity is damaged by sin, they are improvable because God himself, in Jesus Christ, has removed the fatal obstacle to that improvability. Yes, Comenius was optimistic about the effects of education on the refinement of humanity. But only because he believed God's promises.

Comenius's vision of universal reform was based on his distinctive theology of history. This theology of history was substantiated by a very specific interpretation of particular biblical statements in key passages of the *General Consultation* (that is, in the sixth volume of the *General Consultation on the Restoration of Human Affairs*). It doesn't make sense without them. Comenius did not believe that history leads to a happy tomorrow on the basis of some kind of automatic progress. He simply understood the Bible, which he saw as God's revelation, in a very specific way.

In the *General Consultation*, Comenius methodically argued with alternative eschatological scenarios, based on different interpretations of key biblical statements.[5] Especially with so-called catastrophic eschatology, which assumes that the dramatic finale of human history will be marked by thickening darkness and the triumph of evil, by an "apocalypse," before a decisive, supernatural reversal in the form of the definitive triumph of God.[6]

Comenius therefore diligently gathered as evidence biblical verses in favor of, not catastrophic, but transformational, eschatology.[7] That is, in favor of the conviction that the finale of human history will take place in the characteristic spreading of light and successful establishment of God's order on earth. The human world will become "a paradise on earth," before the end of history comes. All biblical promises regarding the bliss of the age to come will be fulfilled on earth, in this world, not beyond the gates of eternity, in "the afterlife."

In this sense, Comenius was a staunch "pre-millenialist." He was an advocate of the view that before the definitive end of the human age, there will be established the "Kingdom of peace and justice" which the biblical

4. Hábl, *Komenského lekce z lidskosti*; Palouš, *Komenského Boží svět*, 66.

5. Komenský, *Všenáprava*, 42.

6. Komenský, *Všenáprava*, 353.

7. Vojtíšek, *Apokalypsa nebo transformace*, 15.

prophets watched for. This ideal state, the kingdom of God on earth, will last one thousand years (Rev 20:1–6). Only then will there be the final eschatological battle between the forces of good and evil, and the final victory of good (Rev 20:7–10).

Comenius also firmly believed in the concrete periodization of human history, which corresponds to the sequence of seven millennia, symbolically foreshadowed in the seven days of the creation week at the beginning of the book of Genesis (Gen 1:1—2:3). Just as creation arose in six days, culminated by the seventh day of rest, so human history takes place in six millennial "days," after which comes the seventh (also lasting a thousand years) "day of rest."[8] After all, one day is as a thousand years with God, argued Comenius with the well-known statement of the psalmist in the interpretation in Second Letter of Peter.[9]

The most important element of this seven-part segmentation of human history was the identification of the current historic moment as the dividing line between the end of the sixth day and the beginning of the seventh. Comenius believed that humanity stood at the very end of the sixth day, that is, at the end of the sixth millennium of history.[10] Therefore he believed in the urgent need for vital reforms and social, cultural, and political transformation, to prepare for the establishment of the millennial kingdom of God. And therefore, he believed in their success and their feasibility. After all, God wanted it. Who could prevent it?

On the one hand, therefore, Comenius dared to express his bold vision for the universal reform of human affairs because, and only because, he believed God's promises and firmly relied on them. He wagered that God wanted it. And that God is the ultimate cause of this sought-after transformation.

At the same time, however, Comenius categorically rejected the passive expectations of God's miraculous intervention, which were usually the result of a catastrophic scenario at the finale of human history. To Comenius, the passive expectation of God's miraculous intervention at the close of history was completely foreign. His theology was rigorously "synergistic."[11] He was convinced that God does not want to assert his will without humanity. A person who knows what God wants, follows the path of his will.

8. Komenský, *Všenáprava*, 50.

9. Komenský, *Všenáprava*, 48; Ps 90:4; 2 Pet 3:8.

10. Komenský, *Všenáprava*, 51, 355.

11. Funda, "Der Gedanke," 155.

What can be achieved through humanity, God does not, on principle, achieve through the miraculous means of the heavenly Ruler. This is his modus operandi. Therefore, Comenius's vision of universal reform was activating, mobilizing, motivational. God acts in human history in such a way that everything which can be done by people, he leaves to them.[12] He invites them to collaborate in his work. In this sense, the implementation of God's will is co-conditioned by the willingness and readiness of people to put their hand to the work, to cooperate in that task of establishing God's order on earth.[13] This was Comenius's theology of history.

The fact that within this magnificent vision he proposed very wise and far-sighted reforms of education, social order, international relations, and so on, cannot be removed from the whole framework of Comenius's thought. The hope he combined with his vision of universal reform rose and fell with his confidence in God as the heavenly director of the transformational changes.

When, for example, Comenius proposed the introduction of a universal language to promote understanding between all nations, he proposed it, in an important sense, chiefly because in this way it is possible to prepare for the establishment of God's universal government.[14] When he proposed the introduction of music education in every school, he proposed it, in an important sense, especially because in this way it is possible to prepare every person to properly praise God's glory.[15]

When he proposed to base the teaching of natural history on the observation of nature, the classification of phenomena and so on, it was not primarily a kind of anticipation of Enlightenment scientific rationality. Rather it was a careful reading of the "book of God's creation." Comenius was a great supporter of empirically based scientific research. But he understood it as a careful study of God's creative manuscript, that is, the study of creative orders which mirror God's wisdom. Where in his proposals he captured the ideals of the coming Enlightenment humanism, it was, in an important sense of the word, actually a bit of an accident, or coincidence.

The question of whether Comenius was rather a "man of the Baroque" or a "man of the Enlightenment" can be somewhat misleading. Especially when it overshadows the fact that he was primarily a "man of the Unity

12. Komenský, *Všenáprava*, 63.

13. Kišš, "Renewal," 160.

14. Komenský, *Všenáprava*, 196; Kučera, "Die Sprache," 102.

15. Komenský, *Všenáprava*, 271.

of Brethren."[16] The deepest reasons for his vision of universal reform were theological.

The core of his arguments, expressed in his vision of universal reform, was, in short, a reliance on God's promises. Specifically, in the spirit of the Czech Reformation, in connection with its program of reform that was looking to reform both the church and also (!) society according to the norms of the Scripture. In this sense Comenius was Hus's successor.[17]

If God so desires, said Comenius, no obstacle is great enough to thwart the fulfillment of God's plan for the human race. And if God so desires, continued Comenius, we cannot wait with our hands folded. We are called to actively support the coming Kingdom. By disseminating and applying its principles, each in its own sphere of influence. In doing so, we will be preparing for his glorious coming by our own efforts.

It is certainly possible to separate Comenius's vision for universal reform from his theological history and from his theological arguments. In this context, let us mention an analogous example from another religious tradition: the unconventional vision of "correction of the universe" (*tikkun olam*), as it was expressed by the Jewish mystic Yitzak Luria, can be understood (in the spirit of Enlightenment humanism) as a difficult task for the common good which has truly motivated many Jewish patrons, scientists, and philanthropists to a lifelong engagement in charity. And it is surely possible to understand *tikkun olam* as a metaphor for any sacrifice for the common good. Within Jewish philanthropy (and Jewish humanism) this also has often been the case.

On the other hand, if we honestly want to understand what Yitzak Luria meant by his eschatological concept of *tikkun olam*, we can only carefully study his magnificent theory of the history of redemption, that is, the initial scattering of sparks of God's holiness in the darkness and the gradual liberating of those sparks, dispersing them throughout the whole world through the religious efforts and mystical passion of believing Jews, with a hopeful view of the glorious redemption at the end of history. That is, the *Shekhinah*, God's presence, which suffers with the suffering members of the Jewish people in exile, will be delivered from exile and all the light of God's glory will again be united with its heavenly source. This is the meaning of Luria's vision of the correction of the universe, *tikkun olam*. This and

16. Říčan, "K bratrským," 89; Molnár, *Českobratrská výchova*.

17. Říčan, *Dějiny*, 391.

nothing else. It is similar to Comenius's vision for universal reform. If we remove the theological basis, it falls apart.

It was no coincidence that Comenius referred to his vision of universal reform as a Universal Reformation.[18] The universal reform of the world begins with the purification and reform of the church.[19] He believed that all reform movements, that is, movements for the reform of church and society, initiated by Jan Hus, Martin Luther, John Calvin, and others, were only partial, inconsistent, and in the end, unsuccessful.[20] He therefore sought a radical reform of world Christianity which would go hand in hand with the purifying of the Christian church and society from all possible filth. And at the same time, with this purification would be the successful spreading of Christianity throughout the globe. An integral part of Comenius's vision of universal reform was the acceptance of Christianity by all hitherto unchristian nations.[21]

Comenius was keenly aware of the tragic division of Christianity and was extremely conciliatory in this area.[22] More than most of his contemporaries. It was clear to him that the prerequisite—and thus the beginning of universal reform—was the unification of feuding Christianity. That is why he looked forward to the worldwide council of representatives from all branches of the Christian church. It was for this council that he wrote his *General Consultation.*

However, although Comenius was a supporter of ecumenical peace, it didn't mean that he was retreating from the doctrinal positions of the orthodox church. He held no vague, theologically foggy position. He was, for example, a completely unambiguous proponent of the Trinitarian concept of God's being.[23] He fundamentally rejected the antitrinitarian teachings of the Socinians and the like.[24] He did not believe that there would be any synthesis of world religions. He held that Muslims and other non-believers would accept Christianity. And that it would happen before the fulfillment of the eschatological vision of universal reform.

18. Komenský, *Všenáprava*, 56, 151.
19. Komenský, *Všenáprava*, 81.
20. Komenský, *Všenáprava*, 275–76, 338.
21. Komenský, *Všenáprava*, 228.
22. Komenský, *Všenáprava*, 117, 126.
23. Floss, *Hledání*, 157.
24. Floss, *Meditace*, 42; Floss, *Hledání*, 166.

Thus, if Comenius's proposals are interpreted as a prelude to the emancipatory vision of Enlightenment humanism, it is a serious distortion of the meaning that Comenius himself ascribed to his vision. When it came to education, it wasn't about any utilitarian value of education itself. For him it was the achievement of God's will for humanity. Yes, about the full realization of the image of God in humanity.

In this way and no other was how Comenius himself understood his pedagogical and reformative proposals. He was, after all, a bishop, priest, man of the church, and deeply religious. His vision held together only in within the biblical and theological coordinates in which it was articulated.

In a sense it can be said that Comenius did not attach any external utility to his pedagogical and reformative proposals. His goal was theological, religious. For him, it was not about the pragmatic usefulness of the teaching method to better prepare for later employment or a profession. Definitely not in the first place. For that matter, not in the second either.

The disarming, heroic optimism with which he looked forward to the realization of his bold proposals actually had nothing to do with Enlightenment or societal optimism. He dared to insist on things which, in his day, appeared unbelievable, impossible, naïve, foolish, and unfeasible. Not because he was so progressive, but because that is how he understood biblical promises.

He was convinced that it was God's wish. Therefore, sooner or later, it would happen. Thus, it called for patient work to carry out God's plan. Basically, Comenius's universal reform cannot be understood at all without a thorough knowledge of the Bible. In fact, he did not even seek the consent of readers who did not know the Bible or who would not, as he did, consider it God's revelation and therefore the starting point for any argument.

In a certain sense, Jan Amos Comenius was the preparer of the Enlightenment, there is no doubt about that. But only in the sense that the Enlightenment implemented the least important aspects of his enlightened and reformative vision. The light that Comenius saw coming was not that of the Enlightenment. Although the light Comenius saw was influenced by Neoplatonic philosophy, that influence was not really so important. The essential thing for Comenius was that the source of that light be Christ.

In that sense, although Jan Amos Comenius was a forerunner and preparer of the Enlightenment, he also saw its one-sidedness. That is, the problematic nature of the European Enlightenment program if it were completely separated from its original theological basis and from the biblical conception of humanity and the meaning of existence. In what sense? Well, if we were left only with evolutional biology to measure what makes a person human, the basic values of Enlightened humanism would be seriously compromised.

Comenius's peace initiatives could also rightly be considered a prophetic anticipation of current peace initiatives.[25] But it is still important to remember that Comenius's peace was primarily the Old Testament *shalom* and the New Testament *irenics*. Thus, the quality is inseparable from the biblical contexts of meaning. It was not just peace as the absence of war, from a purely practical, value-neutral perspective. Of course that's part of it, but Comenius's peace had a constructive value (theologically defined) content, it was not only a ceasefire.

It was the restoration of God's peace, violated by sin.[26] It was the eschatological renewing of the peace which was there at the beginning. Yes it was the restoration of the paradise that was lost by the first Adam. And fought for again by the last Adam, Jesus Christ.[27]

In the finale of history, human affairs are to regain the glory they had at the very beginning, before sin occurred.[28] The state of paradise, which was lost as a consequence of sin, is to be restored. And it should happen here, on this earth.[29]

Precisely because Comenius was firmly convinced that the deciding time at the end of the sixth millennium of history had come, and the arrival of the seventh day of rest was in sight, he took his pen and stirred up all his contemporaries in order to gain their cooperation in the restoration of human affairs. He was writing a book that was to be discussed at the World Council of Christianity, the convening of which he sought.[30]

He believed his vision with all his heart, so he did not hesitate to jeopardize his reputation by referring to all kinds of prophecies from various visionaries,[31] including the suspicious and strange. Namely, everywhere their words confirmed something that Comenius was convinced of, that

25. Krátký and Stejskal, *Apoštol míru.*

26. Komenský, *Všenáprava*, 219, 352–53.

27. Komenský, *Všenáprava*, 61, 95, 197, 320.

28. Komenský, *Všenáprava*, 93.

29. Komenský, *Všenáprava*, 39.

30. Komenský, *Všenáprava*, 328, 335.

31. Komenský, *Všenáprava*, 58–59; Říčan, *Jan Amos*, 29.

corresponded to God's plan for the establishment of the millennial kingdom of peace and justice.

And finally let us be reminded that Comenius's universal restoration was, in an important sense, actually a prayer. It was his trustful reliance on God's management of human history. It was not an accident that, in the final chapter of the *General Consultation*, Comenius turned to God himself.[32] After all, God, you want it, so do it, he said. And he finished with the various petitions of the Lord's Prayer (Comenius's paraphrase), that is, petitions for what *is* the revealed will of God: the establishment of God's rule "on earth, as it is in heaven."[33]

The final paragraph of the *General Consultation* goes like this:

> *Father of us all (from whom all is generated), Who are in heaven by your majesty, but also with us on earth, in Europe, in Asia, in Africa, Sanctify us all through your name, Come at last to all the ends of your earthly kingdom, Your will be done from us all and through us all in everything, Give us all the spiritual bread as you give us the physical, Forgive us all from every possible sin, Do not lead us into temptation, But free us all from all evil! For yours is every kingdom and all power and to you only belongs glory in heaven and on earth; even now in time, and also later in eternity, Amen!*

32. Komenský, *Všenáprava*, 359.

33. Komenský, *Všenáprava*, 25, 27, 52, 281.

## Bibliography


Dobiáš, F. M. "Sociálně teologické motivy u Jana Amose Komenského" [Socio-theological Motifs of John Amos Comenius]. In *Sedm statí o Komenském*, 17–43. Praha: Kalich, 1971.

Floss, Karel. *Hledání duše zítřka* [Searching for the Soul of Tomorrow]. Brno: CDK, 2012.

Floss, Pavel. *Meditace na rozhraní epoch* [Meditation at the Turn of Epochs]. Brno: CDK, 2012.

Funda, Otakar A. "Der Gedanke des Synergismus in der Theologie von Johann Amos Comenius" [The Concept of Synergism in the Theology of John Amos Comenius]. In *Comenius als Theologe*, 155–59. Praha: Pontes Pragenses, 1998.

Hábl, Jan. *Lekce z lidskosti v životě a díle J. A. Komenského* [Lessons from Humanity in the Life and Works of J. A. Comenius]. Praha: Návrat domů, 2011.

Kišš, Igor. "Renewal of the World through Jesus Christ and Human Participation in It by Comenius." In *Comenius als Theologe*, edited by Vladimír J. Dvořák and Jan Blahoslav Lášek, 160–65. Praha: Pontes Pragenses, 1998.

Kolesnyk, Alexander. "Chiliasmus und Rationalismus bei Johann Amos Comenius" [Chiliasm and Rationalism in John Amos Comenius]. In *Comenius als Theologe*, edited by Vladimír J. Dvořák and Jan Blahoslav Lášek, 121–28. Praha: Pontes Pragenses, 1998.

Komenský, J. A. *Všenáprava (Panorthosie) Všeobecné porady o nápravě věcí lidských, část šestá* [Universal Reform, *General Consultation Concerning the Restoration of Human Affairs*, Part 6]. Praha: Orbis, 1950.

Krátký, Radovan, and Václav Stejskal. *Apoštol míru J. A. Komenský* [Apostle of Peace J. A. Comenius]. Praha: Československý spisovatel, 1949.

Kučera, Zdeněk. "Die Sprache öffnet den Weg zum europäischen Universalismus: Bemerkungen zur Sprachphilosophie des Comenius" [Language Opens the Way to European Universalism: Remarks on the Philosophy of Language of Comenius]. In *Comenius als Theologe*, edited by Vladimír J. Dvořák and Jan Blahoslav Lášek, 102–14. Praha: Pontes Pragenses, 1998.

Liguš, Jan. "Funktion und Bedeutung der Bibel im persönlichen Leben und im theologischen Denken von Johann Amos Comenius" [Function and Meaning of the Bible in the Personal Life and Theological Thinking of John Amos Comenius]. In *Comenius als Theologe*, edited by Vladimír J. Dvořák and Jan Blahoslav Lášek, 14–26. Praha: Pontes Pragenses, 1998.

Molnár, Amedeo. *Českobratrská výchova před Komenským* [Czech Brethren Education before Comenius]. Praha: SPN, 1956.

———. "O Komenského jako teologa" [On Comenius as a Theologian]. In *Sedm statí o Komenském*, edited by F. M. Dobiáš, 3–15. Praha: Kalich, 1971.

Palouš, Radim. *Komenského Boží svět* [Comenius's God's World]. Praha: SPN, 1992.

Říčan, Rudolf. *Dějiny Jednoty bratrské* [History of the Unity of Brethren]. Praha: Kalich, 1957.

———. *Jan Amos Komenský: Muž víry, lásky a naděje* [John Amos Comenius: Man of Faith, Love, and Hope]. Praha: Kalich, 1971.

———. "K bratrským motivům a vzorům ve Všeobecné poradě" [On Fraternal Motifs and Patterns in the *General Consultation*]. In *Sedm statí o Komenském*, edited by F. M. Dobiáš, 89–102. Praha: Kalich, 1971.

Smolík, Josef. "Komenského přínos ekumenismu" [Comenius's Contribution to Ecumenism]. In *Sedm statí o Komenském*, edited by F. M. Dobiáš, 45–62. Praha: Kalich, 1971.

Vojtíšek, Zdeněk. *Apokalypsa nebo transformace* [Apocalypse or Transformation]. Praha: Dingir, 2014.

# Comenius's Notion of Happiness and Its Platonic-Aristotelian Connotations

David Krámský

## Blissfulness and Harmony

Every human action has its meaning, goal, and purpose, because it is part of an all-encompassing harmony. *Fundamentum rerum omnium harmonia est*—the basis of all things is harmony. Humanity is nothing other than harmony.[1] The practice of our life is thus framed by a moving towards the main purpose, which is *blissfulness* with God. Comenius thus reformulated the original Aristotelian teleological concept of *eudaimonia*.[2] Like Aristotle, Comenius also understood that "all goals are subordinate to this goal."[3] In addition to piety and reverence for God, like Aristotle, he understood humanity as, at the same time, *zoon echon logon*, as a rational being who, moreover, has the power to rule over other creatures, and is thus an image of God. In the spirit of Comenius's didactics, then, being rational first of all means to be "an observer, a designator," "to know, to name and to understand the world." Having dominion over creation then refers to the ability to "rationally control oneself and things," "to be powerful in things and oneself." In other words to be, in the sense of the Greek adjective *aristos* (derived from *areté*)—to behave "royally—that is, seriously and virtuously." With Comenius as well as with Aristotle, the royal practice of our lives is

1. Komenský, *Didaktika*, V:14–15.
2. Spaemann, *Štěstí*.
3. Komenský, *Didaktika*, 46.

primarily determined by virtues and morals. It seems that Comenius's conception of *blissfulness* as the highest purpose of our lives was defined by the correlative context of the concepts of Greek Platonic-Aristotelian-ethics: *fronésis*, *praxis*, and *areté*.

In the *Great Didactic*, Comenius summed up the prerequisites for a blissful (successful) life, as basically being three: (1) education–wisdom, (2) virtue–morals, and (3) piety. The relationship between all these necessary components of a blissful life is expressed by inner agreement—harmony. "So man is really, in himself, nothing other than harmony!"[4]

In addition to the connection of harmony with the blissful life, harmony for Comenius represented the way of human existence as an image of God. And this is because to be an image of God presupposes the harmony of three things: (1) being educated, (2) being the master of oneself, and (3) turning to God as the source. Thanks to education and knowledge, one becomes Wise. Thanks to self-control then, Virtuous and Moral. Thanks to the all-pervasive relationship to God, Pious.[5]

## Practical Wisdom and Virtue

In his *Great Didactic*, Comenius highlighted the ability to "rule over oneself and things" among the basic characteristics of a virtuous life. It is therefore a kind of life practice in which humanity, through virtuous and moral conduct, heads toward the Good—God. A necessary prerequisite for this movement, then, is the exercise of a kind of "practical wisdom" which Comenius encountered in Aristotle's concept of *fronésis*. So virtuous people are ones who, through *logos* (thought) find the right measure of their actions. Therefore, Comenius repeatedly stressed that discipline and restraint are the basic determinants of the virtuous life.

A person "cannot become a man if he is not led to *discipline*," stressed Comenius. The meaning of humanity is mediated to us primarily through education in virtue and piety! According to Comenius, virtue can be taught in such a way that the people themselves will always behave honestly and follow patterns of virtue.[6] We find a similar definition in Aristotle, for whom the basic characteristic of virtue, that it *discourages* us from evil, we learn mostly by habit. Like Plato, Comenius considered the basic virtues

4. Komenský, *Didaktika*, V:17.
5. Komenský, *Didaktika*, 5.
6. Komenský, *Didaktika*, XIII.

to be Wisdom, Temperance, Bravery, and Justice. Comenius understood wisdom (Plato's *sophia*) as "right reasoning"—*orthos logos*. Temperance (*sophrosyne*) as acting with an awareness of limits, Bravery (*andreia*) as the ability to do everything with reason, not emotion or impetuosity. Justice (*dikaiosyne*), then, coincided with Plato's conception of the highest virtue, which is over everything.

In summary, to act morally meant, for Comenius, to act in harmony with the concept of Blissfulness with the highest Good and Purpose—God. This can be achieved only with a wise, virtuous, and pious approach. The main prerequisite is the ability to find and know the limits of one's actions—that is, to control oneself, to avoid pride, to listen to authority, to be disciplined and pious. Here again Comenius's interpretation reflected the Greek interpretation of the morality of virtue, in which piety—*eusebiea*, which semantically directly refers to the need for limits to one's behavior, to be *sebas*—is able to respect what transcends us as individuals.

The opposite of such "pious" respect is *akratés*—a person who is without virtue because unrestrained. Unrestraint then leads a person to injustice, foolishness, impiety, in other words, to what the ancient person feared most, *hýbris*—arrogance, depravity, vice. In Comenius's conception, a distorted world without piety, respect, or wisdom, a world whose center of gravity lies in pronounced egocentrism—one's closed-ness to who they really are.

## Hýbris, the Labyrinth, and Shame

The loss of virtue, wisdom, and piety entangled Comenius's humanity in a depraved, arrogant world often expressed by the ancient term, *hýbris*. What are the main starting points for entanglement in the maze of the labyrinth, the fall to *hýbris*? Pronounced egocentrism and its correlative "entanglement in the world" were, according to Comenius, caused mainly by two features—"guides"—the first was Deception, which was structured by the "habit" of looking at the world through false knowledge or opinions in the sense of *doxy*. "As I learned later, the lenses were ground from the glass of Assumption, and were set in horn-rims called Habit." The second guide was Self-indulgence, which was personalized in the guide Search-all Ubiquitous and his halter of curiosity. This impertinence of the mind was explicitly, throughout the text, associated with loss of moderation and restraint primarily manifested in a lack of shame, respect, authority, obedience and piety. "I examined the bridle and found it was made of the halter of Curiosity, the bit having been forged of the steel of Tenacity in undertakings. Then I understood that I should no longer journey through the world of my own will, as I had intended, but should be forcibly driven on by my mind's curiosity and my insatiable thirst for knowledge."[7] If we freely interpret the picture of the labyrinth, the whole fall of humanity into *hýbris* can be understood as the consequence of the habit of relating to the world without shame.

"The basis of an honorable life is not a spoiled childhood and youth, but well-trained. . . . He who builds the building of great wisdom and virtue should begin with a deep humility. . . . Learn, my boy, to love praise and to have a love of shame; let praise be your spur, let shame be your reins."[8]

The impertinence of mind presented in the *Labyrinth* as the "bridle of inquisitiveness" is figuratively set in opposition to "the reins of shame." In addition to the "spur of praise" and the "reins of shame" there is also habit (cultivated through upbringing and practice) that makes a person wise, virtuous, and humble, in other words, blissful. According to Aristotle, shame, due to its close connection to habit and restraint, can be understood as a kind of quasi-virtue, even though Aristotle understood it as "a feeling rather than a state of character." Shame is rather a "conditioned moral quality": One is ashamed when doing bad things. Nevertheless, shame is especially important for the upbringing of young people, because "we think young people should be prone to the feeling of shame because they live by feeling and therefore commit many errors, but are restrained by shame; and we praise young people who are prone to this feeling."[9]

## Virtue and Practice

To be blissful means to live, in addition to wisely and piously, also virtuously, morally. In the Method of Morality Comenius wrote "The pursuit of wisdom makes us higher, brave, and generous,"[10] or to be "virtuous and pious."[11] Comenius's ethics, unlike that of other moralists, is directed primarily at behavior, not knowledge. It was no coincidence that Comenius

7. Komenský, *Labyrint*.

8. Komenský, *Obecná porada*, 863.

9. Aristotle, *Etika Nikomachova*, IV:15.

10. Komenský, *Didaktika*, XXIII:33.

11. Komenský, *Didaktika*, XXIII:1.

used the Greek term *ergon* in connection with the teaching of virtues—"everything that preceded was only *parerga* (secondary), not yet followed by *ergon*, action, deed, behavior. Virtue is not cultivated other than by works.[12]

With an emphasis on the relationship between habit, practice, and a virtuous life, Comenius referred to another key dimension of the Platonic-Aristotelian interpretation of virtue, namely, the connection between virtue and *ethos* (habit) and *praxis*. Virtues are learned by habit, said Aristotle. Virtues can be taught by constantly acting virtuously.[13] According to Comenius, virtue is "cultivated by deeds, not speech." Above all, the virtue of justice must be instilled, by which is meant service to others. Comenius added, "For corrupt nature is rooted in a vile flaw, self-love, which causes each one to want respect only for themselves, and completely ignores what happens to others. And that is the source of the various confusions in human affairs, when each one cares only about their own things, and completely ignores the common good."

In the list of specific virtues which create the structure of a virtuous life leading to blissfulness, Comenius primarily recalls Plato's concept of care of the soul, mentioning four basic virtues: *Sophia, sofrosyné, andreia*, and *dikaiosiné*, which correspond to the three basic parts of the human soul, lust (*epithymia*), greed (*thymos*), and intelligence (*nus*). According to Comenius (along with Plato), all four of these basic virtues must be instilled into the youth. Wisdom is therefore necessary "that we would make good judgments about things", Temperance, that we would always act "in moderation." Comenius, again with Plato, implicitly worked with the Aristotelian concept of practical wisdom, *fronésis*, where it is necessary to behave according to correct judgment (*orthos logos*) and according to moderation (*mesotés*). Every extreme is something to be avoided. Following the example of the classic concept, Comenius combined the second basic virtue—bravery—with self-control. As with Aristotle's practical wisdom *fronésis*, the prerequisite here is the mind that controls or dominates our emotions. Comenius exhorted one to "be the king (master) of one's actions." Finally, justice is then interpreted as the social ability with which we strive to not harm others, but be always helpful and merciful to others.

12. Komenský, *Didaktika*, VII.

13. Aristotle, *Etika Nikomachova*, II.

## The Successful Life

The basic prerequisite for a virtuous life that leads to Blissfulness with God was, according to Comenius, *praxe*. This was not, however, some kind of common practicality, as opposed to theoretical learning. Such an interpretation significantly reduces and declassifies Comenius's entire educational-reformative conception of humanity. Comenius understood the practice of life, education and upbringing as well as school, in view of their inherent correlation with the notions of blissfulness and virtue, as much closer to the Greek understanding of *praxis* than the common understanding of practice as natural dexterity and usefulness. Comenius did not understand practice, or practical understanding, and behavior as *techné*, but mainly as *um*, connected to *areté*, which we understand in two ways, as virtue and as competence.

On the first level, it is necessary to understand Comenius's emphasis on the practice of life, education and upbringing, with regard to the broader societal context. To be virtuous cannot be in and for itself, but as MacIntyre pointed out, primarily in "socially based, cooperative activity."[14] In different areas of practice people have different social roles. In a given social context it is usually obvious which competence (virtue) is desirable within the specified social role. For example, we know what it means to be a good person—more specifically, a good student, teacher, or parent. The good we achieve by such virtuous behavior is at the same time good for the whole human community.

In addition to practice, the goal or meaning of life itself is also important for the virtuous person. According to MacIntyre, such meaning is experienced mainly in the narrative order of the whole of our lives.[15] Due to this narrative nature, the life of an individual can, as a whole, be called good. Human life is understood as a story and has a primarily teleological nature, heading towards some finite *telos*. The life of an individual is thus embedded in situations in the social world of individuals having clearly defined roles. Within the framework of a narrative life, virtue is a basic prerequisite for the application of practice leading to the good, to a successful, good life.

People are creatures telling the stories of their lives—they become the story of their own history. The narrative self is the subject of its history. It

14. MacIntyre, *After Virtue*, 220.

15. MacIntyre, *After Virtue*, 255.

is the historic self, living in a specific context of community from which flows a very specific responsibility. In his critique of society, Comenius understood Self as ahistorical, separated from living contexts. The causes of the decline of society could thus be seen, among other things, in the fragmentation of all of life and morality, in which the Self was separated from virtue. It came to the point where the individual roles people played in the Theater of the Universe were separated in the lives of the individuals so that their lives appeared only as a series of unrelated, discontinuous episodes.

A necessary aspect of Comenius's practice, then, was its framing with an overall purpose and good. Therefore, for Comenius, blissfulness with God was the highest purpose. To live a good life meant something different for everyone, depending on social circumstances, because each had a different social identity—belonging to this family, to this professional society, to this nation, etc.

Comenius's understanding of human life as practice set in a society-wide (universally reformed) context of blissfulness is foreign to modern society today. Virtuous and moral behavior is today interpreted primarily psychologically. Virtues do not grow out of a society-wide understanding of practice, but as a psychological disposition about which the psychology of the individual testifies. The consequence of the psychological reduction of virtuous-moral behavior is the replacement of virtuous conduct by a moral norm. Comenius's good-living person (that is, wise, virtuous, and pious), who searched for their place in the world, is in today's modern society replaced by an ahistorical, a-practical individuality embedded in a particular and discontinuous life context, which makes the living world one great, incomprehensible maze–labyrinth.

## Bibliography

Aristotle. *Etika Nikomachova* [Nicomachean Ethics]. Praha: Rezek, 2013.

Komenský, Jan Amos. *Didaktika velká* [Great Didactic]. Brno: Komenium, 1948.

———. *Labyrint světa a ráj srdce* [The Labyrinth of the World and the Paradise of the Heart]. Brno: Host, 2014.

———. *Obecná porada o nápravě věcí lidských* [General Consultation concerning the Restoration of Human Affairs]. Praha: Svoboda, 1992.

MacIntyre, Alasdair. *After Virtue*. 3rd ed. Notre Dame: University of Notre Dame Press, 2007.

Plato. *Ústava* [Constitution]. Praha: Oikoymenh, 2017.

Spaemann, Robert. *Štěstí a vůle k dobru* [Happiness and the Will for the Good]. Praha: Oikoymenh, 1998.

# The Concepts of God and Truth in Comenius's Metaphysical Writings

Zuzana Svobodová

## Introduction

THE TASK OF THIS study is to capture the concepts of truth and God in the metaphysical writings of a man who was, according to Jan Patočka "even more ambitious than Bacon or Descartes,"[1] namely, in the *Writings on the First Philosophy* of Jan Amos Comenius. All of the works of Comenius, a seventeenth-century thinker, were focused on the effort to help bring humanity back to the true order of the world whose foundations were established by the Lord, God the Creator and Redeemer. Precisely because Comenius perceived the mission of humanity in the created world as an exceptional, special possibility to understand their surroundings as a whole, as a world that can be comprehended (that is, the world can be seen by humans as meaningful), it was the mission of those who saw this human possibility as a truly human task, to lead themselves and others to take care of that truly human life. If Comenius's whole conception of the world and humanity was based on God, it is obvious that focusing carefully on Comenius's conception of God would seem to be the key for correctly understanding the whole conception. As the last bishop of the Unity of Brethren, Comenius had, of course, a theological, Christian concept of God. In the following text, however, the notion of God in Comenius's metaphysical writings will be viewed. The reason is the universality of Comenius's restoration project,

1. Patočka, *Komeniologické studie I*, 224.

which was not aimed only at Christians, but at every person. In Comenius's metaphysical writings, three basic essential attributes are ascribed to God, and one of these attributes, namely truth or truthfulness, was chosen for the purposes of this text as another concept which will be given special attention here. The motivation for choosing the concept of truth was frequently seeing the meaning of philosophy in efforts to find truth. If today, in the twenty-first century, the concept of God is not refined in terms of the educational efforts of the public school system, then the concept of truth will still play two roles in the life of society and within it, in the life of the school. But how do we understand truth today? And how did Comenius understand truth? The motivation for the following text grew out of these questions.

## The Concept of God in Comenius's Metaphysical Writings

In Comenius's work *Prima philosophia* (First Philosophy), we encounter the concept of God in the very first lines, that is, in the Introduction (*Prolegomena*), where the first philosophy itself was explained as the science of being in general, followed by an explanation of what was called being. All being was divided into the first being, and being that emerged from the first. The first being was God, whom Comenius also called Jehovah and Being of beings (*Ens entium*). In God is life, and it is the most perfect; in God is also the most perfect movement, that is, one in which the terms "from whom," "through whom," and "to whom" are the same, God himself; in God is also the most perfect deed, and it is done both inside and outside himself.[2] According to Comenius, God creates within himself, by his action, essences, begets and embraces the mutual bond of love; thinks about good and loving goals, sets sufficient means for them, and makes decisions for results by certain and unerring means.[3] God acts outside himself in that he "1. anticipates everything that can be, thinks about order, whether something should be created and how to do it, 2. pronounces revelations, commandments (in which is the foundation of the word of God's will for creation), 3. performs his work by creating, controlling, admonishing (which is the foundation of God's works)."[4]

2. Cf. Komenský, *Spisy*, 645.
3. Cf. Komenský, *Spisy*, 651–57.
4. Komenský, *Spisy*, 649.

Everything that is outside of God, then, is a creature which is, according to Romans 11:36, from him, through him, and in him. All of creation has a common essence with the Creator, or, "real being, with which every being is something and not nothing."[5] Creation also has, in common with the Creator, essential attributes, or accidents, which in the first place are unity, truthfulness, and goodness.[6] Comenius's triad (*unitas, veritas, bonitas*) mentioned here commonly appeared in contemporary compendia of educational metaphysics; Comenius himself connected it with the Augustinian triad *unitas, species, ordo* (unity, form, order) in the publication *Scenographia*.[7]

According to Comenius, each of these three attributes gives birth to another triad: unity gives birth to place, time, and quantity—for whatever is one is within the limits of place, time, and quantity; truthfulness bears quality, activity, and passivity—for everything that is, is somehow and necessarily doing and enduring something; goodness, then, gives birth to order, usefulness, and love—for whatever is good is ordered in some way, and thanks to order it is useful to someone, and thanks to usefulness it is for someone worthy of love. Comenius added here, "Otherwise it is not possible."[8] Indeed, if everything inherently arises from the being of God, then it must be possible to truly see these attributes in all of creation as the footprints of God.

According to Comenius, each article derived in this way from the original trio of accidents has in itself its own essential triad. Place consists of three dualities (front–back, up–down, right–left); time is, for Comenius, a flowing of past, present, and future, or the duration through the terms from which (before), through which (now), and to which (after); quantity is a triad in the sense of amount, size, and heaviness (which is measured by number, extent, and weight). Here Comenius immediately elaborated further, the first among numbers is the trio, the first three kinds of size, or continuous quantity, are straight line, surface, and solid.

Because at this point we want to discuss in particular Comenius's notion of truth, it is important how Comenius proceeded to the first trio in which truth gives birth to quality. Of the visible qualities he stated that shape and color are the most noticeable; the first shape, for Comenius, was

5. Komenský, *Spisy*, 39.

6. Cf. Komenský, *Spisy*, 39, 145.

7. Komenský, *Spisy*, 39n103; cf. 126–27.

8. Komenský, *Spisy*, 627, cf. 143.

the triangle, the most perfect was the circle, which consists of the center, circumference, and area. Comenius further wrote about the quality of activity, thus combining quality and activity, both based (besides patience) on truth; and as the quality of activity he mentioned the very important trio: to be able, to know how, to want (*posse, scire, velle*)—for if these are given then the activity takes place, but if only one is missing, the activity does not happen.[9] In this triad it is possible to see Comenius in the tradition of Augustine, where in the *Confessions* he mentioned the triad *esse, nosse, velle* (to be, to know, to want), as well as in the tradition of medieval Trinitarian metaphysics, for example Hugh of Saint Victor or Bonaventure. And from one who inspired Comenius, Tommaso Campanella, who presented *scire, velle, posse* together with *potential, sapientia, amor* (power, wisdom, love) as God's "primalities" of Power, Wisdom, and Love—which Comenius allowed to speak in the World of Archetypes in a unique conversation about the creation of things. Power (*Potentia*), Wisdom (*Sapientia*), and Love (*Amor*), as attributes of the infinite Being, here consider each other in a dialogical way, namely, what the eternal Power implements, the eternal Wisdom discovers, and the eternal Love encourages. Because in this conversation God, in his eternity, seems to contemplate the creation of things outside of himself, there is a different order: it begins with the prompting of Love, continues with inventiveness of Wisdom, and the conclusion is pronounced by Power. The approach is also more logical from a Trinitarian perspective for Love, as the source of all things, is God the Father; Wisdom, which from Love flows eternally, is God the Son; and Power, which flows from Love and Wisdom, is God the Holy Spirit.[10] To illustrate the uniqueness of Comenius's dialogue, I quote from the very end of the conversation (the individual exchanges between Love, Wisdom, and Power are numbered):

> 106. *Love*: But what will we do to make man, our foremost beloved creature, to be aware of [the laws of eternity] and not sin through ignorance?
>
> *Wisdom*: We will engrave this whole seal of our eternity on his mind, so he can keep looking at these things internally and touch their examples in our works that are all around him, and finally, to tell him many secrets in the voice of our word.

9. Cf., Komenský, *Spisy*, 631.

10. Komenský, *Spisy*, 641.

*Power*: With all this help, man will be able, by the strength of his thought, to analyze and spread out everything for himself in more detail, before his eyes, and wherever he turns, see the light of our light.

107. *Love*: He will be able to do it, our grace will not leave him.

*Wisdom*: Nor our light.

*Power*: Or our help.

108. *Love*: Then let him not be abandoned.

*Wisdom*: But as everything else grows from its beginnings to its perfection gradually, so also let him grow.

*Power*: So that which is highest in him, will attain the highest perfection.

109. *Love*: May it happen!

*Wisdom*: So be it!

*Power*: Amen![11]

Comenius added another triad to the action that gives birth to truth: Action requires an agent, an object, and an instrument; the action proceeds from the agent, through the instrument, to the object. "When I speak to you, words flow from my heart, through the air, to your ear and soul. When I write, words flow from my mind through my hand and pen to the paper."[12]

Another triad is also met in passivity: someone else's activity, its transition to the subject, and its acceptance by the subject. The example of seeing oneself in the mirror, which Comenius presented here, leads one to a comparison with the image of the triad, where one is three and three one (the real face, the face reflecting in the mirror, and the face perceived from the mirror). Comenius concluded, "you could never see yourself without the three images."[13] In the God from whom everything comes there is nothing accidental and nothing outside of him can subsist, for outside of him there is nothing, thus God "sees (and saw from eternity) himself, through himself, in himself. . . . Here everything is simultaneous, everything is

11. Komenský, *Spisy*, 715. Italics are in the original here, as well as in all citations where italics are used.

12. Komenský, *Spisy*, 631, cf. 635.

13. Komenský, *Spisy*, 633.

essential, everything is connected, from itself, through itself, in itself, essentially a one–three and three–one."[14]

Just for completeness I am also mentioning other triads flowing from the good or goodness: Order, which is also in the Deity, has its "from where" (eternity flows from itself), "which way" (through itself), and "where" (eternity lies in itself), and to that, so order could be established in creation, it is necessary to add this triad: "1. that it not be allowed to meddle with *non-homogenous* things, 2. that each of the *homogenous* things be set in their place and 3. that *everything be bound by proper bonds*."[15] The benefit, likewise flowing from the good, is also fulfilled in a triad: to use the thing, to apply it to the proper object, and finally, to use it in the proper way. Likewise, from good birthing (or, for the sake of) pleasantness grows from a threefold relationship of things. Pleasantness first grows from a relationship towards its idea, secondly towards itself, and thirdly towards its object.

At the very end of this division of three basic triads Comenius explicitly pointed out, "What we have presented . . . is such a strong characteristic of things that if the triad were removed for some reason, the thing itself would surely perish. . . . Take the soul out of *man* and you will kill him, rid him of his spirit or mind and you get an irrational animal, strip him of his body and you destroy the whole creature. Prevent the *word* from being born in the heart and none will emerge, or from forming on the tongue and none will be heard; make no ear and in vain will the word sound when there is no place to receive it. . . . *The triad of which the essence of a thing consists surely clings so tightly to itself, that none of it can be removed or the thing itself will be removed.*"[16] Among other things, what follows from above is the triadic perception of humanity as a connection of the soul (*anima*, the principle of life as movement, the soul residing inside, according to Comenius),[17] the spirit (*spiritus*, the ability of the mind to observe reasonably, not only crudely—*brutum*, as the rest of the animals—the ones that are living, living beings: *animal*), and body (*corpus*). Very interesting is the fine distinction Comenius makes between the emerging of words when

14. Komenský, *Spisy*, 633.

15. Komenský, *Spisy*, 633, 635.

16. Komenský, *Spisy*, 635.

17. Cf. Komenský, *Spisy*, 631.

speaking—the words come from the heart,[18] and when writing—the words come from the mind, according to Comenius.[19]

Comenius's metaphysics is fundamentally biblical, Trinitarian, modeled on the Christian conception of one God in three persons. Although many have pointed out that there is very little in Comenius's metaphysics that is original,[20] his creative compilation forms a unique new structure where everything proceeds by inference from the Creator, a system built "*more trinitario seu divino*" (in a trinitarian or divine manner).[21] Comenius's conception is also original because it was not meant to be a complex system for experienced researchers, but expressly tries to avoid complex speculation. Comenius particularly mentioned the work of Jakob Böhm,[22] and, for example, the work of Campanella who, in his Universal Philosophy also directly followed Aristotle's Metaphysics,[23] but none of them were able to avoid speculation; therefore Comenius attempted a new concept.[24] The main reason for Comenius's efforts was to write a metaphysics in such a way that it would be completely understandable even to small children,[25] who were previously "equipped with descriptive knowledge of sensory things,"[26] for which Comenius's *Door to Languages* was to be used, for example. In his *Door to Things Unlocked* (1643), Comenius distinctly warned the reader that his metaphysics would "organize learning in a different way than it has been done so far."[27] Comenius's metaphysics wanted to be a "kind guide in thinking about the first concepts of things and a real key for opening the mind to all objects concisely and at once."[28] He was concerned not only about human wisdom, but for the disciples to find the key to God's, as well as human, wisdom in the new order of knowledge which could grow with the help of God "into the tree of human omniscience.[29] Jan Patočka's

18. Cf. Komenský, *Spisy*, 631, 635.
19. Komenský, *Spisy*, 631.
20. Cf. Komenský, *Spisy*, 8, 10, 14.
21. Komenský, *Spisy*, 9.
22. Komenský, *Spisy*, 643, 651; cf. Patočka, *Komeniologické studie I*, 13–17.
23. Komenský, *Spisy*, 217.
24. Cf. also Patočka, *Komeniologické studie I*, 196–97.
25. Komenský, *Spisy*, 25, 175, 225.
26. Komenský, *Spisy*, 225.
27. Komenský, *Spisy*, 171.
28. Komenský, *Spisy*, 173.
29. Komenský, *Spisy*.

thoughts about the founder of phenomenology, Edmund Husserl, resound in Comenius's desire "to build everything more fully, more orderly, stronger and strictly corresponding to the things themselves, from the very beginning." In this endeavor, Comenius was indeed an original thinker who opposed the subjectivism coming from the thoughts of his contemporary, René Descartes. A similar critique of the Cartesian approach to the subject was also perceived in Comenius's work by Comeniologists dealing mainly with Trinitarianism, such as Erwin Schadel, and from Czech Comeniologists other than Jan Patočka (Patočka was aware how tricky comparing Comenius with Descartes could be)[30] for example, Karel Floss and Pavel Floss,[31] Jaroslava Pešková,[32] Radim Palouš,[33] and Stanislav Sousedík.[34]

Comenius first derived the existence of the unity of the world from God, the Creator of the world: as God is one, so also the world is one and each individual creature has some kind of one being which is in itself undivided[35] and separate from another being. Comenius further derived from God the truth of the world: as God is not imaginary but real, so also the world and everything created has existence—Comenius justified the real existence of the world and things with the words: "that every single thing is truly what it is, because of the truth of God."[36] It is possible to see the influence of Aristotle here when each thing heads for its realization through the dynamism which it has been given. Third, from the fact that God is good in his manifestations—towards himself and towards everyone, Comenius derived that so also God has established every creature "to be useful to themselves and others."[37] Here he derived the usefulness of creation from the goodness of God, with reference to the biblical words, "Everything that God created was very good" (Gen 1:31).

30. Cf. Patočka, *Komeniologické studie I*, 14, 205–16; Patočka, *Komeniologické studie II*, 353–54; Patočka, *Komeniologické studie III*, 175–89, 334–62, 384–93, 465–67).

31. Cf. Komenský, *Spisy*, 31.

32. Cf. Pešková, *Role vědomí*, 44.

33. Cf. Palouš, *Komenského Boží svět*, 23–24, 47, 68–69, 73–74, 95–98, 110–42; Palouš, *Česká zkušenost*, 17, 20–23, 28, 32–35, 41; Palouš, *Totalismus*, 121–22; Palouš, *Světověk*, 173, 176, 180–81; Palouš, *Paradoxy*, 15, 17–18; Palouš and Svobodová, *Homo educandus*, 25, 44–45.

34. Cf. Sousedík, *René Descartes*, 45; Sousedík, *O co šlo?*, 98, 105–8.

35. Cf. Komenský, *Spisy*, 339: "[God] gave each created thing to be one thing, complete in all respects."

36. Komenský, *Spisy*, 41, cf. 125.

37. Komenský, *Spisy*, 41.

In the *Janua rerum reserata* (from the year 1681), *unitas, veritas* a *bonitas* are mentioned as the principles of subsistence. Earlier in that work Comenius stated that every individual being had its essence, and then defined subsistence as "the innermost state of being, by which each being is, for itself, that which it is. (In fact, to subsist means to stand under oneself, outside of relationships to others)."[38]

## The Concept of Truth in Comenius's Metaphysical Writings

If we look for the concept of truth in Comenius's metaphysical writings, we soon come across occurrences of the close terms "truth" and "truthfulness," and both were used to translate the Latin *veritas*. The Latin *verum* was sometimes translated as "truthful,"[39] sometimes as "truth,"[40] the term *essentiam veram* was translated as "true essence."[41] Comenius himself was terminologically inconsistent, as he used *veritas, verum* and *vero* to mean truth as one of the essential attributes.

As has already been mentioned, Comenius's conception of truth was embodied in the basic triad of unity, truthfulness, goodness (*unitas, veritas, bonitas*), one, true, good (*unum, verum, bonum; uno, vero, bono*).[42] *Veritas*, the truthfulness of the creation, is derived from God who is truly (*veré*) and true (*veritatus*).[43]

Truthfulness was defined by Comenius as follows: "*Truthfulness* is what each one is in formal harmony with himself." (*Veritas* est, quâ unum quodque indivisum est in se ipso).[44] In the work *Janua rerum reserata* (from the year 1681) the following definition of truth is given: "Truthfulness is what each being is in formal harmony with itself."[45] From the fact that whatever is, is true, it also follows that even what is but is not true, such as a lie, is a true untruth. The truthfulness being talked about here was called by Comenius in his "World of Archetypes" metaphysical truth.[46]

38. Komenský, *Spisy*, 337.
39. Komenský, *Spisy*, 339n422.
40. Cf. Komenský, *Spisy*, 127n204: *Licet verum*—"Although true."
41. Komenský, *Spisy*, 338.
42. Cf. Komenský, *Spisy*, 38–39, 124–25, 145–47.
43. Cf. Komenský, *Spisy*, 40, 124, 139.
44. Komenský, *Spisy*, 124–25.
45. Komenský, *Spisy*, 337.
46. Komenský, *Spisy*, 627.

Similarly, Comenius concluded that if it is valid that every being is good by the fact that it exists, in the sense that it is in itself an object of desire and of efforts for self-preservation, and because it sees the preservation of itself, development, spreading outward, and associating with others as features of good, then also evil, corruption, and sin are, in their essence, their nature of being, good.[47] It can clearly be seen here how, if everything is derived from the one, true, and good God, because without God nothing that is could be, then there must be some way to speak also of evil, lies, sins or corruption with the help of the triad *unitas, veritas, bonitas*, if the unity of the world, of being, of God, is to be preserved.

It should be noted that if, for example, Thomas Aquinas writes about truth in connection with a concept, then the Latin term *veritas intellectus* is not translated as the "truth of the concept," but as the "truthfulness of the concept." According to Comenius, "the truthfulness of the concept is proportionate to the concept of the thing" (*veritas intellectus sit adaequatio intellectus et rei*).[48]

In his metaphysical writings, Comenius distinguished between ethical, logical, physical, and metaphysical truth.[49] Ethical truth with discourse or speech corresponds to the concept of the mind, logical truth is the concept of the mind in relation to the thing itself, physical truth is the thing in relation to its idea, and metaphysical truth is each individual being, being what it is. There is no opposite of metaphysical truth, because metaphysical truth is inseparable from the thing: "*This truth is also in untrue things, because untruth is truly untruth, a lie is truly a lie, a mistake is truly a mistake, etc.*"[50] The opposite of physical truth is delusion and deformity (according to Comenius it is, for example, a violation of the nature of people, of angels), the opposite of logical truth is error or a false idea (when an illusion or myth is presented as true), the opposite of ethical truth is a lie.

This four-part division of truth survived in some of Comenius's contemporaries, but the traditional component of educational philosophy was a triadic division of truth—a distinction was made between metaphysical, ethical, and logical truth.[51] Comenius wrote about the fourth truth in the context of a treatise on the degrees of unity, truthfulness, and goodness,

47. Komenský, *Spisy*, 627.

48. Komenský, *Spisy*, 127n204.

49. Komenský, *Spisy*, 53, 129, 341.

50. Komenský, *Spisy*, 341.

51. Cf. Komenský, *Spisy*, 52–53n123.

while for the degrees of singular unity (there also exists universal unity) he named three (unity is according to the unification of the parts: natural, artificial, accidental), and the degrees of goodness are also three (goal, means, order). Therefore, the four-part division of truth must have been a really well-thought-out plan of Comenius, since he had to be aware that it disrupted the smooth triadic structure given in the treatise, which he could have preserved if he had only taken the mostly three-part division from the period textbooks (for example, he could also have found a triadic division of truth in his teacher from Herborn, J. H. Alsted).

Comenius presented three axioms about truthfulness (*de veritate*): "Every being, as far as it is a being, is true. (That is, it truly is what it is, is from where it is from, is the way it is, etc.)." As the second axiom on truthfulness Comenius presented: "Whatever truly is not, is not. (As in, if gold is not truly gold, it isn't gold)." The last axiom about truthfulness was: "The truthfulness of things is unchangeable. (That is, it cannot happen that what is, is at the same time not, etc., or was not as it now is; or was not from where it is from, etc.)"[52]

In the word truth, as used, for example, in *Via lucis*, Comenius also expressed his position in the dispute over universals (Comenius's interpretation is that it is precisely *veritas*), "So truth is first of all in things, only in second place in the mind of one who understands the thing correctly."[53]

## Conclusion

The aim of this chapter was to show the structure of Comenius's metaphysical writings and focus on the concept of God and the concept of truth, yet here, as also with Jan Patočka, Comenius's internal affinity with the "magical-mystical thinking" of the sixteenth and seventeenth centuries was not to be obscured.[54] Comenius endeavored to avoid ambiguities, complex speculations, and lack of clarity, as his metaphysical conception was to be arranged in such a way that even small children could understand it. In this sense, Patočka saw Comenius as a man of the seventeenth century who strived after discipline and clarity of thought, and at the same time a man of the school, of his own scholasticism, who strived for the reform of

52. Komenský, *Spisy*, 131.

53. Veritas primariò in rebus, secundariò demum in mente rem dextrè intelligentis, according to Comenius, in Komenský, Spisy, 127n204.

54. Patočka, *Komeniologické studie I*, 18.

human education. But Comenius was not a preparer of the Enlightenment in the sense of the anthropocentric rationalistic conception of the world. On the contrary, Comenius realized that the new conceptions of human beings and the world would lead humanity further away from its origins, from God to increasingly elaborate labyrinths, and from the world as God's creation to the world as a reservoir for the manipulative actions of self-centered humanity. Therefore he tried to write foundations that would be clear, understandable, and acceptable for children. Foundations that would be based on a certainty that no longer needed to be proved, on which the knowledge of every human being could stand, and thanks to which they would be able to find their way back to their purpose, which is inherent in every human being, for as the *imago dei* they share a common essence with their Creator, and thus have the opportunity to live from him, through him, and in him. The result was Comenius's trinitarian metaphysics, presented during Comenius's life in several works which were published in new Czech translations that included the original Latin texts, in 2017 under the title *Writings on the First Philosophy*.

If we today ask ourselves what in Comenius's conception of God could appeal to our contemporaries, then his conception of the triadic conversation between Love, Wisdom, and Power seems like a promising inspiration in a day when conversation often turns into a self-presentation when people enter virtual social networks to find space to "share." In the World of Archetypes, Comenius presented readers with a conversation encouraging Love, understanding Wisdom, and exercising Power, so they would understand what was said in a human way, in a way commensurate with God.[55] If readers listen carefully to this conversation, they will understand much of Comenius's vision of God, the world, and the role of humanity. The form in which this conversation was composed directly calls for a staging which could also appeal to people today.

In Comenius's conception of truth the reader may be particularly appealed to by metaphysical truth, through which Comenius showed how its opposite is nothing, because this truth is inseparable from things and applies to untruths as well. While sooner or later each person will have a direct personal experience with opposites such as delusion and deformity (the opposite of physical truth), error (the opposite of logical truth), or lies (the opposite of ethical truth), metaphysical truth appears as the horizon of all horizons, which can never be removed, yet never fully understood in

55. Cf. Komenský, *Spisy*, 655.

the here and now, although it is the deepest foundation of the universe. Comenius reminded humanity, and with them also all of creation, of the great hope: If metaphysical truth is inseparable from things, then even though physical, logical, and ethical contradictions still exist and act, in metaphysical truth a foundation is established which can be realized and fulfilled by God, "by mercy already prepared to come to light."[56]

56. Komenský, *Spisy*, 655.

## Bibliography


Komenský, Jan Amos. *Spisy o první filosofii* [Writings on the First Philosophy]. Praha: Oikoymenh. Knihovna novověké tradice a současnosti, 2017.

Palouš, Radim. *Česká zkušenost: příspěvek k dějinám české filosofie: o Komenského škole stáří, o Bolzanově významu v našem duchovním vývoji a o Masarykově filosofickém mládí—se závěrečným odkazem k Patočkovi* [Czech Experience: A Contribution to the History of Czech Philosophy: On Comenius's School of Old Age, on Bolzano's Significance to Our Spiritual Development and on Masaryk's Philosophical Youth—with a Final Reference to Patočka]. 2nd ed. Praha: Academia, 1994.

———. *Komenského Boží svět* [Comenius's God's World]. Praha: SPN, 1992.

———. *Paradoxy výchovy* [Paradoxes of Education]. Praha: Karolinum, 2009.

———. *Světověk a Časování* [Age of the World and Timing]. 2nd ed. Praha: Vyšehrad, 2000.

———. *Totalismus a holismus* [Totalism and Holism]. Praha: Karolinum, 1996.

Palouš, Radim, and Zuzana Svobodová. *Homo educandus: filosofické základy teorie výchovy* [Homo educandus: Philosophical Foundations of the Theory of Education]. Praha: Karolinum, 2011.

Patočka, Jan. *Komeniologické studie I: soubor textů o J. A. Komenském*. Edited by Věra Schifferová. Praha: Oikoymenh, 1997.

———. *Komeniologické studie II: soubor textů o J. A. Komenském*. Edited by Věra Schifferová. Praha: Oikoymenh, 1998.

———. *Komeniologické studie III: soubor textů o J. A. Komenském*. Edited by Věra Schifferová. Praha: Oikoymenh, 2003.

Pešková, Jaroslava. *Role vědomí v dějinách a jiné eseje* [The Role of Consciousness in History and Other Essays]. Praha: Nakladatelství Lidové noviny, 1998.

Sousedík, Stanislav. *O co šlo?: články a studie z let 1965–2011* [What Was It About? Articles and Studies 1965–2011]. Praha: Vyšehrad. Moderní myšlení, 2012.

———. *René Descartes a české baroko* [René Descartes and the Czech Baroque]. Praha: Filosofia Parva philosophica, 1996.

# Things Essential, Ministerial, and Incidental in the *General Consultation*

Jan Valeš

## 1. Teachings of the Old Unity of Brethren

Comenius sought reform in the areas of education, politics, and religion. The religious situation of his time was very different from the twenty-first century. Nevertheless, his ideas can find application today, as will be seen in the following text.

When Comenius undertook the realm of religion, a concept known as *teachings of the Unity of Brethren on matters essential, ministerial, and incidental* (hereinafter referred to as EMI)[1] came to light. It is the subject of this chapter—mapping the scope and teaching of the EMI within the framework of Comenius's *General Consultation on the Restoration of Human Affairs* (hereinafter referred to as the *Consultation*).

The older version of this teaching, contained in the orders of the Unity of Brethren, read as follows: Essential are the things in which the essence of Christianity is based, and from which salvation arises; namely, on the part of God, the grace of God the Father, the merit of Jesus Christ, the gifts of the Holy Spirit; on the part of the people, faith, love, hope. Ministerial things are established by God to attain the essentials: the Word of God, the keys, and the sacraments. Incidental things, then, are all the sorts of regulations

1. For a brief, popular introduction to the EMI concept, see Valeš, "Na čem záleží?"; for professional studies see Molnár, *Bratr Lukáš*; Bartoš, *O podstatu křesťanství*.

and ceremonies pertaining to the ministerial things, what should be when, where, from whom, and how to externally conduct them so as to be beneficial.[2] Comenius took over this teaching several generations after its initial formulation by Lukáš Pražský (ca. 1460–1528).

The longest part of this chapter is a commentary on the EMI within the *Consultation*. The third part presents the broader context of Comenius's thinking, directly influenced by the EMI. The fourth part presents Comenius's main application. This chapter aims to cite, or at least refer to, all places where the *Consultation* is relevant for the EMI.[3]

## 2. Essential, Ministerial, and Incidental—Text by Comenius with Commentary

The *Consultation* contains dozens of places where the words EMI appear. Most of them occur in two parts of the *Consultation*, which can be considered as key: the description of the spiritual world (*Pansofia*) and the description of the renewed, new religion (*Panorthosia*).

The overall formulation of the EMI appears in four places: in the *Pansofia*, first in the description of renewed religion (II.325–6), then in the interpretation of relationships in the spiritual world (II.379); in the *Panorthosia*, first in the account of the renewed religion (III.341–42), and finally in the outline of the renewal process for religious matters (III.386–403).

### 2.1 Things Essential for Salvation

The central issue of the EMI is salvation, for it is about the things essential "for the salvation of human beings." In this broadest starting point Comenius harmonized his reformative interests with those of the old teaching. In the introduction to the book *Panegersia*, he roused the general public and in the conclusion he asked for agreement on ten points: "First, that we will all have one goal, THE SALVATION OF THE HUMAN RACE: . . . 1. From party interests; 2. From the multitude; 3. From coercion and violence . . . By this, may all be led to strive for common salvation" (I.127).[4]

2. *Řád církevní*, 12–14; summary wording by the author.

3. Since I will be referring often to the *Consultation*, citations for this reference work only will be given in the body text. All others will appear as footnotes.

4. Similarly, in the address to rulers in the introduction to the *Pansofia* he described his reformative project with the words: "to bring salvation to the whole world at once"

At the same time, Comenius distinguished whether salvation goes beyond earthly life. The EMI has this overlap: "Some [of God's gifts] are about eternal salvation, others are about this earthy life. For example, faith, hope, love, and prophecy" (II.380). Here Comenius, apparently, understood faith, love, and hope as examples of things pertaining to eternal salvation, while prophecy is an example of the second category.

## 2.2 Things Essential on the Parts of God and People

Essential salvation is founded on God's work, which humans accept. On God's side is the crucial grace that awakens in people the response of faith, love, and hope.

Ever since the time of Lukáš Pražský, it has been necessary to look at the essential things on two levels: salvation is based on God's action, but it does not happen without a human response.[5] For Comenius, what is important on God's side is the love expressed primarily in the person and work of the mediator, Jesus Christ. On the human side, the answer of faith, love, and hope are: "This is to cultivate in us FAITH, LOVE, and HOPE, a triad which the Holy Spirit has firmly established as the basis of our salvation" (II.275).

The EMI is formulated in a Trinitarian way on God's side—the Father, Jesus, the Spirit. Comenius preserved this. Nevertheless, he characteristically began from the human perspective: "Faith, hope, and love in God the Father, Son, and Holy Spirit are essential; the Father decided for salvation, the Son was instrumental in it, the Holy Spirit offers and secures it" (III.341).[6] Comenius did not analyze God's work in the sense of specific biblical events in the *Consultation*, he focused on God's attributes. He described only the person of Jesus and his work in detail.

On God's side, mercy is crucial: "Here lies the foundation of religion, and we must strive for it. We cannot otherwise reach the pinnacle of faith,

(I:225). In the introductory paragraphs of the *Panorthosia* he no longer talked about "salvation, rescue," but "restoration, reformation, reparation, restitution, regeneration" (III:259). Naturally, in the details spiritual rescue (salvation) differs from the restoration of human affairs (see a detailed description of the subject, agent, and means of restoration in III.290–92).

5. Molnár, *Bratr Lukáš*, 21–22.

6. Comenius also followed the EMI in the description of renewed, general religion, in which the human response was prominent (III.340). It was similar in his description of the sources of peace (II.408).

the warmth of love, or the security of salvation, but by descending into the abyss of mercy" (III.342).[7] He called the public role of general religion as a whole in society, public service. It consists in the proclaiming of God's mercy, which in people is brought about by faith, love, and hope (II.325).

This raises the question of the relationship between the side of God and the side of the people. It needs to be given attention before a detailed interpretation of faith, love, and hope can be made. Comenius described the dynamics of the relationship between God and people as follows: "The first and fundamental stipulation of this relationship is the continuous cooperation of the human will with the grace of God" (II.278–79). In this cooperation God remains sovereign, and people are United with him by the bond of faith, love, and hope. As will be explained below, the Bible (holy laws) plays an important role in this: "General religion, however, will include all of the meanings (*religio*) previously mentioned, firstly by leaving everything unmerited to God, and secondly by constantly reading and preserving his holy laws, and finally, by fastening oneself to God through the irrevocable bonds of faith, love, and eternal hope" (III.341). Cooperation with God does not interfere with human freedom and initiative. Therefore he criticized the Lutheran emphasis on faith separate from acts of love as a violation of the reciprocity of essential things on God's side and on the human side (II.341–42). Part of the human relationship with God is also the obligation which people owe to God (II.354–55). But it is still about rescue.

Comenius offered a pair of detailed reasons why, on the human side, faith, love, and hope are right: First of all, faith, love, and hope correspond to the trio of God's actions. Revelation teaches faith, the commandments dictate what love does, and the promises promise what hope looks for (II.275, 279). Secondly, faith, love, and hope are based on the offices of Christ: we appropriate his sacrifice by faith; we follow his teachings with love; we attain his kingdom by hope (II.378; III.341); faith, love, and hope are the following of Christ (II.366).

Since the time of Lukáš Pražský, it has been a part of the EMI that faith, love, and hope are both the human response to the essential things from God's side, and at the same time, God's gifts.[8] In the *Consultation*, the level of them as gifts partially disappears, specifically, the cognitive

7. The essence of the religion of Cain was precisely that it did not trust God's mercy, while the religion of Abel was characterized by faith, love, and hope, which are well-embodied in God's mercy (III.344).

8. Molnár, *Bratr Lukáš*, 22.

component of faith overshadows all other aspects (III.343). At one point, however, Comenius said that faith, love, and hope are the result of the state of renewal, and he connects them directly with the Christian message (II.272). Elsewhere he again calls faith, love, and hope a secondary way in which God acts with humans (II.283). "Where faith, love, and hope come from: faith is the enlightenment of the mind, love is obedience to the heart, hope is the purity of the soul" (III.342). This confirms both levels of faith, love, and hope: Comenius did not deny the level of them as a gift, but he gave a greater emphasis to them as a response to God's actions.

It is necessary to stop at the individual words Comenius wrote about faith, love, and hope. Faith is a *theory* about the relationship with God, that is, *knowledge* (II.280). Faith means knowing God, which, however, cannot be separated from love, for love is the measure of knowledge: "But we must know sovereignly, because we must love sovereignly" (II.281).

Love is the *practice* of the relationship with God, that is, *action* (II.280). Elsewhere he used the terms *obedience* (II.278), *obedience of love* (III.58), *acts* (III.342), *piety* (III.362), and *life* (III.389).

Hope is *chresis*[9] in the relationship with God, that is, active participation (II.280). He often calls it *trust*, or *to hope*, and also uses it in connection with "hope and patience" (III.343). It is a description of the beneficial effects, the culmination of which is peace (II.282).

He also spoke of their interrelationships: Faith precedes love and hope (logically rather than temporally). Love is the use of faith. Hope is "the use of sweet love" (II.280).

Religion constructed in this way resembles a tree "whose deep roots are faith. The mighty trunk, whose branches with evergreen leaves rise up and to the sides, is love with its deeds. The blossom and fruit are hope, the sweetness of God's eternal mercy" (II.280). Another image is "faith, hand, and heart" (II.276).

Comenius did not omit the dimension of time either: "Faith looks to the past at all that God has said and done. Love controls the present. Hope looks to the future" (II.378).

The content of faith, love, and hope is illustrated by the opposites: distrust, disobedience, horror, and despair (II.288). Even persecution will not overcome them (II.280).

Faith, love, and hope are traditionally called virtues. At the second or third mention of faith, love, and hope in the interpretation of the spiritual

9. This is a Greek word meaning "usage."

world, the translators explain: "Faith, love, and hope were considered supernatural virtues, given to humanity by the grace of God, and were to strengthen, among other things, the natural virtues, which, in the spirit of Aristotle's ethics, were considered rationality, bravery, moderation, and justice. These four virtues emerged from human nature, but were weakened by inherited sin" (n33 in II.275; II.414).

He correctly presented the scholastic joining of Aristotelian civic virtues with the three supernatural virtues. But this connection did not occur in the *Consultation*! Faith, love, and hope are completely missing in the interpretation of the moral world (II.215–22). One can count at least ten virtues, so they are not the Aristotelian four.

So were faith, love, and hope virtues for Comenius? It is possible to deduce two ways. First, Comenius understood the key role of the virtues but did not recognize their exact hierarchy. This applies to his view of the moral world.[10] In the spiritual world, however, is the second way, that faith, love, and hope are virtues in a completely unique sense—as the means of humanity's relationship with God. And they are exactly these three.

The content and importance of faith, love, and hope come to light where Comenius deduced practical conclusions. It was still about the restoration of human affairs. And Comenius was a theorist who was primarily concerned with applying a good theory. From this perspective, faith, love, and hope also saw due (appropriate, relevant, proper) usage.[11] How do they perform their application?

According to the rules of Bible translation, he concluded that faith, love, and hope are the end of a process—leading from Bible reading and prayer, through contemplation, to action—by which "we are convinced of the truth of all God's words and in safety against attacks of temptation we strengthen ourselves to the fullness of faith, love, and hope" (II.275).

He understood faith, love, and hope precisely as the *means* necessary for their proper use (II.279–82). When he then described the important concept of following, that is, using or enjoying Christ (II.366), faith, love, and hope were again the means of following (also II.314).

The inseparability of faith, love, and hope becomes apparent in their practical application. After describing the renewed religion, Comenius, in a

10. Although they speak of following Jesus (that is, the role of the virtues as in the moral world), again we find a greater number of virtues (summed up in the nine beatitudes) and their hierarchy is not exact (II.368–69).

11. E.g., When describing the benefit of a renewed religion, faith, love, and hope are obvious even without using any words (III.341).

separate chapter of the *Pansofia* presented the development of mature piety in seven steps. Faith, love, and hope form three of them. Their inseparability is demonstrated by the "five golden rules of the mode of exercise," where faith corresponds to religion, love corresponds to command, and hope corresponds to promise or warning: "1. A prayer and a declaration are created from every command of God. 2. A declaration and prayer are created from every article of faith. 3. A declaration and confession are created from any request. 4. From each story in Scripture one can create a personal, practical example in the form of prayer, order, declaration, or vow. . . . 5. From every discourse or agreement of God, unceasing conversations are formed: with God the Father; with Christ; with the Holy Spirit" (II.340).[12] With that, Comenius said that every essential action and speaking of God in himself inseparably combines all three dimensions of the relationship with God. To see these three levels, to be able to pass from one to another, and to perceive them at the same time, belong to mature piety. It is most natural that this become the subject of a conversation with God, prayer.[13]

Another practical benefit of faith, love, and hope emerged in Comenius's text—it is peace, tranquility, calm. He spoke of eternal blissfulness, yet peace penetrated the text within the earthly life. The passive dimension is rest from the flame of the desire for wealth, honor, knowledge, or pleasure. In the active dimension, peace grows from faith, love, and hope: "A Christian rejoices in faith because he knows that God has been his father from eternity, that Christ redeemed him long ago, that the Holy Spirit already consecrated and sealed him for eternal life in his mother's womb, and that everything in the world was determined and is furnished for his salvation. He rejoices in love because he discovers that there is a mutual and unshakeable love between him and God, the angels, and all the chosen creatures. He rejoices also in hope, because he knows that when the futility of all things has gone away, he will survive and consider himself in the inheritance of heaven and earth" (II.408; also mentioned on the next page).

12. He developed the same idea in connection with catechesis (II.378). In another place, "Internally it is necessary for all this to come together in man: 1. Theoretically, that the clear truth be obvious to everyone without heresy; 2. Practically, only the bare commands of God without superstition; 3. In usage, only the true promises of God without deceptive hopes" (III.342).

13. With the indivisibility of faith, love, and hope he argued that the love of God has three levels of fearing God: "It is fitting nonetheless to fear the great, love the good, and obey the wise (faith, love, and hope are one)" (II.347).

Faith, love, and hope are also basic for Comenius: they represent a triple bond between humanity and God. At the same time, they are key resources given by God himself. Nor can methods of usage, imitation, and regulation avoid them.

## 2.3 Ministerial Things

Comenius always called ministerial things *ministerial*. The label means that *they are in ministry to the essential things*.[14] In his words, "Ministering to instill every essential word of God, to maintain order with the keys, and to seal the sacraments" (III.341). Today we could call them service, supportive, auxiliary, instrumental, practical, functional, purposeful, or special measures.

The Brethren Catechism of 1615 lists three ministries of Christ: "The Word of God, the keys, and the sacraments."[15] We can find the same three ministries in the *Consultation*. The Bible is the most common topic. In keeping with the tradition of the Reformed Churches, there is no fundamental difference between the Bible and the Gospel, the Word of God, preaching.

The triad of ministries thus established contain an important symbolism of the three offices of Christ: "by his words Christ feeds us as teacher (shepherd), by the power of the keys he guides us as king, by the sacraments he cleanses us as priest" (III.341). This trio of offices corresponds to the trio of faith, love, and hope (see above).[16]

"The keys and the sacraments strengthen and seal" (II.378). However, God's work is possible even without these instruments if they are missing or not used according to his will (II.326). It is worth noting that in these circumstances he did not mention the Bible, because it truly occupies a privileged position among the ministries.

An interesting idea of Comenius was to apply the distinction between *the side of God* and *the side of people*, as we know them from the essential, to the ministerial as well: from God's side, the instruments of service are

14. Rudolf Říčan interpreted the designation as those things "in which the church performs her ministry" (Říčan, "K bratrským," 95). That is true, but it is not a reason to label them.

15. Smetana, *Katechismus bratrský*, 95.

16. The agreement with the Calvinist branch of the Reformation in the list of marks of the true church: proclamation of the Word, administration of the sacraments, discipline, is also a strong point. Comenius did not note this agreement within the *Consultation*.

the messengers, the Bible is their equipment, and the sacraments are their seals. From the human side, then, acceptance of the messengers, zealous reading of the Bible and participation in church meetings, and reception of the sacraments in truth (II.325).

Comenius noticed symmetry—ministries occur in pairs: in the Bible, the law and the gospel; in the keys, binding and loosing; in the sacraments, baptism and the Lord's Supper (II.327).

Now to the individual ministries. Comenius first described the Bible in *Panaugia*, where, however, he did not consider it one of the three ministerial things, but one of the three books of light (I.158–66; see section 3.1 below).

In the spiritual world, the Bible occupies a privileged place from the very beginning (III.272), and there it has no competition. He coined the principle "nothing but the Scripture" (II.276). And the understanding of Scripture is controlled by the EMI. The interpretation of the Bible does not mean its study. For Comenius, interpretation begins with study, but passes into action, where it leads to faith, love, and hope. Thus, Comenius applied the truth that the Bible is a ministerial thing, that is, that it leads to a life of faith, love, and hope.

It is in connection with the interpretation of the Bible the Comenius listed for the first time in the *Consultation* the three forms of the Word, God's action: revelation, commandment, promise. More precisely: revelation or veiling, commandment or prohibition, promise or threat (II.275). Faith, love, and hope are parallel to know—act—use. Also, faith corresponds to God's revelation—love corresponds to commandment—hope corresponds to promise (II.282, 378), "to believe, to act and to hope in what he taught, commanded, and promised" (II.377). Therefore, the basic Christian texts can be assigned to them: the Apostle's Creed to faith, tithe to love, the Lord's Prayer to hope (II.282, 378). This insight played an important role in Comenius and permeated a number of practical applications; some of them have already been presented, others will be.[17]

Naturally, Comenius remembered the aids and textbooks for translation of the Bible, in which the EMI again plays the role of the main outline. Chiefly in the *Pampaedia* (II.58), but also in the vision for a renewed general religion (III.362).

17. In addition, this also works with the contrast of the Law and the Gospel, which is a feature of Lutheranism (II.327), yet emphasizes its unity, which in turn is a feature of the Calvinist school (II.316–17).

Comenius knew two sacraments—baptism and the Lord's Supper (II.327), which he occasionally called the Eucharist. The role of the sacraments in the ministerial things consists in sealing,[18] affirming the relationship with God, giving strength, and strengthening hope (e.g., II.327, 378). The sacraments are a link, cement, which unites believers among themselves (II.328).

He also viewed the sacraments from the perspective of faith, love, and hope, and emphasized how they serve them: "For the sacraments are 1. the public sealing of our creed in faith; 2. our commitment to obedience to God; 3. God's seal of our hope" (II.378).

The keys, or discipline, are an important part of the concept of the church. The power of the keys, as Jesus declared to the apostle Peter, represent the authority entrusted by Christ himself to those who stand at the head of the church. They correspond to Christ's royal office and serve to develop love, and Comenius entrusted them to the leaders of the church together with the secular lords (II.326–27).

He also cited warnings: moral looseness or the opposite, excessive strictness (II.345; III.345, 361).

There should be enough discipline in the church. On the other hand, the ultimate state of discipline is voluntarism! (III.342). The essence of the keys is watchful supervision. He thus spoke of the necessity of discipline, but it should applied with a minimum of coercion and preferably "without coercive power, that is, binding without the key of discipline, as far as possible. But if it is not possible, then by means of it" (III.361). He named three levels of discipline: admonition, threat, expulsion (III.328). As can be seen, he distinguished between the power of the keys in binding, and in unbinding, which should be applied most often. Discipline should take place without prejudice (III.397).

From knowledge of ministerial things come three tasks for the ministers of the church: to make the Bible accessible, to reassure about the truth of grace, to require conscientious action (II.326–27). Ministerial things are their instruments. The EMIs have been part of catechesis from the very beginning (II.379–80).

18. The meaning of the words *seal, sealing* in the chapters on religion must be distinguished from *seals, stamps* in the chapter on the world of archetypes.

## 2.4 Incidental Things

Comenius called them variously: "secondary" (II.379; III.341–43), "secondary, by case" (II.375), "indifferent (adiafora)" (II.379–80), "ceremonial" (III.342). Overall, they receive the least attention. He named them in the *Pansofia* and in the *Panorthosia* he added important details that show his conception of them was in full agreement with what we know from the Unity of Brethren.

"Secondary means are the regulations and customs concerning these things in the general church or in the local church" (III.342). Ecumenical strength can be seen in this definition: what distinguishes one church from another for the most part falls into this area of secondary means, not essential things. "The means and instruments of religion are the ceremonies of all kinds, according to needs and the opportunities that present themselves, as when, during prayer, we sit, stand, fall on our knees or face, etc" (III.346).

Comenius dealt with the secondary issues in the life of the church. He distinguished between God's commands and human regulations. It is an important function of the EMI, because it concerns the authority of religion: "1. theoretically, so that the clear truth, without heresy, would be obvious to everyone; 2. practically, only the bare commands of God without superstition; 3. usage-wise, only the true promises of God without deceptive hope" (III.342). Thus, Comenius held a Protestant position on church traditions.

In addition to incidental things in the life of the church, Comenius also dealt with incidental things in the personal lives of people. The starting point for him was Christian freedom from the law, which can be expressed theoretically as a "case study of conscience," in which "1. there should be few rules; 2. but enough to solve everything; 3. and do it so obviously, that every pious person must be content with them" (III.341).

## 2.5 Summary of Things Essential, Ministerial, and Incidental in the *Consultation*

This section of the chapter has shown that the distinction between the things essential, ministerial, and incidental, as accepted by Comenius in the Unity of Brethren, is one of the foundations of Comenius's restorative efforts. It is important to remember that by essential and ministerial things he meant a precise list and just that.

It is worth noting that Comenius presented and applied the distinctions in the EMI, but those distinctions are not in themselves a matter for which he would constantly argue.

For Comenius, the relationship with God that a person experiences in the form of faith, love, and hope, is the part of the EMI that got the most use in the *Consultation*. Faith, love, and hope are the other side of the essential things—they are a person's bond with God, which has no power it itself, but in God. It is worth the reminder of the interconnectedness and inseparability of faith, love, and hope. They are not among the common virtues in the area of morality, but on the contrary, they play a key role in the area of spirituality.

Comenius accepted, interpreted, and applied the teachings of the old Unity of Brethren EMI. Comenius's stage in the development of the EMI is important in that he consistently applied his efforts to bridge the gap between the quarreling Protestants, and possibly the Protestants and Catholics. During this activity, Comenius did not lay aside the EMI, nor did he formulate anything better; he was faithful to the traditional EMI. His main contribution was that he deepened the understanding of faith, love, and hope and how they grow out of God's mercy, he developed the ministerial things and placed them in an ecumenical context, he reflected theoretically the practice of the Unity of Brethren in the incidental things, and also placed the EMI in the broader context of education and upbringing. On the other hand, he neglected the work of God the Father and the Holy Spirit in the *Consultation*.

"Let the theory of religion be short, practice be long for one's whole life, making use of (defending) its lovely benefits, lasting without end into eternity" (III.342).

## 3. The Theological Anthropology of Faith, Love, and Hope

The EMI as a whole, but especially faith, love, and hope, influence the image of humanity. Religion was the relationship, to Comenius. It was not the external ceremonies, it was an internal relationship which corresponded to the nature of faith, love, and hope. Only a few external things are in the role of the ministers, everything else belongs to the incidental things.

Faith, love, and hope describe the religious side of humanity: "In the steel chain or circle of faith, love, and hope lies all of religion" (II.338). These three are the bonds between humanity and God (II.278). From the standpoint of development, he distinguished three stages of religion: the innocence of Paradise in its untouched state, the state of abandonment after evil entered the world, and the state of renewal, as the world we know is illuminated by the Christian message (II.272). Faith, love, and hope find a key role in the state of renewal, and by the words faith, love, and hope, Comenius meant the relationship with God in general, religiosity in a Christian perspective (II.272, 278, 448).

Because the EMI is about salvation, it clearly confirms the need for rescue. Humans are beings which need saving in the deepest sense of salvation, but also rescue from specific ailments, confusions, futility. Restoration, reform, is thus to be done towards God, towards people, and to things (III.298–320).

The distinction between the essential things on God's side and on the human side places one in the role of responsibility to God. This response is essential—humans are made in the image of God (*imago dei*). The responsibility is manifested in that faith, love, and hope are the response to God's action. Here it is possible to see the basis of Comenius's emphasis on human freedom, for the response to God has to be in the spirit of faith, love, and hope, and thus free. Comenius projected freedom, as an anthropological quantity pertaining to every person, into the principles of voluntarism and simplicity that accompanied his thinking throughout the restorative project. Within the EMI, human freedom is expressed by a clear separation of the authority of God's commandments from the lower authority of human ordinances. Moreover, Comenius understood authority as a ministerial thing, whose performance depended practically on the nature of the essential things.

An example is the question, "Will we now understand the work of converting people as a skill?" (I.258). Conversion means the complex event in which a person's relationship with God is born. It stands on God's mercy, which the person reciprocates with faith, love, and hope. Comenius asked about the cooperation of a free person with God, and asked whether it is possible to view conversion as a purely human step. For Comenius, a person is wholly active on every level belonging to them. Yet, conversion is not a purely human work for it stands on God's promises. Without them, human effort is in vain, so the result is God's gift, but it requires the whole person.

Faith, love, and hope are the means by which God acts, with the help of secondary causes: "One who wants the end but doesn't want to use the means, is tempting God. The means are the hand of God, extended to us to help us. We are all God's helpers" (II.283).

Faith, love, and hope testify of Comenius's understanding of the psychology of personality, in today's words, and how it is reflected in religion. Faith corresponds to human knowledge in the spiritual world. Here are the applications of the three books. Faith is the unifying principle in the spiritual world—it unites different churches into one (II.280). Love corresponds to intention, the will, the desire for the good. The principle *to want* takes the form of love in the spiritual world, as the focus of desire. It is an expression of authenticity (II.280). Hope corresponds to attainment, power, usage, joy. The principle of *power* attains what is good (II.280). The special conception of the virtues of faith, love, and hope was discussed above.

Faith, love, and hope mirror God's actions, which thus affect the whole person, in Comenius's understanding: "In harmony with God he submits his own mind to the mind of God by faith, his own will to God's will by love, his own strength and ability to divine hopes for help and protection. . . . The first and fundamental provision of this relationship is the constant cooperation of the human will with the grace of God" (II.278). The whole person is also affected by the ministerial things, because they correspond to human nature, "which must be taught in order to know something, encouraged in order to desire something, and steered and prodded in order to be capable of something." That is, the Word teaches what to believe, what to do, and in what to hope. Discipline helps us to want it. And the sacraments strengthen us to be able to do it. Comenius saw the harmony of people with God in how the ministers on the one hand correspond to human nature, and at the same time to the offices of Christ, as well as to three kinds of ministers in the church—teachers, pastors, and elders and lay officials (II.326).

The EMI as a whole regulates the life of the church, not the individual. It is by nature social. Faith, love, and hope also capture the social dimension: "People who will clearly confess and in a holy way cultivate this religion, will, by it, be God's village set on a hill. . . . Its radiance will spring from the brightness of faith, will be adorned with a life of holiness and sweetened by the pleasure of hope" (III.344).

Comenius's text was accompanied by the question of whether this anthropology also spoke to non-Christians. On the anthropological level Comenius understood faith, love, and hope as Christian, "Born as a result of this are 1. faith in Christ; 2. love for neighbors; 3. hope of eternal mercy" (II.272). Their birth requires the Mediator, Jesus (II.299–309). What can be said in defense of the claim that Comenius's anthropology of faith, love, and hope also includes people who do not profess Christianity? Two places in the *Consultation* point in this direction. In the interpretation of religion he stated, "If, then, these basic elements of religion, faith, love, and hope, correspond to natural elements or incomplete substances, the question arises as to what should correspond to the seven degrees of substances arising from the elements. . . . Perhaps it is possible to indicate parallels. (II.280) On the one hand, faith, love, and hope agree with creation, the natural elements; on the other hand, the result of the application of all stages of the natural elements is humanity in the image of Jesus Christ. In another place Comenius presupposed the possibility of the light of God's revelation even in those cases where it is definitely not about the Bible (II.448). The resulting picture is as follows: faith, love, and hope are in harmony and agree with the natural elements themselves, and have universal application. However, Comenius clearly saw their full realization in Christianity.

## 3.1 Features of Human Thinking

This is the place to mention the irreplaceable role of the EMI in the area of what we now call epistemology, noetics, or gnoseology—where and how is the light for understanding the truth carried? Particularly, in two aspects of Comenius's interpretation: the book of Revelation, and faith, love, and hope.[19]

In the *Panaugia*, the Bible is the third source of intellectual light: the book of nature, the book of the human mind, and the book of God's revelation. What is the connection between the three books of knowledge and the EMI? Comenius's teaching on the three books did not follow from the EMI. Nor is there any mention in the *Panaugia* that the Bible is a ministerial thing (chap. VII). The doctrine of the three books is more general than the EMI.

The relationship is reversed—in matters of religion, the two other books are also to be used in addition to the Bible: "The foundation of general religion is the essence of God, uncovered by God's revelation, accepted by faith, but also with the help of inner light and sense experience" (III.341). Also in matters of religion it is necessary to draw from all sources of knowledge! Comenius here boldly called for the light of sensory and

19. A third area could be the method of syncrisis, but this exceeds the possibilities of this chapter.

inner experience, which is necessary for a full understanding of things arising from revelation. In a detailed argument about the process of reforming religion, however, Comenius adhered to biblical arguments.

He took it for granted that the three books of knowledge are not in conflict.[20] The *Pampaedia* presents the idea of a universal commentary on the three books of knowledge, which the Bible integrates. The integration involves the faith, love, and hope triad, according to which examples of people are to be arranged—heroic faith, heroic obedience to love, heroic trust in hope against hope (III.58).

This raises the question of possible applications of the EMI or faith, love, and hope outside what Comenius wrote: in the *Panaugia* he gathered arguments for why the human mind needs light that comes from outside. He also demonstrated the need for external light in the *Pansophia's* interpretation of religion (II.276). This fully agrees with the need for salvation, saving, restoration which stand at the heart of the EMI. Since the days of the reformers Luther and Calvin, it has been standard to question the effects of sin on human knowledge. Comenius's position was deliberately central: the light of knowledge is available through God's promises, when one proceeds cautiously and systematically.

Another impetus is the fact that the book of Revelation (Bible) is defined in the area of religion as a "ministering thing" to the essential things. It plays an instrumental role. If Comenius had not called the three books of light "ministerial things," it would be possible to argue for their instrumental role: the purpose of pansophy (universal wisdom), pampaedia (universal education), and panglottia (universal language) is, ultimately, panorthosia (universal reform).

The three levels Comenius identified in the Bible: revelation, the commandments, and the promises (see above), also provide other inspiration. These levels of communication can also be looked for in the other two books: the first informs, the second encourages, the third motivates.

Faith, love, and hope are, for Comenius, true anthropological starting points. Therefore, they are applied not only in the spiritual world, but have parallels in others of Comenius's "worlds" (grades). He said it clearly in the *Pansophia* in the presentation of the world of the possible: "Parallelism of the principles TO KNOW, TO BE ABLE, TO WANT in all worlds. . . . In

20. In his interpretation of the book of Revelation he stated, among other things, "Fifth, among such remarks of God it is above all necessary to seek every such statement concerning things of which neither the world nor our mind can sufficiently inform us" (I.158). The following text did not further explain this statement.

the spiritual world faith, love, hope" (I.299).[21] In the interpretation of the spiritual world it is more often formulated as *to know—to act—to use.*

Faith, love, and hope correspond to the principles of unity, truth, and goodness (e.g., II.280). Comenius used these three principles repeatedly, not only in the details, but also in the essence of the project of restoration when formulating the *golden rule of return* (III.298).

In one place there is tension between the rational side and faith, love, and hope. He discussed what the renewed religion requires—a personal relationship with God: "And it is three exercises, exercises of faith, love, and hope. Faith: belief in everything revealed, even if it contradicts the senses, even if it seems absurd to reason, and thus enlightening one's mind with the light of faith. Love: doing everything assigned, even if it is very hard on the body and blood, and by it transforming the will within itself so as to coincide in everything with the will of God. Hope and patience: hoping for all that is promised, even if none of what is expected appears. . . . As soon as it reaches there, our faith has reached its peak, for a man so enlightened is impassioned and anchored deep in God, so that he may seem to have attained the depth of God's light, love, and affection" (III.343). This faith, love, and hope, despite reason, experience, and the senses, nevertheless in Comenius's mind, still lead to full, authentic humanity.

Faith, love, and hope are the *means* where Comenius distinguished idea itself, the means, and the method (e.g., II.279–82). Thus even the light of reason itself called the means: "For the whole pile of our confusion is nothing other than the gloomy chaos of darkness, and yet there is no other means of dispelling the darkness than light" (I.141). And as a brief theory for lifelong practice, the EMI is called a means (III.341–42).

The inseparability of faith, love, and hope means that Comenius's gnoseology must be perceived in close interaction with all three levels. Knowledge is not isolated from desire or attainment. Faith, love, and hope belong together just like to know, to want and to be able. Therefore the interpretation of Comenius's religion was derived from the Bible, but mainly from "the idea of God himself, whose every quality is the substance of faith, love, and hope" (III.342).

21. A careful reading shows that the three terms did not always have the same order! The quoted title stated in capital letters: to know—to be able—to want. On the next line of "world of the possible," the order is usually: to know—to want—to be able (see the same part of the *Pansophia* in chapter 1). As in the title, so also in the world of archetypes and the spiritual world it was necessary to switch the other two terms.

It is also possible to learn from Comenius in relation to knowledge as a whole. His "pull to the gate" of the general benefit of the restoration of all human affairs was so strong that systematic practice overshadowed the quality of theory, and faith, love, and hope could suddenly be an expression of practice in contrast to theory: "[General religion] will not be a curious searcher of the mysteries of God, but a fervent practitioner of God's revelation. As so by nothing other than the shortest theory, but on the other hand by the more extensive practice of faith, love, and hope and the most pleasing and enjoyable way of receiving blessings from God" (III.341).

## 3.2 Faith, Love, and Hope and Human Maturity

Comenius's vision of humanity in a lifelong process of maturation also draws on a number of specific details from faith, love, and hope within the EMI.

Not only in the *Pampaedia*, Comenius distinguished three groups of participants in education: beginners, advanced, and perfect. The renewal of the church should also distinguish these three levels (III.386–87). In the renewed church, the teaching starts appropriately with each of the three groups (III.393–95). Thus, as in the EMI, so also the division of people into three groups is an old practice of the Unity of Brethren, which Comenius took over.

This is reflected in the catechism, which is intended for beginners. The goal of catechesis is "to teach Christian novices to believe, do and hope for what Christ taught, commanded and promised, that is, to teach them faith, love, and hope" (II.377). It can be seen in the basic texts: The declaration of faith leads to faith. The Ten Commandments to love. The Lord's Prayer to hope. From the beginning it has been taught, "naturally with the distinction between what is essential, ministerial and incidental" (II.379). What is necessary to know? The basis of salvation—faith, love, and hope, its source is in them—in the word, in the power of the keys, and in the sacraments, how to use them prudently for common spiritual advancement—these are the incidental things (II.379–80).

The application of faith, love, and hope also occurs in schools: The school of early childhood (to age six) includes a class on morals and piety, about which Comenius said, "Above all, however, the foundations of the Christian religion, faith, love, and hope, must be taught to them in good time" (III.90). He planned six levels of textbooks for the school of childhood, the last of which was called Paradise: "the study of Scripture and their summary (with practice), faith, love, hope" (III.95). Faith, love, and hope would also be used in the school of adulthood—the second class has as its first rule: "Those who have left school should be as active in the temple and in the church as they used to be in school, . . . for the multiplying of faith, love, and hop" (III.132).

Faith, love, and hope have characterized the relationship with God from the very beginning and are the goal of the initial catechesis: "to teach Christian novices to believe, do and hope in what Christ taught, commanded, and promised, that is, to teach them faith, love, and hope" (II.377). But even Christian maturity (Comenius called it perfection) is defined with the help of faith, love, and hope. What is mature religion based on? The answer: "if without any kind of doubt or worry you are satisfied with what God has revealed to you, if without any procrastination you wholly give yourself to the fulfillment of his commandments and rejoice over his promises no differently than if you were already in heaven, you are ready to fight for faith and holiness" (II.362). It may be surprising that the beginning and the end of the journey is characterized by faith, love, and hope—but at different stages of development. Growth is not understood as evolution or rebirth into a new form, but as the maturation of the faith, love, and hope which beginners already have.[22]

Comenius described seven stages on the way to mature piety. The first two stages are self-knowledge and repentance. They are followed by faith, love, and hope. The next-to-last stage is constant struggle, then finally comes full surrender to God (II.336–64; cf. 335). Comenius thus aimed to achieve peace, tranquility, rest (also II.280–81). In dying, Comenius left love as the sum of our life on the activity side: "So at last comes the last act, surrender to God through faith and through hope in mercy" (III.142).

Faith, love, and hope form a substantial part of the stages of growth and could be more or less highly developed. He gave a detailed explanation of the stage of love as love for oneself, for one's neighbors, and for God. Nothing else in the picture of lifelong maturing resembles the unique role of faith, love, and hope: "the perfection of religion is founded on the steel chain of the three known, heroic virtues of faith, love, and hope" (II.362).

What are the measures that help growth? It naturally follows from the EMI that the ministerial things help. Among them, the Bible is at the

22. Biblical passages which, according to Comenius, include faith, love, and hope: 1 Kgs 1:30, John 1:12–17, 2 Pet 1:3–4 (II.339).

forefront: "By reading we acquire a literal knowledge of the Scriptures. Through prayer we gain the best interpreter of the Scriptures, the Holy Spirit. In meditation God's speech sweetens us, and the letter joins with the Spirit and the Spirit with the letter. By doing so, we are convinced of the truth of all God's words and in safety against the attacks of temptation we are strengthened to the fullness of faith, love, and hope" (II.275). But Comenius's view was broader. In the case of faith, he named these means for growth: on God's side, the word, the keys, and the sacraments, as well as the Holy Spirit and the cross; on the human side, attention, submissiveness, and true obedience (II.342). Thus, it is not only the ministerial things that he mentioned as the first means on God's side, but also the Holy Spirit, that is, the essential things. The cross, in turn, refers to difficult life circumstances. There has already been talk of the interaction of humans with God, and not only the example of conversion. Faith, love, and hope are active instruments for humans in their growth.

Incidental things play an enormously important role in terms of maturity—in them should be the greatest freedom (III.341).

## 4. Distinguishing the Essential, Ministerial, and Incidental as an Instrument for the Renewal of Religion

We are monitoring the relevance of Comenius's thinking for our time. His goal was the renewal of education, politics, and religion. In the area of religion, Comenius placed the renewal project directly on the EMI, which was, to him, an outline of its construction, the plan for the restoration, and in the end, even its instrument.[23]

Comenius envisioned the restoration of human affairs in three phases: removal of deficiencies, correction (restoration), securing what was restored.

### 4.1 Removal of Ailments

Comenius first mentioned the ills of religion in the introduction to the new religion, where he divided them into three types: deficiencies, excesses, and

23. The roots and stories of Comenius's efforts for reconciliation between the evangelical churches are told by Ferdinand Hrejsa ("Komenský irenik"). In the *Consultation*, however, they are only mentioned in one sentence.

monstrosities (III.345). Eventually he divided them differently: in things essential, ministerial, and incidental (III.387–88).

Ailments in essential things are: "whatever in any way removes or diminishes, confuses or obscures, distorts, or destroys faith, love, and hope" (III.387; also III.345), because it is important for them to be "most fully" at hand (III.342). From this follows, among other things: "For example, all subsystems must disappear from theology, because they are only partial and divisive" (II.485).

It is necessary to remove from the ministerial things polemical preaching, disputations in the church and in the schools, narrow-mindedness in holy things, violence over conscience, celibacy, inquisitions, so that the clergy do not get involved in worldly things, desire for property (some he only named, others he commented on; III.387–88). In short, still from the ministerial things: heresy, superstition, tyranny (II.327). It is worth quoting what distorted religion looks like: "Against the word, the sacraments, and the keys, Satan places 1. ignorance or heresy so he can reign in the dark; 2. superstition or worldliness, hypocrisy; 3. negligence in morals (relaxed discipline) or tyranny and schism" (III.345). For the ministerial area Comenius repeatedly specified the important principles of simplicity and moderation: "Religion unnecessarily suffers from whatever does not help faith, love, and hope. . . . Away with superstitious ceremonies!" (III.345).

Given the nature of incidental things, it's a general formulation: "Whatever can corrupt, desecrate, or even defile the church of God in any way, we must stop and remove, and consider making repairs, and attempt a real restoration" (III.389).

## 4.2 Restoration

Comenius put forward the principle: "Then life should be reformed sooner than teaching" (III.388).[24] But there are also other statements: "So that it goes in order, first faith to remove ignorance, then love to ignite obedience, and finally hope" (III.342). "The beginning must inevitably happen from the essential things," by implanting faith, love, and hope" (III.389). Is this a contradiction? It doesn't have to be: God's mercy and the human response to it, from faith through the acts of love to the courage of hope, are essential—and that isn't any theory, but rather life in faith, love, and

24. We also encounter this principle in Comenius's work *Obnova církve: Haggaeus redivivus* (Komenský, *Obnova*, ch. 13).

hope, and it is what needs to be restored first. So the restoration begins from the essential things, that is, from life. He also stated the reasons: 1. it should start with the easier; 2. from reconciliation with God; 3. from the tree of knowledge of good and evil it is necessary to return to the tree of life; 4. in his judgment, Christ does not ask so much for doctrine as for deeds (III.388–89).

Regarding the ministerial things: "As for the truth and honesty of general religion: 1. it must not contain innumerable dogmas in the area of faith, acts and hope, because it is not through many and subtle problems that God calls us to himself; 2. it must be simple in rituals, both for ease and for the nature of religion; 3. it must keep a powerful order of discipline that is voluntary (interiorized by members)" (III.342). He proceeded freely along the ministerial things: he typically summarized Bible doctrines as faith, love, and hope; instead of the sacraments, he spoke about ceremonies which, however, are always tied to the sacraments; finally he named discipline. In the renewal of religious things, ministerial things should be available "as simply as possible" (III.342). On the one hand, this agrees with Comenius's continual emphasis on the simplicity of true things. But in this specific case, it is that in religion, essential things are easily obstructed by the details and minutia of the ministerial things—to the serious detriment of all. Simplicity, then, means deliberately unpretentious, undemonstrative. It can be achieved only if it is persistently kept under focused supervision.

Comenius paid close attention to the interpretation of the Bible. It is first about understanding (beginning with study and then going on to doing), secondly it is about using Scripture: "Regarding the skilled and beneficial use of the Scriptures thus understood, it is necessary to notice what in the passage is essential, what is auxiliary, and what is supplementary" (II.275). The interpretation of Scripture is thus fundamentally linked to the EMI: "What is essential in divine Scripture is that which is revealed or hidden, commanded or forbidden, promised or threatened. It is to cultivate faith, love, and hope in us" (II.275). Proper interpretation of the Bible is the main tool for the keeping the church in the truth, along with the vigilance of the leaders (II.374).

He was against polemical preaching: As a boxer, if he boxes with himself cannot properly show his students the way to hit, so it is with a preacher who demonstrates a conflict of opinion from the pulpit (III.388). He described in detail the restored state of affairs: preaching and teaching should be rather encyclopedic, and distinguish the methods appropriate for beginners, advanced, and mature (III.390–97).

Restoration of incidental things consists in the use of appropriate designations, protection against abuse of rituals, appropriate church administration, and the celebration of holidays (III.398). So what does fullness mean for incidental things? If for essential things it means the richest possible response to faith, love, and hope, then in secondary matters it is voluntarism (III.342). Comenius's voluntarism was not individualistic, it was the voluntary acceptance of common practices in ceremonial matters in a given local church. One should voluntarily submit to such church order in the awareness that it is a secondary matter, a human provision whose goal is to give space for essential things. Church order was always considered to be an incidental thing in the Unity of Brethren.

Comenius resolved disputes individually, without classifying them into individual phases of restoration. Here they concern essential things, there ministerial, and other times incidental.[25] Comenius presented ten fundamentals of reconciliation which represented a method of careful, rationalistic consideration. The method is to affirm (or deny) only what is obviously true (or false), not forcing the rest on others. In unclear cases, either choose according to what is less harmful, allow both, or decide at the level of practice. And record undecided things (III.308–9). This method agrees with the EMI in that it is a matter of distinguishing the essential from the incidental, and in doing that, to uphold the authority of the incontestable as well as the freedom of personal conviction in many sub-questions.

In the area of resolution of disputes, in addition to the ten fundamentals of reconciliation he also set three paths: universality, simplicity, voluntariness (III.309–10). He gave examples mostly from the area of religion. The EMI was applied here in surmounting contradictions with a deeper unity, in distinguishing between God's and humanity's regulations, in prioritizing the more essential questions "on which hinge wisdom and salvation" (III.310).

The principle of universality led to the recommendation of a middle path. This was previously applied to the ministerial things: "So we must intervene and maintain a middle path everywhere 1. Between neglect and overuse of Scripture; 2. Between impiety and superstitiousness; 3. Between

25. Comenius rated dispute resolution as a third way to remove problems in relationships with people, after erasing the past and mutual tolerance (III.301–9). Also, with regard to the principle of starting with the renewal of life, it is appropriate to place the resolution of disputes in the second phase.

neglecting discipline and harmful strictness" (II.345). The middle way connects partial truths which seem to contradict some things. Comenius made the inner tension in the Bible resonate when he compared the relationship with God to a set of scales—on the one hand, fear and worry (the law), on the other side joy and exultation (the gospel) in that "the center or pointer that joins the two together . . . , is an effective faith in which man, with one eye looks at God and with hope looks at his mercy, and with the other eye looks at himself and mirrors his heart" (II.365). He thus achieved the point that faith, love, and hope cannot be separated from one another. The inseparability of faith, love, and hope helped him to describe facts which appeared to be in rational conflict.

He illustrated, practically, the overcoming of disputes in controversial issues. From the perspective of the EMI, the most interesting example was the dispute over justification, whether it is by faith or by works. After a detailed presentation of the problem, he aimed for the path of universality when he gave space for even contradictory statements: "Only to be able to skillfully connect every testimony of eternal truth and we will indeed have the whole, full and firm truth and an absolute, full and clear understanding of the article on justification." He held faith and works as "from our side two conditions, equally necessary, standing as a whole in relation to the whole result" (III.311–12). Elsewhere he said, similarly, "Faith alone without knowledge and without love does not save, nor works without faith, all these must be present at the same time (II.338).

Against the background of the EMI, we can understand Comenius's approach to the resolving of disputes over rituals "by which some want to adorn the worship of God, others do not want to burden it" (III.315). Both sides rightly refer to the example of Christ, who sometimes used ceremony, other times did not. An important reason for rituals is their ability to move the human senses. Their criteria is the relationship to essential things—to express the essentials, but not to shift their meaning. He hoped for an agreement that "there should be fewer, rather than more" (III.315).

At the same time, Comenius expected a possible agreement of all Christians on the essential things: "I surely hope that we will be brothers if we decide not to seek from God anything other than God's faith, combined with love and crowned with hope. After all, we all have the same source from which these forces must emerge!" (III.308).

The role of the EMI in the restoration can thus be described as key. The whole process revolves around it, without an understanding of the EMI

Comenius's idea of the renewal of the church would not be understandable, let alone feasible.

It is the part of the EMI to distinguish between God's provision (essential and ministerial things) and human (incidental things). This is important for maintaining voluntarism, and it is about protection against excessiveness. This feature of the EMI becomes a direct instrument for resolving disputes over incidental things.

The EMI defines the proper use of authority, preferably "without coercive power, that is, without the discipline of the binding key, if possible. But if it is not possible, then by means of it" (III.361). Care must be taken that abuse of the keys doesn't increase. "Violence perpetrated against truth and conscience instead of discipline is an execution, for example, excommunication, the Spanish Inquisition, aural confession" (II.345).

"We ask that general religion be full, orderly, truthful" (III.343). Fullness and truthfulness depend on essential things. In orderliness, then, is an appropriate solution to incidental things (III.343 and 386–87). In essential things there should be fullness, in ministerial things simplicity, in incidental things voluntarism (III.342). In summary, at this stage the EMI serves restoration directly: it helps to determine what needs to be addressed; it gives priority to essential things. The restoration "will be full if, according to the norms of God's word, the whole of religion is reformed (things essential, ministerial, and incidental, etc.)" (III.386).

The role of people, the ministers of the church, is worth giving attention to summarizing (see ministerial things above). They serve the essential things. Their hierarchy corresponds to the offices of Christ. Many of the ailments are their ailments. Therefore, within the restoration phase, Comenius carefully described the preacher's duties (III.396–99).

## 4.3 Strengthening the Restoration

Essential things are already established, also ministerial things have been restored. In this phase Comenius named only incidental things: The hierarchy of pastors is part of church order, which is an incidental thing. Exercises in worship services have to do with ministerial things, but here they are on the incidental side of worship. He also names synods. Discipline again concerns ministerial things, however Comenius was dealing with the practical carrying out of discipline, which belongs to incidental things. Finally, he named income and church property (III.403–5).

In his corrective efforts, Comenius looked for irreplaceable roles of key people, bodies of light. They determine their extraordinary competencies primarily in the area entrusted to them. Thus the consistory of the world is to, among other things, pay attention to the books on piety and, in addition to the text of the Scriptures and commentaries on all three books, also draw up "the most complete index of incidental things given in the Holy Scripture, whose favors could be promptly and abundantly found in whatever concerns any kind of faith, piety, and hope." They also determine competencies towards the other two bodies of light (III.362). In Comenius's world the authorities—secular and ecclesiastical—have the responsibility of the reparation of the church. It is a distinct, aristocratic feature of his thinking. Josef Smolík said that Comenius overcame the feudal organization of a society divided into church and state by formulating three areas of repair. He added, "Comenius's conception of society is pluralistic and harmonious."[26] The democratic element was in inviting all people to the project of restoration.

## 5. How Comenius's Thinking Can Help us Today

Research has shown that the doctrine of things essential, ministerial, and incidental, as Comenius learned it in the Unity of Brethren, is one of the fundamental outlines of the spiritual world. He expressed the relationship with God itself in the words of the EMI. He also described the church using the EMI. Finally, Comenius portrayed his vision for the renewal of the church with the help of that doctrine. At the end of his *Kšaftu umírající matky Jednoty Bratrské* [Testament to the Dying Mother, Unity of Brethren], Comenius referred this teaching to all the surrounding churches: "Oh, that God would give you an image of the foundations of the things essential, ministerial, and incidental, as he has given it to me."[27]

This section traces the relevance of Comenius's work. First there are three observations in which Comenius's initiatives do not work. Comenius showed that restoration would progress gradually in three phases: removal of deficiencies, restoration, and maintenance. However, it seems more likely that all three phases would actually blend together. The *Consultation* itself also proceeded on many levels without the convening of the general assembly (that the book called for).

26. Smolík, "Komenského přínos," 55.

27. Komenský, *Kšaft*, 18.

Comenius did not propose a change of leadership positions. Of course, his proposals did show "reform within existing personnel," as one might expect in the seventeenth century.

The development of the ecumenical movement during the twentieth century proved Comenius to be right in some things, but on one level decidedly not—the role of the consistory: "Order in religion will be preserved if we make sure that everyone performs the ceremonies in the same way. The heart of Christ's universal kingdom will be the establishment of such an order in all things, as well as in persons of all partial churches, that if you see one you have seen them all, and that you may see Christ ruling in it, and in your faith begin eternal life" (III.343).

The following paragraphs offer a possible application of Comenius's thought today. His specific conception of the virtues fits today in the fact that faith, love, and hope are not normally part of education, nor are the civic virtues, but they are left to religious education.[28]

The EMI revolves around the salvation of humanity, which is associated with many practical confusions, deficiencies and problems in society. Comenius tried to suggest concrete ways for the reparation of individual problems from the sources of Christian faith. Such attempts could be attractive also today if they are prepared with Comenius's thoroughness.

The work of Comenius teaches us, by its scope, to watch for restoration in the "full breadth" of life. In our efforts to restore human affairs, let us require this breadth of focus from our representatives in the government, church leaders, and in education.

As Christianity has passed through the fire of the Enlightenment, and secularization in the twentieth century, the EMI still meets its needs. The role of rituals and other incidental things, the definition of the relationship between church and state, as well as the role of the Scriptures and the sacraments, have been shown to be particularly supportive. This cannot be equally said of all forms of Christianity in Comenius's time.

The mainstay is the inclusion of the Holy Scriptures in the category of ministerial things. This is an essential barrier against unhealthy fundamentalism. That is to say, the Holy Scriptures are not an end in and of themselves, but they serve a higher goal, in this case a personal relationship with God, who in love reaches out to people, and to whom people respond with faith, love, and hope. The role of the Holy Scriptures defined in this

28. When Jan Hábl described Comenius's "method of morals" on the basis of his didactic writings, faith, love, and hope were not a part of it (Hábl, *I když*, 135–47).

way could also be raised in other religions, just as the goal of a democratic society is not merely to abide by the constitution, but to achieve a democratic society by its constitution.

Scripture as a ministerial thing and at the same time one of the three books of light, shows the role of knowledge (or, the area of education) in the whole of social life—knowledge is in the service of holistic practice, for whose goals it is an advantage. It cannot be said that this approach is in conflict with the spirit of our age.

On the level of noetics, faith, love, and hope correspond to the light of truth, which has three forms: "declaration, commandment, promise." If we extend these three levels to the knowledge of nature and the human mind, we reach education, which takes into consideration information, formation, and motivation. Of course, we won't find this in the *Consultation*.

Comenius's conception of religion was based on a specific anthropology. For Comenius, Christianity has the feature that it addresses and affects the whole person. God's action has three forms, revelation, commandment, and promise, which appeal to people on the three levels of rationality, will, and behavior, through which emerge the triple bond between God and humanity—faith, love, and hope.

As a summary of religiousness, faith, love, and hope build on more general anthropological starting points: "Religion [deals] with God and conscience to rouse and preserve people in faith, love, and hope" (III.346). As a result it is very complex and offers great potential. Whatever in our lives concerns the free will of humanity or the chaos caused by that will; the spirit that inspires in people the supreme good that illuminates the inner person so it acquires a truly human form; faith, love, and hope—these are the issues that did not die with the entrance of secularism.

The church needs to be reformed, but the differentiation of the EMI does not need to change for this work. It needs to be emphasized that Comenius was not looking for a different structure for the renewed religion than that which he already knew from his own church. Říčan rightly said, "Although in [the *Consultation*] he almost never mentioned the Unity of Brethren, it is clear that he had it in mind as a model of the future, restored, universal church, yes, that to a great extent, his thoughts on the restoration of human society came from the Brethren assumptions."[29] He considered the differentiations of the EMI to be so fundamental that they did not need

29. Říčan, "K bratrským," 91.

to be reformed in order to fulfill their fundamental role in the restored state of affairs.

In religious renewal, Comenius espoused the principle of starting from life, and only then moving on to theoretical questions. Renewal was to begin with erasing the past, with mutual tolerance, and the fruition of faith, love, and hope. This would bring about a transformation of the whole situation, mutual relationships, and in the end, also a change in thinking. Constructive thoughts were not conceivable in the tense situation, but when reconciliation would come and when faith, love, and hope were applied, conciliatory thinking would begin to gain space and a breeding ground. That was one of the very inspiring moments of Comenius's approach.

Religious disputes are still today a cause of wars and tensions, which are difficult to resolve in a conciliatory way. Christianity has come a long way since the Thirty Years' War, and the twentieth century could be called an ecumenical movement. The so-called ecumenical bottom, or Hans Küng's project of world ethos, confirms Comenius's principle that renewal begins with life (not dogma). Some details of the EMI will probably be limited to ecumenical conversations within Christianity, but others could prove useful in interfaith dialogue.

To the extent that the agnosticism of many citizens of the Czech Republic can be considered a specific approach to the solution of religious issues, it is also possible to apply Comenius's approach to the correction and resolution of disputes.

The EMI has no direct equivalent in the areas of politics or education. Nevertheless, in those areas could be perhaps the most important application of the EMI in the efforts for reform: how important it is to not confuse the rectification of essential things with that of ministerial or incidental things. In essential matters it's about the greatest fullness, while in ministerial issues it's about simplicity and unpretentiousness. And with incidental things it's about freedom. Which issues, for example in the area of education, require the greatest possible fullness, the most developed form? Perhaps creativity, the quality of the information acquired, or the character of the people involved? And which, in contrast, require simplicity? Maybe school rules or pedagogical documentation? And on what issues is it important to preserve freedom and supervise it rigorously? Perhaps methods of teaching and the use of aids? Comenius carefully made the distinctions, then warned against mixing them up.

## Bibliography


Bartoš, František Michálek. *O podstatu křesťanství a dědictví Jednoty bratrské* [On the Essence of Christianity and the Legacy of the Unity of Brethren]. Praha: Kalich, 1948.

Hábl, Jan. *I když se nikdo nedívá: fundamentální otázky etického vychovatelství* [Even When No One Is Looking]. Červený Kostelec: Pavel Mervart, 2015.

Hrejsa, Ferdinand. "Komenský irenik" [Comenius the Irenic]. In *Jan Amos Komenský: soubor statí o životě a díle učitele národů*, by Jiří Václav Klíma, 66–75. Praha: Peroutka, 1947.

Komenský, Jan Amos. *Kšaft umírající matky Jednoty Bratrské* [Testament to the Dying Mother, Unity of Brethren]. Brno: Českobratrské knihkupectví, 1945.

———. *Obnova církve: Haggaeus redivivus* [Church Renewal: Haggaeus Redivivus]. Praha: Kalich, 1952.

———. *Obecná porada o nápravě věcí lidských* [General Consultation on the Restoration of Human Affairs]. Vols. I–III. Praha: Svoboda, 1992.

Molnár, Amedeo. *Bratr Lukáš: bohoslovec Jednoty* [Brother Lukáš: Theologian of the Unity]. Praha: Husova československá evangelická fakulta bohoslovecká, 1948.

*Řád církevní Jednoty bratří českých* [Church Order in the Czech Unity of Brethren]. Praha: Comenium, 1897.

Říčan, Rudolf. "K bratrským motivům a vzorům ve Všeobecné poradě" [On Brethren Motifs and Patterns in the *Universal Consultation*] In *Sedm statí o Komenském: Dva dopisy J. A. Komenského*, edited by Amedeo Molnár, 89–102. Praha: Kalich, ústřední církevní nakladatelství, 1971.

Smetana, Jan K. *Katechismus bratrský: podle vydání z roku 1615* [Catechism of the Brethren: According to the 1615 Edition]. Vilémov: Čepka, 1934.

Smolík, Josef. "Komenského přínos k ekumenismu" [Comenius's Contribution to Ecumenism]. In *Sedm statí o Komenském: Dva dopisy J. A. Komenského*, edited by Amedeo Molnár, 45–62. Praha: Kalich, ústřední církevní nakladatelství, 1971.

Valeš, Jan. "Na čem záleží? aneb Věci podstatné, služebné a případné podle staré Jednoty" [What Does It Depend On? Or, Things Essential, Ministerial, and Incidental According to the Old Unity]. *Brána* 12 (2015) 12–19.

# Conclusion

## *A Reparation of Irreparable Things?*

JAN HÁBL

### Lost and Found *Consultation*

THE MATURING OF COMENIUS'S plans for the restoration of all things was closely linked—among other things—to the political circumstances of his time. From the Battle of White Mountain, or more precisely, the Prague defenestration, Europe had been torn by the horrors of the Thirty Years' War. Comenius was in exile from 1628 on and had been working hard on books to help restore his decimated homeland until—hopefully soon—all the exiles could return. In 1631–32 the Swedish and Saxon armies were advancing, and temporarily had the upper hand against the Habsburg troops; for a short time, they even held Prague. Comenius was working frantically on the *Didactics* and a text entitled "A Brief Suggestion for the Renewal of Schools in the Czech Kingdom." He wrote everything in Czech. However, in 1632 the advance of the anti-Habsburg armies was halted and the Swedish King Gustav Adolf, on whom the exiles had laid their hopes, was killed. In addition, the Czech "Winter King," Frederick V, of whom some Protestants also had some expectations, died that same year. As the hopes of the exiles died one by one, "Comenius buried himself with even greater intensity in his work on the reform of the whole world," commented Pavel Floss. "His interest in didactics and other sciences was gradually and increasingly consciously part of the larger concept of restoration, which, however, gained clearer contours only in the late 1940s."[1] In agreement with Floss's observation, Jan Kumpera added that during this period "Comenius began writing mostly in Latin, as he was clearly aware that the restoration of his country could not be achieved without general and universal reform."[2] From Comenius's correspondence we know that sometime between October 28, 1644, and April 18, 1645, he received a major incentive for the formation of the *Consultation*. In a letter to his friends G. Hotton and L. de Geer, he wrote that he "corrected himself and improved in a thousand ways."[3] Apparently his ideas of wholeness, *pansophia*, harmony, etc. came together, and so he began his great work. His work was interrupted many times because of the many duties and obligations he had with his hosts (in Sweden and Hungary), as well as with his fellow believers in the Unity of Brethren. Nevertheless, whenever he had a chance to relax from his work of creating textbooks, which he called "a drudgery of spirit," he worked hard on the *Consultation*.

In 1655 the new Swedish King, Charles X. Gustav, successfully launched a campaign against Catholic Poland. All of the Protestant aristocracy, including Bohuslav Leszcynski, the lord of Leszno, welcomed him as their new king. However, the Polish Catholic majority considered that a betrayal and it proved fatal both for Leszno and for Comenius. When Denmark, the traditional enemy of Sweden, joined the conflict King Charles suffered a series of defeats and had to withdraw from Poland. Leszno ceased to be protected by the Swedes and retaliation by the Catholic Poles was inevitable. On April 29, 1656, the Polish troops invaded Leszno and burned the town. Comenius and his family barely survived and lost all their property, and even worse, lost his library, including the *Consultation*, which Comenius had considered more or less ready for publication. By that time he had already worked on it for 12 years, and on other writings more than 30 years.[4] "Alas, everything is lost . . . , that was ready for publication," Comenius wrote in despair in a letter to J. Rültz on June 24, 1656.

It is both amazing and admirable that Comenius did not fall into ruin. He reconciled himself to the loss, and by September of that same year he wrote in a letter to his friends that he was going to work to "pick up the

1. Floss, *Nástin života*, 13.

2. Kumpera, "Comenius and England," 93.

3. Chlup, "Zhodnocení Komenského myšlenky," 11.

4. Especially painful was the loss of the *Treasure of the Czech Language* and *The Theater of All Things*, on which he had worked since his student years.

shards of his broken containers and somehow stick them together again." He continued elsewhere, "I will finish without delay, and give to the world what sparks I may still have left."[5] After moving to Amsterdam, Comenius worked intensively on not only the *Consultation*, but also on other texts. In the last year of his life, he implored his son Daniel and close assistant Christian Nigrin, to finish the work according to his notes, and publish it. He died on November 15, 1670. It turns out that it was not possible to complete the work without its author. Over time the *Consultation* was lost.

In 1934 (on Christmas Eve), the manuscript of the *Consultation* was found by the Slavist Dimitrij Čiževskij in the archives of the Orphanage in Halle—after a long period of focused and systematic research.[6] The manuscript came under the care of Comeniologists and was published for the first time in 1966, in Latin, in Prague. The Czech translation came into readers' hands in 1992.

## Questions about "Human Affairs"—Temporal and Timeless

Comenius's *General Consultation on the Restoration of Human Affairs* is one of the most important works in his output. It is a beautiful work, deep and extensive. The original manuscript contained some two thousand pages of text; the translation into Czech was divided into three volumes, each having about five hundred pages. It is a magnificent project, an act of unique thought, a literary treasure, and a source of Czech spiritual heritage. It would be a shame to let it go to waste and not draw on its riches. After all, in it Comenius addressed the deepest human issues—and we are still trying to deal with them today.

From the time of Comenius, humanity has made considerable progress. Primarily technological. Humanity is still, however, a precious commodity. The more intensively we are aware of its deficiencies, the more precious it is. From the time of the Enlightenment, Western civilization believed that humanity would move forward along with rational knowledge and science. However, it has proven to be more complicated. Knowledge in and of itself does not guarantee humaneness. Comenius's appeal for a consultation on the restoration of human affairs is still on the table. Everyone who cares about the state of humanity is invited to the consultative table.

5. Chlup, "Zhodnocení Komenského myšlenky," 13.
6. For more details see Patočka, "Jan Amos Komenský," 7–63.

The purpose of this monograph was a hermeneutic questioning—how to read a text that was written more than 350 years ago, productively and with understanding. As has already been said, Comenius's *Consultation* is an extensive yet unfinished work. Comenius worked on it for more than thirty years, reworking and editing the text many times, and he had to reconstruct some parts after he lost them in the Leszno fire. It is obvious that over the years he developed his thinking and gained new stimuli, ideas, and inspiration. At the same time, he often repeated many of his thoughts. If we look for the "essential," the principal, or the realistic from Comenius's *Consultation*, the fundamental question for the editor is not only *what* to look for, but first and foremost, *how*? According to what key? Are we to look for what is foundational for Comenius, or for us? Less than a hundred years ago F. X. Šalda felt that Comenius was "a great man who was strangely ahead of his time, yet also behind it."[7] Later, Marxist interpreters like Jiří Tichý, Robert Alt, Jiřina Popelová, and many others who saw Comenius as a revolutionary, a people's reformer, or a skilled didactic, agreed. Jan Patočka commented on this with the shrewd insight that Comenius scholars of every historical period have had the tendency to read into Comenius "their own perspective," and that it was usually a sophisticated strategy of self-admiration.[8] We wanted to avoid that, so we chose a universal interpretive key of the time: We ask, what are human affairs? Not from "our" perspective, or Comenius's, but in general? What are the key issues that determine or move human society? What are the main drivers of humanity as a whole?

A reader seeking answers to these questions can read a 350-year-old treatise on humanity in two ways. As a researcher, from a distance—as a documentary about the history of thought. This approach is desirable and entirely appropriate. We are grateful for all the comeniologists for their expertise (philological, philosophical, pedagogical, etc.), thanks to which we can hold the work in our hands. But equally legitimate is a reading "without distance," that is, "engaged," or "immersed" in the intentions with which Comenius wrote the text. It is about me, about humanity, about my future and the future of my neighbors with whom I share the one "world stage." Such a reading raises the question: What does a truly good or functional community of people look like? Or, What kind of society has a future? What

7. Šalda, "O literárním baroku," 302.

8. Patočka, *O významu všeobecné porady*, 271–72.

form of humanity is viable and livable? And above all, how do I participate in such a society?

## The Essence of the *Consultation*

Comenius observed that our humanity is contradictory. We have excellent potential, we know a lot, we know how to do a lot, we can do a lot, our will to act is great. So why are our unique human abilities the greatest threat to humanity? Why are we able to abuse everything we have? We are the only beings that have the potential for self-destruction. It is, therefore, of paramount importance that we look for a way to realize our potential, humanely. In his *Consultation*, Comenius carefully considered the causes of all human disorders and called humanity to a discussion on how to remedy them. All of his restorative efforts are based on the premise that "humanity is not quite alright, but it is not completely lost." There is a solution, there is hope.

It is necessary to understand that in Comenius's time Europe found itself on the verge of destruction as a result of war, and religious and political rampages (how many times already?) People seek their own well-being without regard to that of the whole of society. But the well-being of any individual is not possible without the well-being of the whole. Therefore, Comenius invited all people, especially the "Lights of Europe," that is, those who had the power to control human affairs—the rulers and scholars, to the discussion. An emphasis on the entirety, or universality of the *Consultation*, is evident from the prefix *pan-*, which he attached to the names of all his restorative efforts. Comenius divided the *Consultation* into seven parts:

1. *Panegersia* (Universal Awakening): If any remedy is to come, people have to wake up and realize that they have a real, global problem. We are all busy with our own affairs, and we miss the complete picture. Individuals cannot do well if society as a whole is not doing well. That is why Comenius is calling us to wake up and become sensitive to our common problems. First, he explains what "human affairs" are—how people relate to (a) the things around them, (b) themselves, or other people, and (c) God. In short: education, politics, and religion. In this section, Comenius illustrated the violation of these things in the history of humankind and outlined the possibilities for their reparation.

2. *Panaugia* (Universal Enlightenment): Here Comenius started playing with the symbol of light as an instrument for overcoming human darkness and confusion. The human mind needs "light" to make clear what needs to be known, wanted and done to correct, or even save, human affairs. People have been given three sources of light or "lamps": the world, humanity, and the Bible. The Macrocosm, the Microcosm, and the Word. Or we can say (a) the natural world bearing traces of the creative wisdom, (b) the human spirit as the bearer of God's image, and (c) the Scriptures, explaining God's will for human beings. Comenius sometimes called these "the three books" from which one can read everything one needs to know for a good life.
3. *Pansofia* (Universal Wisdom): It is a special encyclopedia of all human knowledge and effort. It has eight parts, which Comenius called stages, or also worlds or layers. Seven worlds are conceived as a record of the historical drama of our cosmos—from the creation of a perfect world through its corruption, the fall of humanity into evil, to the material world, the natural world and from there again ascending to a new spiritual perfection. The eighth, the "World of the Possible" is both the foundation and the pinnacle of all worlds—the ideal that must be pursued. Understanding the world and its history as a harmonious whole, which has a saving purpose, direction and goal, is the foundation of that universal wisdom. It is not about knowing everything, but about knowing everything that it is needed for a good life, or rather, what needs to be remedied. *Pansofia* is the most extensive part of the *Consultation*, taking more space than all the other parts combined.
4. *Pampaedia* (Education in everything): Or, universal education. This plays a key role in the whole of the *Consultation* because the purpose of education is the transmission of the above-mentioned universal wisdom. It is an original, holistic philosophy of education, that is, a philosophy of the lifelong formation of each person. The goal of that formation is to bring all people to a mastery of pansophic knowledge naturally, i.e., without violence or coercion, because violence is contrary to the essence of the Creator and creation. Comenius expressed his educational theory with the principle of *omnes, omnia, omnio*—everything, to everyone, in every way. It is the answer to the three fundamental pedagogical questions: who to teach, what, and how? Teach every person, everything needed for a good life, using all possible appropriate means.

5. *Panglottia* (Universal Speech): As the aim of the consultative work is a society-wide remedy, Comenius proposed, very pragmatically, that the nations unite in one language that would be intelligible to all. He did not intend for it to replace native languages, but recommended that the native languages be refined in such a way as to be able to express all the wisdom available to humankind. In addition, he recommended that everyone learn the universal language, which could be used to communicate with others.
6. *Panorthosia* (Universal Reform of All Things): In this section Comenius presented a concrete procedure for reparation. It begins with oneself, with an individual, and the correction must spread through families, schools, churches, and countries, to the whole of society. The timeless insight of Comenius was the institutional anchoring of his restorative effort: if restoration is to take place, it necessitates the cooperation of key administrative and scientific (educational) institutions, local, national, and international. The goal was to establish understanding and peace among individuals and nations.
7. *Pannuthesia* (Universal Admonition): As the first book of the *Consultation* looked to the past for the causes of the problems of humanity, this last book looks to the future—to the future possibilities of humanity. The book is unfinished, in fact it is only notes. But even so one can feel the intensity and urgency with which Comenius appealed to all people without exception, to participate in the restorative effort.

Comenius demonstrated the key role of education in the way he structured the content of the work—the *Pampaedia* is at the center of a triad that opens and closes with a three-part introduction and a three-part conclusion. Comenius's schematic layout looks as follows:[9]

9. See Komenský, *Obecná porada*, 69.

FIGURE 1

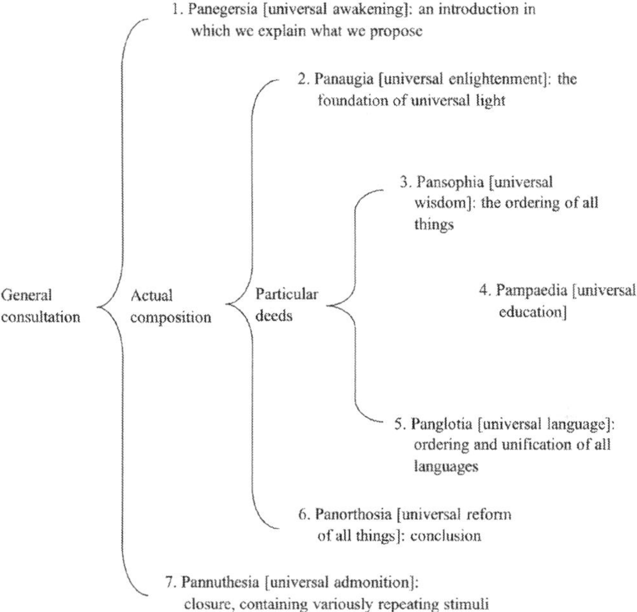


Why, exactly, education is the center of the restoration of human affairs is obvious. "Such will be the next era, as its next citizens are educated," said Comenius. Schools as a whole should serve as "workshops of humanity" where not only "true knowledge," but also character (moral and spiritual) will be cultivated. Sometimes Comenius could sound as if the restoration lay only in knowledge, but it is necessary to read the "whole" Comenius. It is true that he often spoke of the need for the schools to lead to "true" or "honest" knowledge, because much of human confusion comes from mistakes or simple ignorance (he himself was wrong in many ways). At the same time, however, he was aware that the violation of humanity is not just about reason. It is necessary to correctly know, want, and be able (*scire, velle, posse*), as he often repeated. Or to know the good, to want the good, and to do the good, and do so "even when no one is looking." In contemporary pedagogical language, the restoration of human affairs must be holistic and include cognitive, moral, and spiritual components in an individual and social context.

The systematicity and coherence with which Comenius dealt with educational topics (not only in the *Consultation*) led some interpreters to the conclusion that Comenius was the founder of modern pedagogy. It's only possible to agree with this to a certain extent. Although Comenius brilliantly foreknew all the essential topics that pedagogy deals with today (methods, content, forms, goals, organization of the educational system, etc.), his ideological world was subject to different principles than ours. Rather than science in the modern sense of the word, Comenius's pedagogy was an art: *ars*,[10] as he himself called it. It is a specific and subtle skill to deal with things in accordance with their given nature, to not distort it, not do violence to it, not misuse it (*abusus*). For example, speech is to be used to communicate truth, not to deceive one's neighbor. Or, fire is to be used to warm a house, not for war; singing to worship God, not as a pagan ritual, etc. This motif has far-reaching implications for the educational treatment of humanity. It is a fundamental, ontological assumption—namely, that being has order, and that this order is essentially harmonious. The "man-made" (i.e., skillful) work of the teacher consists in introducing humanity (children) to this order. Of course, this cannot and must not be done in a violent way, despite the fact that humans suffer from the self-serving tendency to "behave annoyingly outside the order of being," that is, to be brats. From this came Comenius's motto: *Omnia sponte fluant, absit violentia rebus.*[11]

## What about That after 350 Years?

So, back to the key questions of this book: Is it a utopia? Like Moore's, Campanella's, or Bacon's? Just daydreaming? What can we take from it? Theologizing metaphysics? Or mosaic analogies? Numerical speculations? (Comenius loved triads.) Quasi-sensualistic a priori-ism? Pedagogical alchemy? Or perhaps, chiliastic passion? Did Comenius make the old and fundamental mistake that if people have the correct knowledge, they will also act correctly?

Yes, it was Comenius's big dream of a much longed-for world that would be fit to live in, harmonious, in current speech, sustainable. In many ways it is definitely naïve, even fantastic, as Patočka said, and yet it has a place in our

10. Not in the aesthetic sense of the word.

11. "Let everything flow naturally and without violence." This motto was written on the first page of Comenius's work *Opera Didactica Omnia*. See also Comenius, *Didaktika analytická*, 42. For more details on Comenius's philosophy of education see, for example, Palouš, *Komenského Boží Svět*, or Hábl, *Aby člověk neupadal*.

world, he added in one of his Comeniological studies.[12] To illustrate, there are several proposals that, from today's perspective, seem not only unworkable, but also undesirable. In the *Panorthosia*, for example, Comenius called for the elimination of all opportunities in the nation to encounter sensual stories and secular literature, as well as the removal of pubs, bars, dives, and drinking houses. He went on to specify "let the loan sharks, speculators and those like them, bloodsuckers, and other parasites be removed. With that, fewer should have to suffer gamblers, fortune tellers, jugglers, comedians, tightrope walkers and other charlatans and useless squanderers of money." That monopolies and oligopolies should be removed is economically prudent and rational, but Comenius did not say how. Completely seriously, Comenius also recommended that all people "return to original simplicity in everything, especially in food, dress, titles, etc." Even though we try to understand Comenius's social solidarity and his love for simplicity and order that he probably acquired in the Unity of Brethren, still, some of his proposals border on a totalitarian organizing of society. Comenius would like to have seen the government control births, married life, order in families—he really talked about "supervisors over marriages"—uniforms for different age groups, and official "censors of morals" who would carry out visits to families, schools, churches, and even individuals.

Comenius's desire for a better world also applies to ours. We do not have to identify with all of Comenius's answers, but we can allow ourselves to be confronted by the questions that serve self-reflection and self-understanding. Jaroslava Pešková, an outstanding expert on Comenius put it well: in her judgment, Jan Amos was not great only for his answers to the questions of his time, he was important primarily "for his questioning, which was able to express the key problems of the day."[13] Who are we, really? What makes a person human? How is humanity formed educationally? How to harmonize the well-being of the individual with that of the whole? How to take care of freedom? How to cultivate peace among the nations? Where are we, as humanity, going? Comenius's answers will sound archaic to the modern or postmodern ear, but not everything that is old is necessarily outdated.[14]

12. Patočka, *O významu všeobecné porady*, 282.

13. Pešková, "Aktuální aspekty," 5.

14. This position was well illustrated by C. S. Lewis in the term *chronological snobbery*. He defined it as follows: "The uncritical acceptance of the intellectual climate common to our age, and the assumption that whatever is not current is, on that basis, to be questioned." See his autobiography *Surprised by Joy*, 195.

# Bibliography


Chlup, Otokar. "Zhodnocení Komenského myšlenky pansofické" [Evaluation of Comenius's Pansophic Thought]. In vol. 4 of *Vybrané spisy Jana Amose Komenského*, edited by Otokar Chlup, 5–57. Praha: Státní pedagogické nakladatelství, 1966.

Floss, Pavel. *Nástin života, díla a myšlení Jana Amose Komenského* [Outline of the Life, Work, and Thought of Jan Amos Comenius]. Přerov: Vlastivědný ústav, 1970.

Hábl, Jan. *Aby člověk neupadal* v *nečlověka. Komenského pedagogická humanizace jako antropologický problem* [So That Man Would Not Fall in a Non-human: Comenius's Pedagogical Humanization as an Anthropological Problem]. Červený Kostelec: nakl Pavel Mervart, 2015.

Komenský, Jan Amos. *Didaktika analytická* [Analytic Didactic]. Praha: Samcovo knihkupectví, 1946.

———. *Obecná porada o nápravě věcí lidských* [General Consultation concerning the Restoration of Human Affairs]. Vols. I–III. Praha: Nakladatelství Svoboda, 1992.

Kumpera, Jan. "Comenius and England." In *Comenius in World Science and Culture*, C-III, edited by Jaroslav Pánek, 91–97. Praha: Historical Institute of Academy, 1991.

Lewis, C. S. *Surprised by Joy: The Shape of My Early Life*. London: Harcourt, Brace, Jovanovich, 1955.

Palouš, Radim. *Komenského Boží Svět* [Comenius's God's World]. Praha: SPN, 1992.

Patočka, Jan. "Jan Amos Komenský: nástin životopisu" [Jan Amos Comenius: A Biographical Outline"]. In *Komeniologické studie I*, edited by Věra Schifferová. Praha: Oikoymenh, 1997.

———. *O významu všeobecné porady* [On the Importance of Universal Consultation]. In *Komeniologické studie II*. Praha: Oikoymenh, 1998.

Pešková, Jaroslava. "Aktuální aspekty filosofické argumentace v Komenského 'Konsultaci'" [Current Aspects of Philosophical Argumentation in Comenius's *Consultation*] *Filosofický časopis* 40.1 (1992) 51–56.

Šalda, F. X. "O literárním baroku cizím i domácím" [On the Literary Baroque, Foreign, and Domestic]. In vol. 1 of *Z období zápisníku*, edited by F. X. Šalda, 282–307. Praha: Odeon, 1987.